MANDATE MADNESS

MANDATE MADNESS

HOW CONGRESS FORCES
STATES AND LOCALITIES
TO DO ITS BIDDING
AND PAY FOR THE PRIVILEGE

JAMES T.
BENNETT

Transaction Publishers
New Brunswick (U.S.A.) and London (U.K.)

Library of Congress Catalog Number: 2013039458
ISBN: 978-1-4128-5372-9
Printed in the United States of America

Library of Congress Cataloging-in-Publication Data

Bennett, James T.
    Mandate madness : how Congress forces states and localities to do its bidding and pay for the privilege / James T. Bennett, George Mason University, Fairfax, VA.
        pages cm
    ISBN 978-1-4128-5372-9 (cloth : alk. paper) 1. Unfunded mandates--United States. 2. United States. Congress. 3. Federal government--United States. 4. Central-local government relations--United States. 5. Intergovernmental fiscal relations--United States. I. Title.
    HJ275.5.B465 2014
    336.73--dc23
                                                            2013039458

TK

Contents

Acknowledgments

I am grateful to many for their assistance with and support of the research and editing of this book. The research would not have been possible without the generous financial support of the Sunmark Foundation. Trey Carson provided excellent research assistance. I also owe profuse thanks to my editor, Bill Kauffman, for I am indebted to him for significant contributions to this study.

1

Introduction:
The Mandate Temptation

The unfunded federal mandate is a policy that politicians of both parties profess to oppose, yet they often find it irresistible as a means of forcing state and local governments to do their bidding—and to pay for the privilege. It is the sly means by which politicians provide benefits to their constituents while foisting off costs on lower levels of government.

Democrats do it, Republicans do it, and liberals and conservatives do it: the temptation to issue mandates that cover oneself in glory—while beggaring the fellow somewhere down the line—is one that few politicos of any stamp can resist. Mandates may well transgress the Constitution—though, as we shall see, the Supreme Court is of several minds on the matter—and by imposing a one-size-fits-all solution on social and political problems they are a prime example of the folly of centralized control. Yet they persist. How did they come to be, and why do they show no real signs of going away? Those are among the questions explored in *Mandate Madness*.

The book begins with an overview of the history of unfunded federal mandates and a survey of the political debate and gamesmanship surrounding them. Then in a series of chapters that mix history, analysis, legislative and legal details, and even a bit of humor (for if we cannot laugh at federal blundering and overreach, we would surely cry), we will explore the growth, revision, and development of the unfunded federal mandate by concentrating on several of the most controversial and colorful of the laws. They include

- The **55 mile per hour national speed limit** imposed in 1973 (and since repealed). This mandate, based on the absurd universalist conceit that the highway laws in Montana should be identical to those in Rhode Island, was widely reviled and even ignored by drivers. Uncle Sam told the states to either adopt a 55 mph maximum speed limit or

1

forfeit a percentage of their federal highway money. Lacking a clear constitutional sanction to impose certain laws on the states, the federal government instead conditions federal aid on the performance by the states of actions desired by Washington—for instance, the imposition of a 55 mph speed limit to be enforced by state and local law officers and whose enforcement is to be paid for by state and local governments. Such sanctions have generally passed muster in the federal courts. After all, as federal judges are wont to observe, the states could always *refuse* to take the aid, in which case they are not bound by the federal conditions attached to that aid. (But just try finding a state that will actually refuse federal funds.)

- The **national twenty-one-year-old drinking age**, a project of the allegedly federalist Reagan administration, under which states that refused to adopt the national standard were punished with a reduction in federal highway aid. This law further advanced, under cover of the "spending power" granted to the federal government by the Constitution, the proposition that Congress can impose unfunded mandates upon the states—in this case, a twenty-one-year-old drinking age that state and local police were required to enforce—because, after all, a state has the "choice" of refusing to go along (and thereby forfeiting its federal aid).

- **No Child Left Behind** (NCLB), the George W. Bush education reform that forced upon the nation's schoolchildren a regimen of standardized tests and threatened local school districts with federal sanctions if their students did not pass those tests in sufficient numbers. This was, perhaps, the most brazen and wide-reaching federal power grab in recent memory: the Bush administration, prime backers of NCLB, succeeded in nationalizing educational policy to an unprecedented degree. States complained loudly about this aggression and about the unfunded nature of the mandate, for although federal education aid increased under No Child Left Behind, the boost is nowhere near what is necessary to meet its unrealistic goal of ensuring that every child in America achieves a minimum level of academic proficiency by 2014.

- The **Help America Vote Act** (HAVA), enacted in the wake of the 2000 "hanging chad" election farce in Florida. This bipartisan effort forced states and localities to overhaul their election machinery, discarding not only faulty chads but also the venerable (and reliable) lever-system voting machines. Although the feds offered grants to pay for this wholesale technology shift and the training necessary for poll workers to adapt, the monies were insufficient to meet the added expense to states and localities. Using the Florida mess as pretense, the federal government usurped a function that had heretofore always been the responsibility of state and local governments. And of course those state and local governments had to foot the bill for a law that stemmed from incompetent electoral administration in a single state. Thanks to the Sunshine State, the other forty-nine states were squeezed like a fresh orange by HAVA.

- **REAL ID**, the post-9/11 attempt by the federal government to effectively nationalize the historic state responsibility of issuing driver's licenses. Once again, the feds offered modest and inadequate grants to the states to cover the cost of meeting the new national requirements for the issuing of driver's licenses. But REAL ID is also a fascinating case of successful state-level resistance to an unfunded federal mandate: though it has not been repealed, vigorous anti–REAL ID action by defenders of privacy as well as opponents of unfunded mandates has left the act in a kind of operational limbo for now. There may be some lessons therein for anti-mandate rebels.
- Such failed or abortive unfunded mandates as **national seat-belt** or **motorcycle helmet laws**. Like the federal mandates mentioned above, these laws would have pushed the cost and duty of enforcing nationally mandated laws upon states and localities. But unlike the other cases, these would-be mandates were defeated or derailed. (In the case of the seat-belt mandate, the "victory" was thin gruel indeed. Almost all of us are required to buckle up anyway.) These cases, too, hold lessons for those who would challenge current or future unfunded federal mandates.

Mandate Madness also examines legislative efforts to rein in or repeal unfunded federal mandates, most notably the Unfunded Mandates Reform Act (UMRA) of 1995, which addressed the problem, at least superficially—or perhaps only superficially. Although the act purported to "curb the practice of imposing unfunded Federal mandates on States and local governments," in practice it has been almost wholly ineffectual, riddled as it is with loopholes and exemptions for all manner of federal laws.[1] The Unfunded Mandates Reform Act has been about as effective in achieving its purpose as the posting of the Sixth Commandment on the wall of a strip club would be.

Finally, the book looks at the treatment of unfunded federal mandates by the federal courts, which have, in recent years, shown glimmers of sympathy for federalist arguments based on the Tenth Amendment to the US Constitution. Although the courts have deferred to Congress and the president in challenges to No Child Left Behind and even the drinking age (*South Dakota v. Dole*), those who find wisdom in the federalist political arrangement maintain—perhaps with more wistfulness than realism—that the unfunded federal mandate has not joined death and taxes as an immovable part of the modern political landscape.

****

In 1998, Paul L. Posner, then the director of federal budget issues at the US General Accounting Office, published *The Politics of Unfunded*

3

Mandates: Whither Federalism?, which immediately became the standard text on this woefully understudied issue. Posner remarked upon the "dearth" of works on the subject, and the last fifteen years has not exactly seen an avalanche of new works.[2]

Posner saw the proliferation of unfunded mandates as a sign of the failure of the system. It was out of balance, out of whack, and federal officeholders could not resist the temptation to get credit for creating new programs or initiatives while passing the buck down to lower levels of government, whose beleaguered solons would have to figure out a way to pay for the party. Or in Posner's piquant phrase, unfunded federal mandates broke "the link between the joy of enacting benefits and the pain of paying for them."[3] Pleasure and pain—Congress basks in one and inflicts the other.

Posner describes six types of mandates, and his typology, borrowed from the federal Advisory Commission on Intergovernmental Relations, remains the standard: *direct orders*, under which the federal government dictates policy to states or localities, which face civil or criminal penalties for disobeying (e.g., the application of federal minimum wage laws to employees of state or local governments); *crosscutting requirements*, which apply to most or all federal grants to states and localities (e.g., the requirement that handicapped persons have access to the relevant facilities); *crossover sanctions*, whereby the feds threaten to eliminate or reduce grants if states do not adopt certain policies (e.g., laws related to driving while intoxicated); *partial preemption*, under which federal law preempts state laws while permitting states to share in the enforcement of those laws (e.g., workplace safety regulations); *total preemption*, whereby federal laws entirely supplant state laws, as with the economic regulation of airlines; and *major program-specific grant conditions*, whereby the feds require "significant fiscal and policy actions by state and local government recipients," as with the requirement that handicapped children receive a "free and appropriate" education.[4]

Thus mandates come in various shapes and sizes. They may be funded or unfunded; they may be in the form of conscription that leaves the states no choice but to obey or they may promote "voluntary" participation under which the states risk the penalty of forfeiting federal aid. In all cases, they represent a frank assertion of national supremacy over the states and localities, even to the point of dispensing with the Tenth Amendment as casually and thoughtlessly as one would toss a used tissue paper.

Mandates, funded and unfunded, have their defenders. As one such argued in a 1988 conference on mandates at the Urban Institute in—where else?—Washington, DC, "the federal government should not be held hostage to the states whenever it attempts to accomplish goals of clear national importance."[5] Just how to define "clear national importance" is no easy task. It seems to encompass everything from securing the voting rights of African Americans in the 1960's South to telling the states how fast their motorists may drive and how much alcohol they may consume before driving. The mandate slope is nothing if not slippery.

This subject is too sprawling and the data too dispersed for a comprehensive picture of unfunded federal mandates. Our focus will be on the history, politics, and implications of some the most controversial mandates of the last generation. The intention is to provide a series of detailed but succinct histories that, in the aggregate, paint a picture of the birth, growth, and development of mandate madness.

Our subjects range afield, policy-wise, from transportation to education to public safety to anti-"terrorism." They are primarily crossover sanctions and grant conditions, which often reveal the unfunded federal mandate in its most egregious form, but they are of a piece in that they illustrate the ways, subtle as a subordinate clause or thumpingly obvious as a hammer to the head, by which the federal government mandates actions to states and localities, haughtily neglecting to even fully pay for them.

This book will largely (but not entirely) focus on those unfunded federal mandates that fall under the *crossover sanctions* category. This has been the form that some of the most controversial of recent mandates have taken; it is also largely outside the narrow application of UMRA, which applies primarily to direct orders. As Posner notes, and as we shall explore at length later, crossover sanctions—for instance, reducing a state's federal highway funding if it does not adopt a federally mandated drinking age or motorcycle helmet law or minimum blood alcohol concentration standard—have been regarded by the federal courts as voluntary. A state can theoretically refuse the federal monies and set its own drinking age. In practice, this is almost unheard of because states have come to rely on federal funds to so great an extent that stepping away from the trough is seen as an act of sheer madness. Why sacrifice money over principle?

What this reality says about the perverse nature of federalism and intergovernmental relations in the early twenty-first century is unflattering in the extreme, but there it is. And here we go.

Notes

1. Unfunded Mandates Reform Act of 1995, Public Law 104–4.
2. Paul L. Posner, *The Politics of Unfunded Mandates: Whither Federalism?* (Washington, DC: Georgetown University Press, 1998), p. 10.
3. Ibid., p. 6.
4. Ibid., pp. 13–14.
5. Michael Fix and Daphne A. Kenyon, "Introduction," *Coping with Mandates: What Are the Alternatives?* (Lanham, MD: University Press of America, 1990), p. 12.

2

From Federalism to Coercion: A Brief History of Mandates

The use of federal mandates to guide state policy was a twentieth-century innovation. It grew concomitantly with the central state; as Washington expanded to a previously unimaginable size and sphere, so did its power to order about lesser jurisdictions. As Paul Posner notes, "Prior to the 1960s . . . a presumption against coercive federal mandates on the state and local sector had been accepted as one of the rules of the game by all actors in the system."[1]

But rules change.

The spending clause within Article 1, Section 8, has provided much of the necessary cover for the vast expansion of the federal realm, including its use of mandates. It reads: "The Congress shall have power to lay and collect taxes, duties, imposts and excises, to pay the debts and provide for the common defense and general welfare of the United States, but all duties, imposts and excises shall be uniform throughout the United States."

You will notice that the "spending clause" nowhere uses the word *spending*. That power is said to be implicit. Yet the cautious interpretations thereof in the early republic barred the federal government from undertaking such activities as the subsidization of canals, bridges, and roads.

When James Madison vetoed an act providing for the federal subsidy of internal improvements in 1817, Thomas Jefferson explicated his view of the spending clause in a letter to his former treasury secretary, Albert Gallatin:

> [Y]ou will have learned that an act for internal improvement, after passing both Houses, was negatived by the President. The act was founded, avowedly, on the principle that the phrase in the constitution

which authorizes Congress "to lay taxes, to pay the debts and provide for the general welfare," was an extension of the powers specifically enumerated to whatever would promote the general welfare; and this, you know, was the federal [that is, the supporters of a strong central government a la Alexander Hamilton and Gouverneur Morris] doctrine. Whereas, our tenet ever was, and, indeed, it is almost the only landmark which now divides the federalists from the republicans, that Congress had not unlimited powers to provide for the general welfare, but were restrained to those specifically enumerated; and that, as it was never meant that they should provide for that welfare but by the exercise of the enumerated powers, so it could not have been meant they should raise money for purposes which the enumeration did not place under their action; consequently, that the specification of powers is a limitation of the purposes for which they may raise money. I think the passage and rejection of this bill a fortunate incident. Every State will certainly concede the power; and this will be a national confirmation of the grounds of appeal to them, and will settle forever the meaning of this phrase, which, by a mere grammatical quibble, has countenanced the General Government in a claim of universal power.[2]

Mr. Jefferson proved far too optimistic. President Madison's veto did not "settle forever" the meaning of the spending clause. In fact, those who wished for a looser construction of that clause redoubled their efforts, focusing at first on measures with a degree of popularity, especially the construction of roads and bridges and canals in the West. Later, such activities as the federal subsidization of education would be added. The wall had been breached. In time, the very notion that there are any effective constitutional limitations on federal spending would be nearly a joke.

The courts have long found conditional federal aid to be within the bounds of constitutionally permissible acts. Since the Morrill Act of 1862, as Columbia Law School professor Albert J. Rosenthal noted, Congress had required "the teaching of agricultural science in certain colleges it subsidizes," although, as Rosenthal adds, "in the absence of the federal spending such a requirement would probably be beyond any of the powers granted to Congress."[3] Congress may direct these colleges to offer prescribed courses of study as a condition of receiving federal aid, but it may not do so—or so it appears—without the provision of such aid. Carrot, *sí*; stick, no.

The Morrill Act "was the first continuing grant program," as Bruce J. Casino of the Georgetown University Law Center writes in his history of grants-in-aid in the pages of *Urban Lawyer*.[4]

Still, the advance of federal grants-in-aid was slow, as befitting a constitutional republic. They didn't really begin to take off until the federal income tax, born in 1913, brought to the federal treasury the windfall that made government expansion (and a century of wars, beginning with World War I) possible. Under the Smith-Hughes National Vocational Education Act of 1917, for instance, the federal government offered grants to states for vocational training in the schools. By 1920, Casino notes, eleven cash grants to the states had consumed about $30 million annually. Throughout the Roaring Twenties, highways were the primary vehicle for the transfer of cash from Washington to the states.

The Great Depression and subsequent New Deal of President Franklin D. Roosevelt saw an expansion of federal grants to the states, or even directly to municipal governments. Such grants ballooned from $100 million in 1929 to $1 billion thirty years later. But there have always been Americans suspicious of taking "free" federal money. As the mayor of Hartford, Connecticut, said in 1931, "We believe in paying our own way. It is cheaper than to bear the cost of federal bungling."[5]

These early examples of federal aid were subsidies—bribes, if you are cynical—to get lower levels of government to act in ways desired by the federal government. This was subvention, not coercion. There might be conditions placed upon this aid, but these were not unfunded federal mandates as we understand them.

The US Supreme Court acted, briefly, as a check upon this federal expansion into state and local activities. In *United States v. Butler* (1936), the court struck down a controversial tax under the Agricultural Adjustment Act (AAA) of 1933. Proceeds from the tax went to "subsidize farmers who agreed to take land out of production."[6] If a farmer did as the feds instructed, he would receive payment. The court opined that "if, in lieu of compulsory regulation of subjects within the states' reserved jurisdiction, which is prohibited, the Congress could invoke the taxing and spending power as a means to accomplish the same end, clause 1 of [Section] 8 of article 1 would become the instrument for total subversion of the governmental powers reserved to the states."[7]

The court based its *Butler* decision on an old-fashioned reading of the Tenth Amendment, which reserves to the states (or the people) the "powers not delegated to the United States by the Constitution, nor prohibited by it to the States." It defined the spending power broadly but found that the tax in question was not anchored to an enumerated

9

power: in other words, the Tenth Amendment protected the states against federal encroachment, in this case in the form of the federal regulation of agriculture.

Butler was one of the last of the court's anti–New Deal rulings. For the next year, President Roosevelt, emboldened by his landslide victory over Republican Alf Landon in 1936 and frustrated that the Supreme Court was obstructing his New Deal, proposed to "pack" the court under a bizarre formula: for each sitting justice over seventy years of age (six at the time), the president would appoint a new justice. In fact, FDR adduced the *Butler* case as evidence that the court was insufficiently truckling to the New Deal agenda. Although the Senate ultimately demurred and the court was not packed, it was intimidated, and would no longer produce rulings with the tenor of *Butler*. When the very next year the court, chastened by FDR's attempted packing of its membership, considered the federal tax on employers that was central to the Social Security Act, it upheld that tax and "effectively demolished some of the premises of the *Butler* case," as Rosenthal argues.[8] Henceforth, Congress had a more or less free rein encompassing the limits of what it might spend money on—including conditional grants to the states. (The chastened, or intimidated, court diminished the Tenth Amendment to a mere "truism that all is retained which has not been surrendered" in the 1941 case of *United States v. Darby*.[9] Federalism was in for a big sleep.)

Although in *Butler* the court overturned the AAA tax as a violation of the Tenth Amendment, it did open the door to a broader conception of the spending clause. As legal scholar Jeffrey T. Renz notes in the *John Marshall Law Review*, the court in *Butler* held that if a federal government tax passes constitutional "muster, Congress may spend in any way that it deems in furtherance of the general welfare, even for purposes not set forth in the enumerated powers"—a paradigm that "was the key to the New Deal's expansion of congressional and federal power."[10] So *Butler*, while on the surface a blow to the national leviathan, helped to set the stage for the use of Congress's spending power to further all sorts of national and nationalizing goals. Congress decides what the general welfare is, and if it needs to threaten the withdrawal of federal monies from those states that block that interest, so be it.

The issue crystallized over highway billboards, of all things.

The catalyst was US senator Richard Neuberger of Oregon, a liberal Democrat and former journalist—or do I repeat myself? Senator

Neuberger was the father of highway beautification, or billboard abhorrence. As political scientist James L. Sundquist explained in his opus *Politics and Policy*, at the subcommittee level, Senator Neuberger inserted language into the bill that would later become the 1956 law establishing the National System of Interstate and Defense Highways. Neuberger's amendment provided that billboards be banned from the interstate. The full committee modified Neuberger's language so as to authorize "the federal government, acting as agent of the states, to acquire advertising easements along the interstate highway system as part of the land acquisition process when the states so desired." The federal/state split to acquire these easements was 90/10, but the provision contained no penalties for states that did not wish to participate. Nevertheless, Neuberger's amendment was dropped when the bill hit the Senate floor.

As Sundquist notes, this battle was being fought in the states before it came to Congress. The billboard lobby, with its supporters in the advertising and sign-painting business, grappled with the garden clubs and civic groups who wished to keep highways free of elevated clutter. As Sundquist cynically notes, newspaper editorialists were usually keen for billboard prohibition, though their editorial tributes to natural beauty lacked "reference to the newspapers' own self-interest in suppressing a competitive advertising medium."[11] Speaking up for the rights of motel, restaurant, and tavern owners to hawk their wares along the interstate were the labor unions representing carpenters, painters, and sheet-metal workers, who argued that billboards can contribute to "the actual beautification of the countryside."[12] This might have been a stretch, but it was an interesting example of the unions defending the rights of free enterprise and advertising.

Senator Neuberger and his anti-billboard allies kept at it. In 1957, the federal highway administrator Bertram D. Tallamy and Secretary of Commerce Sinclair Weeks proposed to punish those states that failed to keep their sections of the interstate highway system free of billboards (whether by buying easements or enacting bans). The punishment: the burden of an offending state's share of interstate construction projects would increase from 10 to 15 percent. Unfortunately, Tallamy and Weeks seemed to have not cleared this with their boss, President Dwight D. Eisenhower, who said in a news conference that "while I am against these billboards that mar our scenery, I don't know what I can do about it." This was one of the last instances of an American president conceding that he just might lack the power to do something.

The advertising lobby agreed. As Harley B. Markham, chairman of the Outdoor Advertising Association of America, Inc., told the Subcommittee on Public Roads of the Senate Public Works Committee, "The states now have authority to enact any regulatory legislation which they desire or decide they need. Legislation for federal control would not only preempt and usurp this right, but would assume that the states are unaware or unconcerned about their own resources."[13]

The Senate modified the approaches of Neuberger and Tallamy/ Weeks, offering to boost from 90 to 90.5 percent the federal share of interstate projects in states that controlled billboards. The measure passed, 47–41, after heated debate. The House concurred, and so in 1958 it appeared that natural beauty along the nation's interstates was just over the next bend in the road.

Not quite. After seven years, only 194 miles of the 41,000-mile interstate system had been cleansed, or freed, from the threat of advertising. Only about half the states had bought into the program. The law was widely regarded as a failure. Carrots had failed; now was time for the stick. Under President Lyndon B. Johnson, compulsion became the preferred method of dealing with refractory states.

Moreover, Lady Bird Johnson, the First Lady, had taken as her cause the beautification of the nation's highways. (That these areas were more beautiful before the federal government seized them, often by eminent domain, and built roads upon them did not enter Mrs. Johnson's calculations.) The measure now had that momentum that only a bullying husband pushing his wife's favorite cause can attain. In fact, the 225,000 miles of the federally aided "primary roads" system was added to the mix, though the billboard lobby did succeed in removing commercial and industrial areas from coverage. The administration's measure was modified in Congress, but the bill that passed the Senate by 63–14 and the House by 245–138 and was signed into law by President Johnson on October 22, 1965, authorized the secretary of commerce (later transportation) to withhold 10 percent of a state's federal highway monies if it did not comply with the federal billboard control statute. The immediate price of disobedience—or the assertion of state preferences; the cost of the mandate, that is—ranged from $1.36 million in Rhode Island to $36 million in California.[14] "Crossover sanctions" had entered the room.

Whether one admires or despises billboards or whether one thinks their regulation should be a matter for state, federal, or local government, the important thing about the Highway Beautification Act of

1965 is that it set a precedent by withholding federal funds from states that did not comply with and enforce federal law. Speed limits, motorcycle helmets, seat-belt laws, a national minimum drinking age, and so many other (transportation-related, interestingly) federal mandates or would-be federal mandates copied this template. And the mandate *was* unfunded, or at least only partially funded. States were directed to remove billboards or face the forfeiture of 10 percent of their highway monies, and they were also required to compensate the owners of the stricken billboards. The feds, in turn, only reimbursed the states 75 percent of the cost of the billboard owner's compensation—leaving those states with the bill for the other quarter.[15]

The Highway Beautification Act "represented a dramatic shift" in federal-state policy, as a February 1984 report of the Advisory Commission on Intergovernmental Relations put it.[16] Its use of crossover sanctions established a precedent for future unfunded federal mandates: Threaten states with the deprivation of anticipated monies. They'll cave—heck, they'll even pay the bill.

A few words about the aforementioned commission: The Advisory Commission on Intergovernmental Relations, or ACIR, was an entity created during the Eisenhower administration by Congress to study relations between the federal, state, local, and tribal governments. It monitored the growth of federal mandates, among other complications and features of federalism. The mission of the ACIR, as laid out in its establishing legislation, was to "strengthen the American federal system and improve the ability of federal, state, and local governments to work together cooperatively, efficiently, and effectively."[17] Its twenty-six member board, appointed by both houses of Congress and the president and consisting of state, local, and federal officials, Cabinet members, and private citizens, soldiered on for decades in the decidedly unglamorous task of seeking to right the intensifying imbalance in the federal system. The ACIR was one federal entity that was not enamored of federal mandates.

The ACIR was a legislative progeny of Senator Robert Taft (R-OH), the federalist who was known as "Mr. Republican." Senator Taft proposed, shortly before he died, that a federal commission evaluate the state of federal-state relations. So cogent was the commission's report that by 1959 it was made permanent, or as close to permanent as a government commission is supposed to be. In its youth, federal grants-in-aid were multiplying like baby-boom children, but the strings attached were not considered overly onerous by most recipients, who were happy to let the federal faucet run. But then came the mandates and direct federal orders. In scholar Timothy Conlan's words, grants and incentives gave way to "instruments that impose sanctions on, preempt, or co-opt state and local authority."[18] Over the span of its lifetime, from 1959 to 1996, the number of federal mandates counted by the ACIR skyrocketed from two to sixty. (Conlan says that ACIR's estimate is conservative; at about the same time, the National Conference of State Legislatures counted 185 federal mandates.)[19]

John Kincaid, who served as executive director of the ACIR from 1988 to 1994, explains that an era of "cooperative federalism" reigned from approximately 1954 to 1978. The reach of the national government was expanding far beyond what our ancestors could ever have conceived, but this was accompanied by "major increases in federal aid to states and localities." Cooperation was the basic theme; the feds, while clearly enjoying a preeminence among the varying levels of government, sought to "compensat[e] state and local officials for federal intrusions into their authority with fiscal assistance" as well as "federal assumption of policy decisions too painful to be made by some state and local authorities," for example, the enforcement of civil rights for African Americans in the South.[20]

But as Kincaid writes, the federal government grew used to having its way with states and localities. Cooperation, with its implied consent, seemed unnecessary. Why not just force states and localities to do the bidding of Washington? And if Washington failed to provide these other levels of government with sufficient funds to carry out its orders, well, tough luck. Thus was born the unfunded federal mandate. And also born was an era of coercive federalism, which would reach its peak, or nadir, in the presidency of George W. Bush, under whom relations between Washington and the governors of the states were described as "poisonous."[21] The carrot was all the rage; the stick was obsolete.

"Regulatory federalism" was the term used by Advisory Commission on Intergovernmental Relations staff to describe the new dispensation of federal-state relations beginning in the 1960s. The federal government enacted a sweeping range of new laws covering everything from civil rights to clean air, clean water, and labor standards and even endangered species. Most of those early mandates covered environmental and civil rights matters. Twelve such mandates were enacted in the 1960s, twenty-two in the 1970s, and then they proliferated unabated, indeed in ever greater numbers, during the allegedly federalist Reagan administration, for as we shall see, Republicans have proven to be just as willing as Democrats to impose mandates and due bills upon states and localities.[22] And they have been even less willing than the Democrats to foot any portion of the bill: during the Reagan-Bush decade of the 1980s, the real value of federal aid to states and localities declined by 33 percent, even though federal mandates sprouted like weeds after a rainstorm.[23]

As for the Advisory Commission on Intergovernmental Relations, "permanence" just ain't what it used to be. In 1996, the "Contract with America" Republican Congress snuffed the ACIR. You see, the Unfunded Mandates Reform Act of 1995 had been passed in all its symbolic (or shambolic) glory, and so nothing much was left to do in this area. The stable had been cleaned out. Senate Majority Leader Bob Dole had pledged that the first thing the new Congress would do would be "to relieve states from unfunded federal mandates."[24] And with UMRA it did just that. Or such was the conceit.

The commission had come to seem stale. After all, as Conlan notes, it dated back to the Eisenhower administration, which seemed practically antediluvian to many of the young Republicans elected in 1994. Eisenhower, wasn't he a World War II general? What possible relevance could anything he said or did or supported have in the age of Newt Gingrich? Its staff had been reduced "from a high of 37 in the 1970s to just 13 in 1995."[25] The Contract with America crowd never did abolish those superfluous departments it had rhetorically targeted—the Departments of Education, Energy, and Commerce—but it succeeded in wiping out this very small commission. It did not, however, wipe out federal mandates, funded or otherwise.

(Actually, ACIR's death cannot be laid solely at the feet of the Republicans. It died shortly after its members engaged in a bitter partisan fight over the commission's potential recommendation, embodied in an ACIR draft report, that the Congress modify "thirteen politically sensitive mandates," most notably the labor-cherished Davis-Bacon Act, the Fair Labor Standards Act, the Occupational Safety and Health Act, the Family Medical Leave Act, metric conversion laws, and the mandate that handicapped children receive free and appropriate educations from localities.[26] A coalition of 150 special interest groups, gathered under the anodyne moniker of Citizens for Sensible Safeguards, attacked these recommended reforms as daggers aimed at the heart of all that is good and decent about the American welfare state. Although the chair of the commission was William Winter, a former Democratic governor from Mississippi, Democrats on the ACIR revolted—and the commission wound up in the graveyard of defunct governmental agencies.)

****

The unfunded federal mandate came into its own in the 1970s and exploded in the 1980s as an example of a "new, more coercive era in our federal system," as Paul Posner writes. They frequently were directed at policy areas in which the federal government had in recent years become more active: "air and water pollution, equal employment and service access to protected minorities, wage and hour standards, educational opportunities for the handicapped and women, criminal justice, and transportation policy."[27] (The tendency of higher levels of government to dictate behavior to lower levels was not unknown, even in early America. Alexis de Tocqueville, in his 1835 classic, *Democracy in America*, wrote of the typical New England state that its "general laws . . . impose a certain number of obligations on the selectmen," which are not compensated by the state.[28])

These mandates of the 1960s, '70s, and '80s encountered scattered resistance. The assumption was, after all, that politicos in states and localities were not as wise as federal lawmakers. Given their druthers, the conventional thinking went, states would fail to fund worthy programs aimed at ameliorating pollution or fostering education and civil rights. Moreover, politicians were "anxious to take credit for legislation that appeals to broadly shared values championed by an all-pervasive media."[29] Given the opportunity, for instance, to trumpet one's credentials as an opponent of drunk drivers while passing the tab for enforcement onto lower levels of government, what irresponsible publicity-hogging legislator could resist? Few things are more alluring to a politician than the chance to take credit for something that other, unseen persons will have to pay for. There is no downside—unless the politician is a man or woman of principle or conscience, but . . . well, exceptions do not a rule make.

Sure, politicos, particularly Republicans in our age, may pay lip service to federalism or to the wisdom of permitting those closer to the people to make the laws under which those people should live, but again, the chance to appear in the gaze of an adoring media as a noble scourge of drunk drivers or teenaged drinkers or terrorists with counterfeit driver's licenses or any number of unsavory characters is difficult to resist. Opinion polls almost invariably show wide public support for federal action against a whole range of "problems"—some media-generated—which in the past were thought better addressed at the state or local level. But, hey, federalism is passé: national hegemony is the new law of the land. Mandates, now part of the mainstream of the policy conversation, "came to be seen as a logical and appropriate tool to promote greater national uniformity."[30] Whether that national uniformity was a good thing seemed to be a discussion entirely off the table. One size fit all. Regional differences and local flavor were out. A single national standard, applicable from Nome, Alaska, to Miami, Florida, was in. *Everything* has become a federal concern—a federal case, to use the now anachronistic phrase. No problem was too small to be a subject of interest to Washington and the well-heeled pressure groups to which policymakers responded. If such policymakers were overly worried about the degradation of federalism, its decay in the era of unfunded federal mandates, and rampant nationalization, they hid that worry well.

Martha Derthick, in the *Brookings Review*, put it well. Congress, she said, "is not much inclined to contemplate the deeper issues of federalism and to ask, self-critically, whether or where it should exercise restraint in its use of mandates. If it can expand the benefits of government while imposing much of the cost on other governments in the system, why not do it?"[31]

The "waning informal influence state and local officials" exert on national politics is one cause of the profusion of mandates.[32] Federal officeholders are much less beholden to state and local parties than they were in the days before television and the effective nationalization of the two major parties. State and local party chairmen are mere voices in the mix, less important to most federal officeholders than the moneymen and interest groups. The county Republican or Democratic boss counts for very little indeed in an age of Fox News, the *Huffington Post*, and national political action committees (PACs) and fundraisers who channel campaign funds to candidates from Idaho to Alabama. There is no longer, except in rare cases, a strong symbiotic relationship between a member of Congress and local party officials. Yes, he or she will listen to those officials, but only as one group in a plentiful set of advisors and supporters. A town supervisor complaining of the effect that a federal mandate might have on his little town is barely heard by a member of Congress whose primary focus is on satisfying his major donors and those media figures whose approval he craves.

The independence of modern politicos from their local parties makes them much less responsive, and certainly less sensitive, to complaints from local party officials.

And as Posner and others point out, state and local officials these days are hardly the parochial home-turf-defending localists they once may have been. They watch the same television programs and are swept along by the same policy fads, whether hysteria over a new illegal drug or a sudden impulse to clamp further regulations on drivers of automobiles. As was the case with the Reagan-inspired national unfunded mandate that the states raise their legal drinking ages to twenty-one, support for such mandates is often broad, if not especially deep. No one—not a congressman and not a town councilman—wants to be seen as defending teenaged drinking or opposing educational opportunities for handicapped youngsters. Once such proposals reach a critical mass of public acceptance, often egged on by media hype, even turf-protecting local officials are swept along.

And of course state and local officials can also shirk their responsibilities to defend local prerogatives by shrugging that "you can't fight city hall (or, in this case, Washington, DC)." At most, mayors, supervisors, and even governors might carp and cavil over details or tone. They don't like being bossed around, but they don't particularly object to the things they are ordered to do. They are acquiescent, even passive. As Louisville Mayor Jerry Abramson, then president of the US Conference of Mayors, explained his group's reservations about mandates, "We're all in favor of cleaning the environment, helping the disabled and making the world a better place. What we object to is this ham-handed, one-size-fits-all approach that costs huge amounts of money and often accomplishes very little."[33]

Ronald Reagan, for one, spoke of an era of "new federalism" during his first term in the presidency—and yet that term was marked by lunges toward coercive federalism in such areas as transportation, product liability, and communications. The Reagan White House consistently overrode state and local preferences and laws when they conflicted with the administration's national policies. Direct orders, preemption, and of course unfunded federal mandates—many were the arrows in the Reaganite quiver. Most often the issue was deregulation, where the administration found that it was far easier—if problematic for one who professes a federalist faith—to deregulate by overriding state laws with a single national law than it is to deregulate an industry (e.g., cable television) on a state-by-state basis. As federalism scholar Timothy J. Conlan

18

writes, "When it comes to regulations, business generally prefers not only fewer requirements to more, but uniformity to diversity."[34] A single set of national rules, in the eyes of most big business muckety-mucks, is superior to a federalist patchwork of state laws. It's so much easier for the big guys—and harder for the little guys—to adapt to one single standard from the Atlantic to the Pacific.

No recent president has spoken more effusively of federalism than Ronald Reagan. "My administration is committed—heart and soul—to the broad principles of American federalism," he assured a gathering of state legislators in 1981. His aide Richard S. Williamson called Reagan's "new federalism" a "quiet revolution" in which the scales of the federal-state balance would be restored to a more equitable distribution.[35] And yet Ronald Reagan, putative federalist, chose time and again to assert the superiority of national dictates over state preferences. Federalism, while perhaps soothing to the ears of an audience, proved to be barely an afterthought to its frequent panegyrist. US Advisory Commission on Intergovernmental Relations executive director John Kincaid remarked in 1990 that Reagan did nothing to halt the onslaught of coercive federalism, instead supporting "federal restraints on state regulation of business" and federal mandates for "health, environmental, and public-safety" issues.[36]

But Reagan was not alone in ignoring federalism. As Timothy J. Conlan observed in 1986, "It appears that hardly anyone today believes that maintaining the integrity of the federal system is sufficiently important to justify sacrificing other important values."[37]

In chapter 3, we shall take a closer look at a coercive and unfunded federal mandate that the Reagan administration forced upon recalcitrant states: the national twenty-one-year-old drinking age, which united such disparate states as South Dakota, Vermont, and New York in defense of states' rights and against the nationalizing and centralizing policy of Reagan and his transportation secretary, Elizabeth Dole. (In a supreme irony, Secretary Dole's husband, Republican senator Bob Dole of Kansas, declared in 1995 that in the coming Congress, "we plan to dust off the Tenth Amendment and restore it to its rightful place in the Constitution."[38] A year later, he would run for president of the United States while carrying in his pocket a copy of the Tenth Amendment to the Constitution, which provides that "the powers not delegated to the United States by the Constitution, nor prohibited by it to the States, are reserved to the States respectively, or to the people." Almost any nonsophistical reading of the Tenth Amendment would find the

Reagan-Dole national drinking-age law to be unconstitutional. Yet in one of the signal constitutional cases involving federal mandates, the US Supreme Court upheld the Reagan-Dole law, without any audible peeps of protest from the family Dole.)

President George W. Bush widened federal involvement in what had theretofore been state and local matters to a jaw-dropping extent, but in fairness, earlier Republican presidents had not exactly been strict constitutionalists when it came to federal-state relations. As federalism scholar Timothy Conlan pointed out in 1998, "conservative Republicans are often tempted to use and even expand federal authority when they have the opportunity to do so"—the Reagan administration, as we will see, offers plenty of evidence for that charge. Neither Republicans nor Democrats, Conlan continued, "is willing to sacrifice the opportunity for federal involvement in state and local activities that hold political appeal."[39] In other words, there are precious few scrupulous and principled decentralists when the lure of federal power is at hand.

On a wide range of issues the administration of George W. Bush pushed centripetal schemes to centralize power in Washington. On issues that we will consider in this book—national ID cards (REAL ID), voting practices (the Help America Vote Act, or HAVA), education (No Child Left Behind)—and in other areas as well (welfare, tort law, energy), the "compassionate conservative" Bush sought to bend the states to the national will. This "coercive federalism" was explicated by Paul Posner in a seminal 2007 essay in *Publius* titled "The Politics of Coercive Federalism in the Bush Era."[40]

"Coercive federalism" covers a range of nationalizing actions, from direct orders to the states to crossover sanctions to conditional aid. Unfunded federal mandates are a significant feature thereof, but not the be-all and end-all. Although the Unfunded Mandates Reform Act of 1995 predated the George W. Bush administration by six years, it had almost no deterrent effect upon Bush's agenda of coercion. No Child Left Behind, for instance, with its conditional federal assistance, was exempt from UMRA, as was the Help America Vote Act. REAL ID, advertised as a national security measure, probably evades UMRA because of the act's broad national security exemption, though some have urged a court challenge on just these grounds.

But the states, which had been relatively quiescent in the face of earlier incursions upon the state-federal balance, became somewhat more assertive during the second President Bush's big-government, conservative administration.

"Cooperative federalism" faded in the wake of 9/11. President George W. Bush, Vice President Dick Cheney, Secretary of Defense Donald Rumsfeld, and others at the helm of the American state seemed to think that deference to the traditional roles and prerogatives of the states was "weak"; an aggressive national response to terrorism had as its domestic corollary an aggressive nationalism in apparently unrelated policy fields such as education. Elected on a platform of "compassionate conservatism" and promising humility in foreign policy, George W. Bush turned out to be the most power-centralizing president since a previous Texan, Lyndon B. Johnson, who had called his efforts at expanding federal subsidization and the direction of state and local actions "creative federalism."[41] But even LBJ betrayed a modest sensitivity to state and local concerns. He had been Senate majority leader, after all, in the twilight of that era in which long-serving Southern Democrats, especially, looked out for the rights of their home states—at least on some matters. The second President Bush, by contrast, was heedless of those rights, real and purported, of the states. The exigencies of the War on Terror trumped the Tenth Amendment rights of the states not only in ostensibly security-related areas such as the licensing of automobile drivers but also in education, which since the 1950s has been slowly nationalized—and that nationalization has often been supported with the rhetoric of national security.

Just why the second President Bush was so "dismissive of federalism concerns and frequently an agent of centralization" is a question taken up by Tim Conlan and John Dinan of George Mason University and Wake Forest University, respectively.[42] They observe that in addition to Bush's Republican Party pedigree, he was also an ex-governor, and his party controlled both houses of Congress, a recipe, one might think, for at least timid gestures in the direction of decentralizing power. And yet he wound up as perhaps the most centralizing president of modern times. What happened?

The easy answer is 9/11, or the terrorist attacks of September 11, 2001, which provoked a "war on terror" whose policy initiatives tended to concentrate power in Washington, DC, running roughshod over the states and former conceptions of federalism. The REAL ID Act, which we shall consider in chapter 8, was one such policy.

But 9/11 cannot be blamed for No Child Left Behind, the Help America Vote Act, the 2003 expansion of prescription drug coverage under Medicare, the strengthening of the president's ability to federalize the National Guard, or several other Bush "accomplishments" that served to empower the national government and weaken the states. (At the request of the states, the Democratic Congress of 2007–8 repealed the National Guard law, which had been inserted by Bush allies into the FY 2007 Defense Authorization Act and enacted over the "strenuous objections" of the National Governors Association.[43] In brief, the new law enabled the president to nationalize state guard troops to respond to national disasters without the consent of the governor. As committed to a strong national government as the Democrats are, no one could possibly out-nationalize Bush Republicans.)

Conlan and Dinan remark, somewhat charitably, on President Bush's "lack of any philosophical commitment to federalism."[44] (An accounting of philosophical commitments lacked by President Bush would run to a very long list indeed.) The president had neither a rhetorical nor an operative dedication to dispersing power among the states; while others in his party might propose devolution, Bush almost inevitably chose consolidation and concentration of governmental functions in the nation's capital. "President Bush has proved remarkably willing to sacrifice state and local policy interests and, if necessary, substantially expand the federal government's fiscal and functional profile," concluded Conlan and Dinan.[45]

The onset of coercive federalism, with its "federal preemption of state and local authority accompanied by unfunded federal mandates," has "occurred across several Republican administrations," as Professor Christopher J. Deering of George Washington University has noted.[46] If one judges politicians by their rhetoric, this might be surprising. After all, Republicans since the New Deal have had at least a rhetorical commitment to federalism and to the rights of states to shape their own policies on social programs, especially. Not so anymore.

In any event, "the party of local control has become the party of the federal mandate," as Paul Peterson has written in his study of federalism.[47] During the presidency of George W. Bush, one was much more likely to hear complaints of onerous federal mandates from Democrats than from Republicans, although, in keeping with the basically unprincipled nature of party politics, that alignment has reversed itself to an extent during the presidency of Barack Obama. Yet, although Obama has nary a kind word for devolution, he can't compete with his predecessor in the unfunded federal mandate game.

****

One of the first voices of protest against unfunded federal mandates came from an unlikely source: New York City mayor Ed Koch. In 1980, writing in the neoconservative journal of social sciences *The Public Interest*, Mayor Koch explained how "the mandate millstone" weighed down his fair city. He pointed to "47 federal and state mandates" that would in the coming year cost Gotham "$711 million in capital expenditures, $6.25 billion in expense-budget dollars, and $1.66 billion in lost revenue."[48]

Mayor Koch posited four maxims that, he said, seemed to guide the "mandate mandarins" of Washington, DC:

1. "Mandates solve problems, particularly those in which you are not involved."
2. "Mandates need not be tempered by the lessons of local experience."
3. "Mandates will spontaneously generate the technology required to achieve them."
4. "The price tag of the lofty aspiration to be served by a mandate should never deter its imposition upon others."

Detect a hint of bitterness there?

Mayor Koch was no babe in the political woods. He had been a member of Congress before his election to the mayoralty, and a very liberal member at that. He confessed to having voted for numerous mandates. "After all," he said, "who can vote against clean air and water, or better access and education for the handicapped?"[49] The temptation to take the easy way—to vote for sexy or worthy projects and pass the bill on to state and local governments—is overwhelming. Yet Mayor Koch had the unusual experience of moving from federal to municipal government: from the realm of mandate givers to that of mandate receivers. What he found appalled him.

The mayor instanced the examples of unfunded federal mandates for the transportation and education of the handicapped. With impeccable motives—or so we assume—federal lawmakers had dumped upon the politicos back home responsibility for, in the former case, "total accessibility" for handicapped persons to transit *systems*. The expense staggered the mayor: the Congressional Budget Office estimated that the cost of complying with the handicapped accessibility regulations worked out to $38 per trip for the severely disabled, while the cost of a transit trip by a person who was not severely handicapped was about 85 cents.

Surely there must be a cheaper way. There was—in theory.

The exasperated Mayor Koch explained that the US Departments of Transportation and Health and Human Services would not accept the City of New York's proposal to provide a "paratransit" system—door-to-door service—for those who are severely disabled. "It would be cheaper for us to provide every severely disabled person with taxi service than make 255 of our subway stations accessible," wrote the mayor.[50]

Mandates had gone wild. Members of Congress and the president issued them almost blithely, carelessly, without thought for those who wound up paying the bill. "A new mandate may appear to its authors to be a bold experiment in behavior modification for a worthy goal," wrote Koch. "But I do not think they view themselves as accountable for the hardship they may inflict on a particular locality."[51]

It was not easy to demonize Koch as a regulation basher or free-market fanatic, as mandate mandarins liked to characterize their critics. And those critics multiplied like a calculator sum stuck on X.

October 23, 1993, was denominated National Unfunded Mandates Day. This was not exactly a contender to knock Mother's Day or Valentine's Day or even Arbor Day off the list of major secular holidays, but it served its purpose. Across the country, and in Washington, DC, too, state and local governmental officials representing the US Conference of Mayors, the National League of Cities, the National Association of Counties, and the International City/County Management Association held press conferences to shine the harsh light of publicity upon the treasury-draining and sometimes draconian mandates imposed upon them by an arrogant and unresponsive federal government.

One sponsor of this anti-holiday, the US Conference of Mayors, released a study (based on a survey of city officials from 314 cities) estimating the cost of compliance in 1993 with ten federal mandates (underground storage tanks, Clean Water Act, Clean Air Act, the Resource Recovery and Conservation Act, the Safe Drinking Water Act, asbestos abatement, lead paint abatement, the Endangered Species Act, the Americans with Disabilities Act, and the Fair Labor Standards Act) at $6.5 billion. Significantly, not a single one of these mandates would be affected by the Unfunded Mandates Reform Act.[52]

As Timothy J. Conlan, James D. Riggle, and Donna E. Schwartz of George Mason University remarked of Unfunded Mandates Day and the legislation that followed, "For the first time, state and local government officials made issues of federal regulation—rather than federal-aid subsidies—their top priority in Washington."[53] These officials came to Washington not to beg for a bigger place at the trough but to demand that their shackles be loosened. And as the trio of authors further note, the press was at last somewhat sympathetic to the complaints from the cities and the states. A Nexis search revealed that while only 22 newspaper articles mentioned "unfunded federal mandates" in 1992, 836 did so in 1994.[54] The spotlight had been turned on a little-known corner of the federal leviathan.

Even members of Congress were speaking a language of defiance. In September 1993, Representative Pat Roberts (R-KS) wrote the new vice president, Albert Gore, that "We face the real prospect of outright rebellion by Americans unwilling or unable to comply with the growing mountain of unattainable, unfunded mandates."[55] (The early Clinton years were noted for two mandates highly unpopular with Republicans: the Brady Act and the National Voter Registration Act of 1993, known commonly as the "Motor Voter" law, which forced the states to set up voter registration procedures for those applying for driver's licenses or social services. The latter was widely seen, correctly, as a way to register a disproportionate number of Democrats, as the demographics of those applying for social services skew Democratic.)

Defenders of unfunded federal mandates gathered to fight off, or at least water down, attempts to constrain them. These defenders tended to be statist liberal academics or activists for labor and civil rights causes. Because he who controls the language controls the terms of the debate, these champions of nationalism over federalism sought to find a less invidious phrase than "unfunded federal mandate." That term was so *loaded*. The Advisory Commission on Intergovernmental Relations, shortly before its demise, actually suggested "federally induced costs" as an alternative.[56] The name change died aborning.

Champions of a strong national government see mandate critics as disingenuous libertarians who are attempting to repeal, by insidious means, "a panoply of statutes designed to assure all Americans equal access to safe and healthy homes, schools, workplaces and communities, and in some cases, basic civil rights." (One might ask, after surveying the state of our nation's inner cities, just how effective these longstanding guarantees of "safe and healthy" homes and schools have been.) To these critics, such as Makram B. Jaber in the *Emory Law Journal*, the very phrase *unfunded federal mandate* is nothing more than a "brilliant sound bite."[57]

Daniel H. Cole and Carol S. Comer, writing in the *Stanford Law & Policy Review*, assert that federal aid to the states "more than compensate[s]" for the inconvenience of mandates, and besides,

25

mandates are generally in pursuit of "noble social goals."[58] Good intentions excuse everything! Mandate critics are said to paint "a mythical picture of the federal government as a voracious and uncontrollable monster" instead of the presumably benevolent helpmeet it really is.[59]

Centralizers are unable to see—or they see but do not mind—the enervating effect of mandates on civic life. When policy is dictated from the top down, the grass roots are devitalized. Ordinary people feel as though they are powerless, even impotent. They withdraw from civic life because what's the use? Joseph F. Zimmerman notes that the decline in town-meeting attendance in New England is "associated with the proliferation of mandates." He declares, "Participatory democracy clearly suffers when national mandates are imposed upon local governments."[60]

Democracy suffers when decisions are made at the top of the pyramid and handed down—along with the bill for carrying out those decisions—to the folks at the bottom.

****

The Unfunded Mandates Reform Act (UMRA) of 1995 addressed the problem, nominally. But nominally didn't do the trick.

President Clinton signed the act into law on March 22, 1995. The president, a former governor of Arkansas who had been on the receiving end of mandates in his former position, said, with considerable hyperbole, "Today, we are making history.... We are recognizing that the pendulum had swung too far [toward Washington], and that we have to rely on the initiative, the creativity, the determination, and the decision-making of the people at the state and local level to carry much of the load for America as we move into the twenty-first century."[61]

UMRA had begun life as a rather more assertive attempt—with a mouthful of teeth—to tame mandates. Senator Dirk Kempthorne (R-ID), a former mayor of Boise, introduced in 1993 the Community Regulatory Relief Act, which proposed that any federal mandate must supply to state and local governments "all funds necessary to pay the direct costs incurred."[62] The senator did not exempt civil rights laws from this requirement, making it a nonstarter for many Democrats. But enough senators were hearing from the frustrated folks back home that mandate reform picked up something approaching momentum.

Senator Kempthorne's forthrightly anti-mandate approach was watered down during its journey from bill to law. He worked with

Senate Governmental Affairs Committee chairman John Glenn (D-OH) to fashion a measure that stood a chance of passage in a Democratic Senate. Exemptions were written in, as were floors for the estimated cost of mandates that would be subject to congressional disapproval. A point-of-order scheme that appeared in the eventual law was drawn up. Yet despite widespread support—a majority of both the House and Senate had cosponsored the mandate reform bills—neither chamber had the chance to vote on the legislation during the 103rd Congress. It was stalled primarily by opposition from sclerotic liberals protective of their turf and Washington's lengthy reach. As Representative Henry Waxman (D-CA), the high priest of nanny statism in the House, said in opposition to mandate reform, if it were enacted, "We could no longer pass essential laws to address urgent social problems or to protect human health and the environment."[63] Basic standards of decency would simply collapse were Washington barred from ordering states and localities to carry out and pay for laws sent down from on high.

But then the 1994 GOP congressional landslide happened. The Republican leaders in the House were committed, at least as a rhetorical strategy, to federal mandate reform. In the Senate, the Kempthorne bill was given the symbolic title of S. 1. After extensive debate—including the Democrats' "cleaning out their wastebaskets trying to find amendments," as Senate Majority Leader Bob Dole said; one such amendment would require "reports concerning mandate impacts on homeless children"—the Senate passed the bill on January 27, 1995, by 86–10.[64] The nays were all Democrats. The surnames of these hardcore nationalizers were Bumpers (D-AR), Boxer (D-CA), Lieberman (D-CT), Sarbanes (D-MD), Levin (D-MI), Bradley (D-NJ), Lautenberg (D-NJ), Hollings (D-SC), Leahy (D-VT), and Byrd (D-WV).

Passage in the House of the companion legislation, whose primary sponsor was Representative William Clinger (R-PA), was also delayed by numerous attempts by Democrats to gut what was already, from one perspective, a gutless bill. It finally won approval on February 1, 1995, by a vote of 360–74. Every nay vote came from a Democrat, with the exception of Representative Bernie Sanders, the Vermont socialist who identifies as an Independent and usually votes with the Democrats.

Those considerable margins belied the extended discussion over the measure; as David Broder, long the barometer of conventional wisdom in the nation's capital, noted in the *Washington Post*, the Senate debated UMRA for fifteen days and held forty-four roll-call votes, while the House of Representatives parleyed for eight days and took thirty votes. Broder marveled that so modest a piece of legislation "was bitterly resisted by Washington-knows-best legislators."[65]

As stated in the act, its purpose was to

> curb the practice of imposing unfunded Federal mandates on states and local governments; to strengthen the partnership between the Federal Government and State, local and tribal governments, to end the imposition, in the absence of full consideration by Congress, of Federal mandates on State, local, and tribal governments without adequate funding, in a manner that may displace other essential governmental priorities; and to ensure that the Federal Government pays the costs incurred by those governments in complying with certain requirements under Federal statutes and regulations, and for other purposes.[66]

This sounded good. As Paul Posner wrote shortly after its passage, the Unfunded Mandates Reform Act of 1995 "signals recognition of the need to hold federal officials more accountable for the intergovernmental consequences of national actions."[67] Symbolically, it delivered a message. Symbolically. But as Nelson Lund noted in the *National Review* shortly after UMRA's passage, its "toothlessness" is perhaps its distinguishing feature.[68]

First, the definition: UMRA stated that "the term 'Federal mandate' means any provision in a statute or regulation or any Federal court ruling that imposes an enforceable duty upon State, local, or tribal governments including a condition of Federal assistance or a duty arising from participation in a voluntary Federal program."[69]

In effect, UMRA is limited to the fairly small number of mandates that fall under the category of direct statutory orders, and then a wide swath of these is also excluded. Mandates in the form of crossover sanctions—for example, threats to withhold highway monies unless states adopt federally dictated drunk-driving standards—are also exempt. This was an absolutely critical omission. The refusal of Congress to include crossover sanctions or conditional federal aid in the Unfunded Mandates Reform Act amounted to a "monstrous huge loophole," in the words of Marjorie Miller of the Congressional Budget Office.[70] These programs, as we shall see, are front and center in today's unfunded federal mandate debate—but UMRA simply looks the other way.

Those acts passed during and with the support of the George W. Bush administration—the significant, even historical, federal mandates that provoked some states to resistance, such as No Child Left Behind and REAL ID—are by and large not covered by UMRA. Toothless? Why, the Unfunded Mandates Reform Act is as edentate as anything you would find this side of *Deliverance*.

Covering only a select group of bills under consideration by Congress, UMRA required that the Congressional Budget Office assess the uncompensated cost of proposed federal mandates on state and local governments. If such cost exceeded $50 million (later raised to $60 million) annually for those levels of government or $100 million for private businesses, any member of the House or Senate could halt action on the bill by raising a point of order. This point of order was not raised automatically; a member of Congress had to pick up this ball and throw it. Subsequent to the point of order, the body could vote to override the point of order. It would only be sustained by a majority vote. So UMRA *did not ban unfunded federal mandates*. Far from it. But it did at least halt the runaway train long enough for skeptics to demand an accounting from the conductor. Or, to use a calmer metaphor, UMRA might act as a "speed bump" to slow, at least temporarily, a heedless Congress as it races to slap yet another unfunded federal mandate upon the fifty states.[71]

In the eyes of its sponsors, UMRA's sanctioning of this point of order put Congress on notice that unfunded mandates could not pass quietly into law without *some* consideration, however cursory, being given to the burden placed on lower levels of government.

On the surface, if one didn't probe too deeply, the new Republican Congress was finally addressing the aggravating and perhaps even unconstitutional practice of the federal government of mandating action by the states and localities and sticking those other jurisdictions with the bill. But beyond the name, beyond the federalist rhetoric that draped the new law, the Unfunded Mandates Reform Act of 1995 was to unfunded federal mandates what a tin of Band-Aids is to a man standing before a firing squad. The gesture is so ineffectual that the Congress may as well not have even bothered with it.

For one thing, all previously existing federal mandates, funded or not, are exempt from UMRA. It is not retroactive, which means that it does nothing to free states and localities from the oppressive burdens of the prior mandates that fueled the anti-mandate movement. So if the Americans with Disabilities Act is imposing serious costs upon your local transportation system, as it did in Philadelphia, where "ADA regulations required the city to make 320,000 curb cuts for wheelchairs at 80,000 intersections at a cost of $180 million over two years when the City's entire capital budget was only $125 million"—tough luck.[72] This is a classic legislative case of closing—or threatening to close—the barn door after the cows are long gone.

For another, as Nelson Lund writes, "Huge and vaguely defined categories of new unfunded mandates are exempted even from the mild requirement that they enjoy majority support in a separate floor vote."[73]

UMRA exempts any bill containing a mandate that "is necessary for the national security or the ratification or implementation of international treaty obligations." The "national security" exemption is large enough to drive a tank through—or, as we shall see, a national ID card. In response to knee-jerk opposition from labor and civil rights groups, it also exempted bills involving civil or constitutional rights or measures addressing discrimination—which, as Professor Edward A. Zelinsky notes, is so broad an exception that "virtually any mandate can be justified" thereunder.[74] And of course a mandate carrying a price tag to state and local governments of $49 million annually or less was home free. As Conlan, Riggle, and Schwartz conclude in their study of the politics of UMRA, "the multiple exclusions provide a variety of ways for the Congress to circumvent the act's intent."[75] In the act's first decade of existence, only once—in a House vote on a minimum wage hike—was a point of order both raised and sustained. The US Advisory Commission on Intergovernmental Affairs—which was abolished shortly after the mandate act was passed—estimated that up to two-thirds of the previously existing mandates would have been exempt from the act anyway.[76]

And in fact, since 1981 the Congressional Budget Office had already been supplying to Congress estimated costs of proposed mandates of $200 million or more that had been reported from congressional committees, thanks to the State and Local Government Cost Estimate Act of that year. True, the UMRA-dictated estimates were to be more detailed, but as Zelinsky asked, "Why should the reports produced by the CBO now discourage Congress from imposing new unfunded mandates when the reports produced by the CBO during the previous fifteen years had no discernible effect?"[77] This was a case of the wish being father to the thought.

In 1996, UMRA's first year, the CBO prepared estimates for sixty-nine bills that included intergovernmental mandates. Only eleven of them met the $50 million minimum, and of these just one (a minimum wage increase) actually made it to the floor. As Paul Posner writes, other mandates were "modified when sponsors learned that they might prompt a point of order."[78] Upon being informed that their bill both qualified as a mandate and would impose a cost of $50 million or more in uncompensated demands upon state and local governments or $100 million for private businesses, the sponsors of these measures amended them—or jiggered the numbers—to slip in under the threshold. Thus was UMRA evaded. Other post-1995 unfunded mandates that side-stepped UMRA include the Help America Vote Act and the No Child Left Behind Act. These acts we shall examine in detail later.

A May 2001 joint hearing of the Subcommittee on Technology of the House Rules Committee and the Subcommittee on Energy Policy, Natural Resources, and Regulatory Affairs of the House Government Reform Committee assessed the effectiveness of UMRA half a decade into its meek existence. While witnesses generally agreed that Title I, which directs the CBO to draw up cost estimates for mandates exceeding the specified floors and subjects those bills to points of order, had done what it was intended to do (which is emphatically *not* to say that it stopped or even significantly deterred the feds from mandating), Title II, which directs federal agencies to "undertake the same kind of cost analysis of mandates imposed in their regulations that the CBO undertakes in Congress," had been relatively useless. According to a study by the General Accounting Office, federal agencies hadn't even bothered to draw up the required "fiscal impact statements" for three-quarters of the 110 rules GAO identified as requiring such statements.[79] No entity is quite so far above the law as a federal agency.

Like the mandates that come before Congress, federal regulations to be promulgated by various agencies are only covered by UMRA if they were published after October 1, 1995. Thus the "scores" of previous mandates are scot-free, as John C. Eastman observes in his analysis of UMRA in the *Harvard Journal of Law & Public Policy.*[80]

As Edward A. Zelinsky, professor of law at the Benjamin N. Cardozo School of Law at Yeshiva University and a cogent critic of mandates, insisted after the passage of UMRA, the problem of unfunded federal mandates "remains unremedied." These mandates are still an "attractive device by which legislators advancing their own political interests opportunistically dispense public largesse to importuning constituencies while deflecting to officeholders at lower levels of government the political costs of taxing to pay for that largesse."[81] With UMRA, federal lawmakers gave the appearance of responding to cries for relief from state and local officials—they gave the all-important appearance of *doing something*—while leaving this most attractive and insidious option available.

Zelinsky points out that similar laws at the state level requiring that legislation imposing mandates disclose the costs thereof have been spectacularly ineffective. For one thing, they exempt a wide swath of mandates. And Zelinsky doubts that the premise of such laws—that their authors and potential supporters don't understand the costs of such mandates—is even accurate. In most cases, mandaters know *exactly* what they are doing. In fact, *that's why they're doing it.* Moreover, even the frequent requirement that mandates require a supermajority for passage has failed to brake this runaway train: the state legislators "simply vot[e] to suspend such prohibitions."[82]

While one of UMRA's primary authors, Senator Dirk Kempthorne, claimed to David Broder on the act's tenth anniversary that UMRA "fundamentally changed the relationship" between the federal, state, and local governments and also "changed the culture on Capitol Hill"—that's a lot of change for a toothless act—for the most part even its boosters concede that it has been a disappointment. It "hasn't done nearly as much as we might have hoped," Senator Lamar Alexander (R-TN) diplomatically told Broder. If "as much as we might have hoped" is a synonym for "not a damn thing," then senator Alexander might have been onto something. The senator did analyze, keenly and frankly, the real problem, which is that "Democrats, still stuck in the New Deal, are reflexively searching for national solutions to local problems [and] Republicans, having found ourselves in charge, have decided it is more blessed to impose our views, rather than to liberate Americans from Washington."[83]

There were exceptions to Alexander's rule. For the most part, Republicans continued to proclaim their undying opposition to unfunded mandates, or at least those mandates proposed by the Democratic Party. Senator James Inhofe (R-OK) said that unfunded federal mandates "are the product of an assertive, greedy Government that has arrogantly injected itself into the dictatorial position that was feared most by our Founding Fathers."[84] (The senator, to his credit, would later vote against President Bush's crowning achievement in unfunded mandates, the No Child Left Behind Act.)

But Americans in the provinces, and some of their state and local representatives, had grown tired of scraping and bowing to Washington, of both enforcing and paying for the mandates their mandarins handed down to them. They doubted that any real relief was coming from Washington. So they set out to defend themselves.

The studies of those defenses are what Priscilla M. Regan of George Mason University and Christopher J. Deering of George Washington University—their schools constituting a Founding Fathers tag team?—refer to as a "growing body of work on state resistance to federal initiatives."[85] This resistance expanded as federal mandates and usurpations of traditional state and local functions expanded.

****

States resist unfunded federal mandates—when they do resist—in various ways. They may fight it in the courts, in the legislatures, or even in the arena of public opinion. When leviathan is pressing down upon you, any handy weapon will do.

In the case of REAL ID, several states launched vigorous protests, passing resolutions of noncompliance. Such an instance is "a more unusual, formal, overt and direct challenge" than are the other methods of resistance.[86] In those other cases, or in states with less confrontational political cultures, states and their agents may lobby to win funding for the unfunded mandates; that is, their beef is not so much with the mandate as with the lack of funds. States employ lobbyists in Washington, DC, and while those lobbyists are often either drawn from the usual lobbyist pool or quickly adapt to the mores of Washington, they do seek to modify what state officials regard as onerous or unfair federal laws. Conciliation-minded or nonconfrontational states may seek waivers or exemptions from the objectionable policy. This tactic was among those used by states reluctant to conform to No Child Left Behind and REAL ID. Or states may bring suit against federal mandates, as South Dakota did in the case of the Reagan administration's national twenty-one-year-old drinking age.

States with large Hispanic populations were more likely to object to NCLB, as it was thought that English as a second language speakers would have a more difficult time passing the required reading tests. (The same was true in the case of REAL ID: states with relatively large Hispanic populations were found disproportionately among those rejecting the national ID.)

As Christopher J. Deering notes, one standout finding is "the consistent significance of union membership." States with larger unionized workforces were less likely to dissent from NCLB and REAL ID. Yet he found a lack of "common factors" uniting those states that rebelled, to varying degrees, against these Bush-era unfunded mandates. States, like the heart, often have reasons of their own.

The mandate trap, once laid, is hard to avoid. When states become dependent upon a funding flow from Washington, it becomes politically, even fiscally, difficult to turn off the tap. Even though the citizens of those states have contributed, proportionately (or even disproportionately, in the case of some states with respect to the fuel and excise tax raised Highway Trust Fund), to the federal revenues that are then kicked back to the states, their contributions are discounted when the feds opt for coercive federalism. No matter that the automobile and truck drivers of South Dakota contribute more, per capita, to the Highway Trust Fund than do, say, the residents of Manhattan—South Dakotans still faced the loss of federal highway money when their state resisted the Reagan-Dole mandate that states raise their legal drinking ages to twenty-one. (New York, in fairness, also fought that mandate, though the strongest opposition came from legislators representing the outer boroughs and upstate.)

Infusions of federal monies can serve as a lifeline—or perhaps as a leash. The entity that controls the money can jerk the leash in whatever fashion it wishes, and the supplicant on the other end must dance to whatever tune is called.

****

The feds can use the spending clause, the courts have found, in a somewhat roundabout way to influence state and local policies. They can place conditions upon the receipt of federal aid, thus achieving the desired effect without the sledgehammer (a probably unconstitutional sledgehammer) of a direct order.

Lacking a clear constitutional sanction to impose certain laws on the states, the federal government instead conditions federal aid on the performance by the states of actions desired by Washington: for instance, the administering of standardized tests to fourth graders. Attaching conditions to federal aid is an excellent way to bend the states to the desire of the federal government. Conditional aid has generally passed muster in the federal courts. After all, as federal judges are wont to observe, the states could always *refuse* to take the aid, in which case they are not bound by the federal conditions attached to that aid.

In practice, this option barely registers on the probability meter. As Michael S. Greve of the American Enterprise Institute observes, "Even if the states can reject federal funds as a matter of law, they will be unable to bolt: each state's voters will be compelled to pay a portion of the federal funds, irrespective of the state's participation."[88] It would take an unusually principled act to refuse monies toward which a state's taxpayers have already pitched in. They would, in a sense, be paying twice for a program toward which taxpayers in the other states are only paying once. In addition, these mandated programs typically have aggressive, even zealous, constituencies at the local level that would make life miserable for any politico who dared suggest that his or her state forgo the money.

(Reliance on the commerce power, by contrast, is a more precarious strategy by the feds. In *U.S. v. Lopez* (1995), for instance, the Supreme Court struck down the Gun Free School Zones Act of 1990, which made it a federal crime for "any individual knowingly to possess a firearm at a place that [he] knows . . . is a school zone." By this act, Congress had sought to ban the presence of firearms near public school campuses, yet the court found this an overreach of the federal commerce power. Miracle of miracles! This was the first time in more than half a century that the court had found real limits to the seemingly infinitely elastic interstate commerce clause of the Constitution. Yet in *Gonzales v. Raich* (2005), the court interpreted the commerce clause to permit the federal government to ban the growing of marijuana at home for personal consumption, even for medicinal use, and even if a state—in this case, California—has expressly legalized such practice. The *Gonzales* case seems to envision a commerce clause that is so endlessly elastic as to empower the federal government to regulate almost any aspect of an individual's life. The court is nothing if not capricious.)

If it is easy for the federal government to shuck off its responsibility to pay for the programs it creates, it is devilishly hard for states to reject federal aid—especially when every other state is receiving such aid and when the purported beneficiaries of such aid do not understand why some niggling constitutional issue should keep them from enjoying the subvention.

Having one's cake and eating it too is a universal desire, as is the preference to have someone else pay for the cake. As William T. Gormley Jr. of the Georgetown Public Policy Institute observes in *Publius*, "The more money the federal government makes available to the states, the happier the states tend to be. The more mandates the federal government imposes on the states, the unhappier the states tend to be."[89] Give us the dough, but don't tell us how to spend it: the states, like teenagers, have a strong preference for no-strings-attached gifts.

But the giver of these "gifts" had plenty of strings in mind.

For if the spending clause is more or less open-ended and the enumerated powers of the federal government have been, shall we say, transcended, can Congress go one giant step further and "compel the recipients of its largesse, the states included, to refrain from acting in ways only loosely related to the purpose of the appropriation and wholly unrelated to its enumerated powers"?[90] Can Congress, say, in providing federal tax dollars to states and localities for road work, force those states and localities, as a condition of aid, to set speed limits or minimum drinking ages at a level deemed proper by Congress? And can it also pass along the enforcement costs of these mandates? Yes, yes, a thousand times yes, stated the Supreme Court—and Congress has accepted the invitation.

Mandates, in particular the crossover sanctions branch of the family, became an irresistible temptation. As Albert J. Rosenthal wrote in the *Stanford Law Journal* in a 1987 analysis of the constitutionality of conditional federal spending, Congress found mighty alluring the prospect of attaching "strings to its expenditures, to coerce recipients into conduct which it might not be able constitutionally to compel if it sought to do so by direct regulation."[91] The states and localities were hard-pressed to refuse compliance with such conditions, and the courts had left open the path by which Congress could impose its will by acts other than constitutionally suspect direct orders.

The modern mandate legal muddle, which has been described charitably by Jonathan Duncan as falling "far short of clarity and even farther short of consistency," starts with *National League of Cities (NLC) v. Usery* (1974), in which states and localities sued to keep from having the federal Fair Labor Standards Act, with its wage and hour provisions, applied to them. By a vote of 5–4, the US Supreme Court sided with the lower jurisdictions, as Justice William Rehnquist, in his majority opinion, declared that the federal government could not regulate the states "in their capacities as sovereign governments."[92] The Tenth Amendment was peeking up from its grave.

The *NLC* case, a high-water mark of resurgent federalism, spurred new—and "largely unsuccessful"—challenges on Tenth Amendment grounds to federal overreach.[93] But *NLC* was overturned by the court in *Garcia v. San Antonio Metropolitan Transit Authority* (1985), which permitted the feds to force state and local governments to apply the Fair Labor Standards Act to their employees. The impact was enormous: more than seven million public employees were affected. Additional costs in 1986 alone were estimated at $1.1 billion.[94] And, perhaps even more importantly, the Tenth Amendment was shoved back down its rabbit hole. Justice Sandra Day O'Connor dissented from the *Garcia* decision, wryly remarking on Congress's "underdeveloped capacity for self-restraint," betokening her eventual emergence as the court's principal defender of federalism.[95]

In *New York v. United States* (1992), the US Supreme Court cited the Tenth Amendment in striking down one of three waste-disposal incentives in the Low-Level Radioactive Waste Policy Amendments Act of 1985. The goal of the act was to ensure that states lacking low-level radioactive waste disposal sites remedied that deficiency. The deficiency, it should be noted, was widespread: at the time of the bill's passing, only South Carolina, Nevada, and Washington had operative disposal sites.

Two of the act's incentives for the unsited states to take responsibility for such waste generated within their borders—monetary and access incentives—passed muster, but the third, a "take title" incentive, did not. This nullified provision forced states to take title to low-level radioactive waste generated within their borders if other arrangements for the disposal of such waste had not been made, for example, by constructing such a site within their borders or joining a regional compact. If a state had not arranged for the disposal of such waste by a specified time, that state, "upon the request of the generator or owner of the waste, shall take title to the waste, be obligated to take possession of the waste, and shall be liable for all damages directly or indirectly incurred by such generator or owner as a consequence of the failure of the State to take possession."[96] Congress was dictating to the states that they either build a disposal site within their borders or take title to all such waste generated therein. With typical discourtesy, this mandate was not to be funded by the feds. (The take-title provision was "a favor to the generators of radioactive waste," writes Edward A. Zelinsky.[97] The favor was granted by the feds but was to be performed by the states.)

The act was challenged by the state of New York and its counties of Cortland and Allegany. The US Court of Appeals for the Second Circuit upheld the act, but the US Supreme Court, in an opinion written by Justice Sandra Day O'Connor, struck down the "take title" provision. Justice O'Connor described the take title provision as "lying outside

Congress' enumerated powers or as infringing upon the core of state sovereignty reserved by the Constitution's Tenth Amendment." Congress was forcing upon the states a choice—some choice!—between taking title to the waste ("which would in principle be no different than a congressionally compelled subsidy from state governments to radioactive waste producers") and obeying Congress's dictate to build radioactive waste disposal facilities. Forcing either of these acts upon the states "would be beyond the authority of Congress," wrote Justice O'Connor for the majority. (Stevens, Blackmun, and White dissented.)

Justice O'Connor understood the significance of this case. It raised questions "as old as the Constitution" itself, namely, "discerning the proper division of authority between the Federal Government and the States." And for once, the states were not found to be wholly and abjectly subordinate to the national government. By forcing states to take title to low-level radioactive waste generated within their borders, Congress had "crossed the line distinguishing encouragement from coercion." It had commandeered the states to act as administrators of a federal mandate and crossed a constitutional bridge too far. Congress may not, said the court, "conscript state governments as its agents."[98]

That clapping heard dimly in the distance was probably George Mason and James Madison, the authors of the Bill of Rights, applauding a rare judicial nod to the Tenth Amendment. Perhaps it was not a "mere truism," as the New Deal had diminished it, after all.

As Jonathan Duncan observed, the *New York* decision was an emphatic pronouncement that "States do not exist as regional offices or administrative agencies of the federal government."[99] What a pity, however, that the federal government barely noticed *New York*. It was too busy barking orders to those hapless and beleaguered regional offices known as the fifty states. Still, as Michael C. Tolley and Bruce A. Wallin of Northeastern University argue in *Publius*, the *New York* case is "probably the best example of how the 'anti-coercion' principle might be used by states to challenge federally mandated action."[100]

In *New York*, the court opined, with a nod to its critical national drinking-age decision *South Dakota v. Dole*, that conditional aid is a perfectly legitimate way for the feds to encourage desired behavior by the states because "the residents of the State retain the ultimate decision as to whether or not the State will comply. If a State's citizens view federal policy as sufficiently contrary to local interests, they may elect to decline a federal grant."[101] Sure they will. Those residents have paid into the federal treasury at the same rate as residents of other states;

is it not an invidious distinction to keep from them the same grants received by the governments of those other states simply because they reject a one-size-fits-all policy prescription of the federal government?

If *New York v. United States* provides a foreshadowing of anti-mandate jurisprudence, a more visible case was soon to follow. In 1997, the US Supreme Court, in *Printz v. United States* (1997), struck down a central provision—an unfunded federal mandate—of the gun-control law known as the Brady Act (nee Brady Bill).

The Brady Handgun Violence Prevention Act of 1993, as its proper handle went, took its name from Jim Brady, the White House press secretary to Ronald Reagan who was crippled by a stray bullet that struck his head when John Hinckley tried to assassinate the president with a .22 caliber revolver on March 30, 1981. Mr. Brady's wife, Sarah Brady, became a leading crusader for more restrictive gun-control laws and the chairperson of Handgun Control, Inc.

The result was the Brady Bill, signed into law by President Clinton on November 30, 1993. The Brady Handgun Violence Prevention Act of 1993 established a five-day waiting period for the purchase of specified handguns. The purpose, according to its authors, was "to prevent convicted felons and other persons who are barred by law from purchasing guns from licensed gun dealers, manufacturers or importers."[102]

Prior to this law, as Dylan Finguerra noted in the *Journal of Law and Policy*, "only fourteen states had mandatory waiting periods, nine states required a permit to purchase a handgun, and two states required a telephone background check."[103] Members of Congress and the president, who know best, or so the conceit goes, judged these efforts insufficient. A waiting period and background check were imposed on all fifty states.

The Brady Act also, and most controversially, dumped on state and local law enforcement officers the responsibility for conducting background checks on the purchasers of specified handguns. (The Gun Control Act of 1968 had required purchasers of certain firearms to swear that they were neither felons nor mentally unstable—that is, that they were legally permitted to possess the weapon in question. Their word of honor, in the form of a signature on a federal form, was sufficient. No background check was necessary.)

Under the Brady Act, the purchaser of said handguns was required to fill out a form (issued by the Bureau of Alcohol, Tobacco, and Firearms) providing identification information as well as answering questions that would possibly reveal disqualifying traits (under felony

39

indictment, dishonorably discharged from military service, an illegal alien). The purchaser would deliver this form to the gun dealer, who would verify the would-be purchaser's identify and then send it along to the chief law enforcement officer (usually the sheriff or perhaps the chief of police), or CLEO, of the county of residence of the purchaser. "The instant the form is received," wrote Jonathan Duncan in the *Kansas Law Review* shortly after the Brady Bill had been enacted, "the CLEO proceeds under mandate from the federal government and the Brady Act proceeds into severe constitutional trouble."

For the CLEO is given five days to "ascertain . . . whether receipt or possession" of the handgun would violate the act. The CLEO is required to undertake "research in whatever State and local record-keeping systems are available and in a national system designated by the Attorney General."[104] If the purchaser is ineligible under the Brady Act, the sheriff must notify the individual of the reasons for the denial. In other words, the sheriff is turned into an enforcer—and an enforcer in tedious detail—of this federal mandate. He and his county are not reimbursed for their time or expense. Not one red cent. The cost of carrying out the mandate had to be paid for by either raising local taxes or transferring money from other, presumably more urgent or relevant, needs. It was a case of Washington knows best.

There was language in the act foreseeing the eventual establishment of a national computerized system under which gun dealers could conduct their own instant background checks, bypassing the CLEOs, but this was to take place somewhere in the hazy future—like maybe 1998, or maybe not. For the foreseeable future, however, the burden of background checks fell upon the sheriffs.

This was seen at the time of debate as an unfunded mandate. (It was not covered by UMRA, which grandfathered in all previous federal mandates.) Representative Steve Schiff (R-NM) called it such and offered an amendment (which failed) to give local law enforcement officials the option of not performing a background check. Senator Larry Craig (R-ID) asserted that the mandatory background check violated the Tenth Amendment.[105]

As Robert K. Corbin, president of that bogeyman to all good liberals everywhere, the National Rifle Association (NRA), put it, "The U.S. Congress didn't just roll another unfunded federal mandate down the Capitol steps. The U.S. Congress violated the U.S. Constitution. Knowingly." He added that under the Brady Act, the feds were taking "control of state and local police from the communities they serve . . .

divert[ing] them from their primary duties . . . [a]nd tell[ing] state and local officials, 'Oh, by the way, it's our program, but you foot the bill.'"[106]

Local law enforcement officials filed several lawsuits against the new law—not, signally, on the expected Second Amendment grounds, but rather on Tenth Amendment grounds. First out of the box was Richard Mack, the sheriff of Graham County, Arizona, who declared that "the federal government has no jurisdictional authority to order or command me or any other sheriff in this country to enforce federal law. I am not a federal agent. . . . I work for Graham County and was hired by the people to do their bidding." The Brady law, said Sheriff Mack, "imposes a greater burden on a very limited sheriff's office manpower, budget, and resources." In effect, the federal government was conscripting Sheriff Mack, and all the sheriffs of all the counties in the United States, to enforce a very time-consuming provision of the Brady Act that required background checks on all buyers of handguns. As Sheriff Mack told one newspaper, "a citizen of Graham County bought a gun in Tucson [Pima County], and, under the law, I'm required to do background checks wherever citizens of my county go" to buy such guns. "The gun shop owner and I spent an hour and a half faxing things back and forth. . . . In effect, I spent an hour and a half working for the gun shop."[107] The Arizona federal district court, in *Mack v. United States*, sided with the sheriff in the matter of background checks, asserting: "The issue is not . . . whether Congress possesses the raw power to regulate the transfer of handguns. Clearly it does. The thorny question is whether the Tenth Amendment limits the power of Congress to regulate in the way it has chosen."[108] The district court said that it did.

Robert W. Lee, in the pages of the right-wing magazine *The New American*, surveyed the range of sheriffs who had taken on the Brady Act. They were from Vermont, Wyoming, Texas, Louisiana, Mississippi, and, most notably, Montana, where Sheriff Jay Printz of Ravalli County lent his name to what became one of the Tenth Amendment's greatest—and, alas, few—judicial triumphs over an unfunded federal mandate. Sheriff Printz had refused to carry out the required background checks. Sheriff Printz's challenge to the Brady Act was first supported by District Court Judge Charles C. Lovell, who struck down the background check mandate on Tenth Amendment grounds as well as the broader constitutional framework. In fact, federal courts struck down parts of the law in Arizona, Louisiana, Mississippi, and Vermont; the only federal court to uphold the act's most notorious provisions was in Texas (*Koog v. United States*).

As Jonathan Duncan points out, the *Koog* court found that the background check imposed only a "minimal" burden on CLEOs.[109] Yet across the country, sheriffs had testified that the cost in personnel hours to do even one background check could be substantial. For instance, a sheriff in Orange County, Vermont, Samuel Frank, said that such checks took between fifteen minutes and six hours—no small portion of time for an office that typically had a grand total of two persons on duty. Sheriff Frank testified that he "spent approximately six hours on a single search of a [National Crime Information Center] records check in which a 1963 felony conviction was discovered, but was not complete enough for a final decision for the pending gun sale."[110]

Background checks were not a mere matter of plugging a few ID numbers into a computer and waiting ten seconds for the result. Many of these records were not computerized; sheriffs, especially those in sparsely populated rural areas, had to travel many miles to examine the records firsthand. Of course, the people who write and agitate for laws such as the Brady Act hardly know that sparsely populated rural areas even exist, and if they are aware of such areas they often view them disdainfully as backwaters whose benighted serfs have nothing better to do than carry out the dictates of better-educated authorities in the nation's capital.

The Brady Act distorted the allocation of time and money by local law enforcement. Compliance with the background check mandate meant that much less time and money could be spent on other tasks—tasks that, in the absence of the mandate, these sheriffs would have performed. This diversion of resources is a consequence of mandates that their authors somehow never even foresee, let alone acknowledge.

The district courts frequently referred to the *New York* decision. State and local officials under the Brady Act were being commandeered, just as states had been by the take-title provision of the low-level radioactive waste disposal law. "No commandeering" became a guiding principle—much to the distress of the federal government, whose functionaries somehow cannot see that there might be anything constitutionally troublesome or practically bothersome about the feds commandeering what to them seem inferior levels of government. Justice O'Connor's "no commandeering" language had "signaled the revival of constitutional federalism," as Professors Tolley and Wallin averred.[111] And it set the stage for a potential judicial scaling back of unfunded federal mandates.

In Justice Scalia's majority opinion in *Printz*, the federal government, by forcing state and local law enforcement officials to perform

Brady Bill background checks on purchasers of handguns, in effect conscripted them to act as agents of the federal government. Wrote Justice Scalia: "the power of the Federal Government would be augmented immeasurably if it were able to impress into its service—and at no cost to itself—the police officers of the 50 States." Scalia added the observation that "By forcing state governments to absorb the financial burden of implementing a federal regulatory program, Members of Congress can take credit for 'solving' problems without having to ask their constituents to pay for the solutions with higher federal taxes."[112]

The Brady Act in its entirety was not struck down, it is true, but its most controversial section—an act of federal mandating and commandeering that seemed to view county sheriffs as uncompensated agents of the all-wise and all-powerful federal government—was gone. It had been judged to have run afoul of the Tenth Amendment, one of those fundamental pieces of the Bill of Rights that seemed to have disappeared for decades before its rediscovery at the end of the twentieth century.

Robert W. Adler, a defender of federal mandates as wise social policy, notes in the *Vanderbilt Law Review* that neither the *Printz* nor the *New York* decisions made a distinction between funded and unfunded mandates: it was the compulsory nature of the mandate upon state and local governments that violated the Constitution, not the manner of funding. Adler contends that these are narrow rulings that bar federal commandeering of a state's regulatory apparatus but leave standing direct orders, full and partial preemptions, and aid conditions—the vast bulk of mandates, that is.[113]

The courts may provide, at best, a very partial and unsatisfying way out of the mandate muddle. The pro-mandate legal writer Makram B. Jaber argues that except for direct orders from Washington to the states, which are rare, "'relief' from unfunded federal mandates is not likely to come from the courts."[114]

As we shall see in our discussion of *South Dakota v. Dole*, the court has held that states are not entirely without recourse when squeezed by federal mandates: they can always turn down the federal money and thus not be bound by the mandate. As long as states have that as an "out," mandates seem to fall on the permissible side of the constitutional ledger. Yet in many cases and under many programs, the states are so enmeshed in the web of multilevel governmental funding that a rejection of federal funds might amount to an abandonment of the program in question. And in the case, say, of the Highway Trust Fund, from which federal highway construction and repair monies have been disbursed, those revenues are being raised by a gasoline tax paid by drivers in all fifty states. For the feds to cut off a state from this appropriations flow would be an act of invidious discrimination.

The states, having traded their sovereignty for the federal security blanket, are stuck. Despite General Revenue Sharing (1972–1986), which was a brief flirtation with cutting those nettlesome "strings attached" to federal aid to state and local governments, the tie that binds has become ever more taut, even strangling. Under revenue sharing, states enjoyed relative freedom to set their own priorities. More than $85 billion was transferred from DC to the states and localities under this program, which frustrated interest groups and their congressional advocates no end—what's the use of doling out all that money if one can't force the dole taker to do one's bidding?[115] (Today, federal grants-in-aid account for about 26 percent of state revenues—the largest single share from any source. This is down from 31.7 percent in 1980. But "no strings attached" is decidedly *not* the operating principle.)[116]

As Elvis once sang, the states are caught in a trap, and they can't walk out.

Help is unlikely to come from the Obama Democrats, who operate within the party's now eight-decades-old centralizing paradigm, or the modern Republicans, who occasionally talk the talk but almost never walk the walk.

Paul Posner analyzed every federal mandate-related roll call vote in Congress from 1983 through 1990. There were sixty-nine in all; the most common forms, with eighteen each, were direct orders and crossover sanctions. His findings were a surprise—but only if one is bewitched by the airy speechifying of politicians.

Everyone knows that Republicans talk a good game when it comes to federalism. But in the years under study by Posner—critically, years when Republicans held the White House—congressional Republicans supported federal mandates at a higher rate (57 percent) than did Democrats (52 percent). And it should be noted that the Democratic percentage was not particularly affected by the votes of Southern Democrats, who supported the mandates at a 51 percent level.[117]

Parsing the data further, Posner reveals that Republicans and Democrats alike are ready and willing to shove mandates down the throats of state and local governments when those mandates comport with their own policy preferences. When the measure at hand "furthered the conservative social policy agenda of moral issues, preempted states from stronger regulation of the environment and other business issues, and restricted or placed conditions on welfare payments," Republicans were most likely to support federal mandates. Democrats, meanwhile, were most likely to fall in line behind federal mandates when they involved the "national imposition of liberal social agendas, such as strengthening the application of civil rights requirements on grantees."[118]

Neither party shows anything like a principled commitment to federalism or skepticism of federal mandates, funded or unfunded. The majority of partisans simply wish to impose their policy preferences on as large a constituency as possible, nationally, if feasible. But if political realities restrict the realm to the states, then they'll take that. The number of political figures who adhere to even a rough consistency on these issues is minuscule. A central, indeed essential, feature of the American republic—federalism—is dead or dying. And the widespread support for unfunded federal mandates is Exhibit A. In the succeeding pages, we will examine several unfunded federal mandates in depth—and perhaps look for traces of federalism amid the ruins.

Notes

1. Posner, *The Politics of Unfunded Mandates*, p. 22.
2. Thomas Jefferson to Albert Gallatin, June 16, 1817, *Letters and Addresses of Thomas Jefferson*, edited by William B. Parker and Jonas Viles (New York: Wessels, 1907), pp. 259–60.
3. Albert J. Rosenthal, "Conditional Federal Spending and the Constitution," *Stanford Law Review* (Vol. 39, No. 5, May 1987): 1107.
4. Bruce J. Casino, "Federal Grants-in-Aid: Evolution, Crisis, and Future," *The Urban Lawyer* (Vol. 20, No. 1, Winter 1988): 28.
5. Ibid.: 32, 30–31. For an analysis of pre–Great Society federal grants to the states, see Phillip Monypenny (no relation to the secretary in the James Bond movies, we assume), "Federal Grants-in-Aid to State Governments: A Political Analysis," *National Tax Journal* (Vol. 13, No. 1, March 1960): 1–16.
6. Donald J. Mizerk, "The Coercion Test and Conditional Federal Grants to the States," *Vanderbilt Law Review* (Vol. 40, 1987): 1164.
7. *United States v. Butler*, 297 U.S. 1 (1936).
8. Rosenthal, "Conditional Federal Spending and the Constitution": 1127.
9. *United States v. Darby*, 312 U.S. 100 (1941).
10. Jeffrey T. Renz, "What Spending Clause? (or the President's Paramour)," *John Marshall Law Review* (Fall 1999): 83.
11. James L. Sundquist, *Politics and Policy: The Eisenhower, Kennedy, and Johnson Years* (Washington, DC: Brookings Institution, 1968), p. 341.
12. Ibid., p. 344.
13. Ibid., pp. 343–44.

14. *Regulatory Federalism: Policy, Process, Impact and Reform*, Advisory Commission on Intergovernmental Relations, February 1984, p. 78.
15. Mizerk, "The Coercion Test and Conditional Federal Grants to the States": 1187.
16. *Regulatory Federalism: Policy, Process, Impact and Reform*, p. 80.
17. www.library.unt.edu/gpo/acir/Default.html.
18. Tim Conlan, "From Cooperative to Opportunistic Federalism: Reflections on the Half-century Anniversary of the Commission on Intergovernmental Relations," *Public Administration Review* (Vol. 66, No. 5, September/October 2006): 667.
19. Ibid.: 674. Estimates of the total cost of federal mandates have varied wildly. Early efforts to slap a price tag on mandates ranged from $8.9 billion (1993) to $500 billion (1991). Marcella Ridlen Ray and Timothy J. Conlan, "At What Price? Costs of Federal Mandates since the 1980s," *Publius* (Vol. 28, No. 1, Winter 1996): 7. There was also disagreement over what were the most expensive or onerous mandates. A 1980 Urban Institute study of the impact of six federal mandates (the Davis-Bacon Act, the Clean Water Act, the Education for All Handicapped Children Act, the Bilingual Education Act, the handicapped access to public transportation regulations, and 1976 amendments to the unemployment compensation system) on six American cities and one county fingered the Clean Water Act as far and away the most expensive, and it also found these mandates to be regressive in that "they tended to impose proportionately higher costs on jurisdictions with the lowest fiscal resources." Michael Fix and Daphne A. Kenyon, "Introduction," *Coping with Mandates: What Are the Alternatives?* (Lanham, MD: University Press of America, 1990), p. 13. A 1979 survey by scholars at the University of California at Riverside, while admitting that a wide gap existed between "data needs" and "data availability," found estimates of the cost of state and federal mandates ranging from 10 percent of a local government's expenditures to 85 percent thereof. Now *that's* a range. *Regulatory Federalism: Policy, Process, Impact and Reform*, p. 160.
20. John Kincaid, "From Cooperative to Coercive Federalism," *Annals of the American Academy of Political and Social Science* (Vol. 509, May 1990): 140.
21. Dale Krane, "The Middle Tier in American Federalism: State Government Policy Activism during the Bush Presidency," *Publius* (Vol. 37, No. 3, 2007): 454.
22. Timothy J. Conlan, James D. Riggle, and Donna E. Schwartz, "Deregulating Federalism? The Politics of Mandate Reform in the 104th Congress," *Publius* (Vol. 25, No. 3, Summer 1995): 24.
23. Ibid.: 26.
24. Daniel H. Cole and Carol S. Comer, "Rhetoric, Reality, and the Law of Unfunded Federal Mandates," *Stanford Law & Policy Review* (Vol. 8, No. 2, 1997): 103.
25. Conlan, "From Cooperative to Opportunistic Federalism: Reflections on the Half-century Anniversary of the Commission on Intergovernmental Relations": 669.
26. Posner, *The Politics of Unfunded Mandates*, p. 203.
27. Ibid., pp. 4–5.
28. Alexis de Tocqueville, *Democracy in America*, Vol. 1 (New York: D. Appleton, 1899), p. 51.

29. Posner, *The Politics of Unfunded Mandates*, p. 23.
30. Ibid., p. 213.
31. Martha Derthick, "Federal Government Mandates: Why the States Are Complaining," *Brookings Review* (Vol. 10, No. 4, Fall 1992): 53.
32. Posner, *The Politics of Unfunded Mandates*, p. 79.
33. Ibid., p. 168.
34. Timothy J. Conlan, "Federalism and Competing Values in the Reagan Administration," *Publius* (Vol. 16, No. 1, Winter 1986): 37.
35. Ibid.: 29.
36. Kincaid, "From Cooperative to Coercive Federalism": 148.
37. Conlan, "Federalism and Competing Values in the Reagan Administration": 46.
38. Jonathan Duncan, "Looks Like a Waiting Period for the Brady Bill: Tenth Amendment Challenges to a Controversial Unfunded Mandate," *Kansas Law Review* (Vol. 43, 1994–95): 866.
39. Timothy J. Conlan, *From New Federalism to Devolution: Twenty-five Years of Intergovernmental Reform* (Washington, DC: Brookings Institution Press, 1998), pp. 313, 303.
40. Paul Posner, "The Politics of Coercive Federalism in the Bush Era," *Publius* (Vol. 37, No. 3, Summer 2007): 390–412.
41. Lyndon B. Johnson, "Memorandum on the Need for 'Creative Federalism' through Cooperation with State and Local Officials," November 11, 1966, www.presidency.ucsb.edu/ws/index.php?pid=28023.
42. Tim Conlan and John Dinan, "Federalism, the Bush Administration, and the Transformation of American Conservatism," *Publius* (Vol. 37, No. 3, Summer 2007): 279.
43. John Dinan, "The State of American Federalism 2007–2008: Resurgent State Influence in the National Policy Process and Continued State Policy Innovation," *Publius* (Vol. 38, No. 3, Summer 2008): 383.
44. Conlan and Dinan, "Federalism, the Bush Administration, and the Transformation of American Conservatism": 279.
45: Ibid.: 297.
46. Christopher J. Deering, "State Resistance to Federal Mandates: A Cross-Case Analysis," paper presented at the annual meeting of the American Political Science Association, Toronto, Canada, September 3–6, 2009, p. 1.
47. Patrick McGuinn, "The National Schoolmarm: No Child Left Behind and the New Educational Federalism," *Publius* (Winter 2005): 67.
48. Edward I. Koch, "The Mandate Millstone," *The Public Interest* (No. 61, Fall 1980): 42.
49. Ibid.: 43–44.
50. Ibid.: 45–46. For problems in implementing a modern civil rights mandate, see Kathryn Moss, Scott Burriss, Michael Ullman, Matthew Johnsen, and Jeffrey Swanson, "Unfunded Mandate: An Empirical Study of the Implementation of the Americans with Disabilities Act by the Equal Employment Opportunity Commission," *University of Kansas Law Review* (Vol. 50, 2001): 1–110.
51. Koch, "The Mandate Millstone": 55–56.
52. Makram B. Jaber, "Unfunded Federal Mandates: An Issue of Federalism or a 'Brilliant Sound Bite'?" *Emory Law Journal* (Vol. 45, No. 1, Winter 1996): 292.

53. Conlan, Riggle, and Schwartz, "Deregulating Federalism? The Politics of Mandate Reform in the 104th Congress": 24.
54. Ibid.: 27.
55. Paul Gillmor and Fred Eames, "Reconstruction of Federalism: A Constitutional Amendment to Prohibit Unfunded Mandates," *Harvard Journal on Legislation* (Vol. 31, 1994): 397.
56. *Federally Induced Costs Affecting State and Local Governments* (Washington, DC: Advisory Commission on Intergovernmental Relations, September 1994).
57. Jaber, "Unfunded Federal Mandates: An Issue of Federalism or a 'Brilliant Sound Bite'?": 281.
58. Cole and Comer, "Rhetoric, Reality, and the Law of Unfunded Federal Mandates": 104.
59. Ibid.: 111.
60. Joseph F. Zimmerman, "Financing National Policy through Mandates," *National Civic Review* (Summer-Fall 1992): 366.
61. Conlan, Riggle, and Schwartz, "Deregulating Federalism? The Politics of Mandate Reform in the 104th Congress": 23.
62. Ibid.: 28.
63. Ibid.: 30.
64. Ibid.: 33.
65. David S. Broder, "Those Unfunded Mandates," *Washington Post*, March 17, 2005.
66. Unfunded Mandates Reform Act of 1995, 104th Congress, www.govtrack.us/congress/bills/104/s1.
67. Posner, *The Politics of Unfunded Mandates*, p. 2.
68. Nelson Lund, "The Mandate Hoax of 1995," *National Review* (November 27, 1995): 52.
69. Unfunded Mandates Reform Act of 1995.
70. Laura S. Jensen, "Federalism, Individual Rights, and the Conditional Spending Conundrum," *Polity* (Vol. 33, No. 2, Winter 2000): 274.
71. Posner, "The Politics of Coercive Federalism in the Bush Era": 402.
72. John C. Eastman, "Re-Entering the Arena: Restoring a Judicial Role for Enforcing Limits on Federal Mandates," *Harvard Journal of Law & Public Policy* (Vol. 25, 2001–2002): 948.
73. Lund, "The Mandate Hoax of 1995."
74. Edward A. Zelinsky, "The Unsolved Problem of the Unfunded Mandate," *Ohio Northern University Law Review* (Vol. 23, No. 3, 1997): 772.
75. Conlan, Riggle, and Schwartz, "Deregulating Federalism? The Politics of Mandate Reform in the 104th Congress": 38.
76. Daniel E. Troy, "The Unfunded Mandates Reform Act of 1995," *Administrative Law Review* (Vol. 49, 1997): 143.
77. Zelinsky, "The Unsolved Problem of the Unfunded Mandate": 773–74.
78. Posner, *The Politics of Unfunded Mandates*, p. 183.
79. Eastman, "Re-Entering the Arena: Restoring a Judicial Role for Enforcing Limits on Federal Mandates": 938.
80. Ibid.: 942.
81. Zelinsky, "The Unsolved Problem of the Unfunded Mandate": 742.
82. Ibid.: 744.

83. David S. Broder, "Those Unfunded Mandates."
84. Duncan, "Looks Like a Waiting Period for the Brady Bill: Tenth Amendment Challenges to a Controversial Unfunded Mandate": 845.
85. Priscilla M. Regan and Christopher J. Deering, "State Opposition to REAL ID," *Publius* (Vol. 39, No. 3, 2009): 477.
86. Ibid.: 478.
87. Deering, "State Resistance to Federal Mandates: A Cross-Case Analysis," pp. 11, 14.
88. Michael S. Greve, "Big Government Federalism," American Enterprise Institute, March 2001, p. 4.
89. William T. Gormley Jr., "Money and Mandates: The Politics of Intergovernmental Conflict," *Publius* (Vol. 36, No. 4, 2006): 525.
90. Renz, "What Spending Clause? (or the President's Paramour)": 84.
91. Rosenthal, "Conditional Federal Spending and the Constitution": 1104.
92. Duncan, "Looks Like a Waiting Period for the Brady Bill: Tenth Amendment Challenges to a Controversial Unfunded Mandate": 852.
93. "Readings of Particular Interest," *Regulation*, September/December 1984, p. 69.
94. Adam M. Zaretsky, "A Gift Horse for the States: Federal Mandates," *The Regional Economist* (April 1993): 9.
95. Derthick, "Federal Government Mandates: Why the States Are Complaining": 51.
96. *New York v. United States*, 505 U.S. 144 (1992).
97. Zelinsky, "The Unsolved Problem of the Unfunded Mandate": 770.
98. *New York v. United States*, 505 U.S. 144 (1992). In a related vein, the court had held, in the earlier case of *Hodel v. Virginia Surface Mining & Reclamation Assn., Inc.* (1981), that Congress may not "commandeer the legislative processes of the States by directly compelling them to enact and enforce a federal regulatory program."
99. Duncan, "Looks Like a Waiting Period for the Brady Bill: Tenth Amendment Challenges to a Controversial Unfunded Mandate": 859.
100. Michael C. Tolley and Bruce A. Wallin, "Coercive Federalism and the Search for Constitutional Limits," *Publius* (Vol. 25, No. 4, 1995): 78.
101. *New York v. United States*, 505 U.S. 144 (1992).
102. P.L. 103–159.
103. Dylan Finguerra, "The Tenth Amendment Shoots Down the Brady Act," *Journal of Law and Policy* (Vol. 3, 1994–95): 640.
104. Duncan, "Looks Like a Waiting Period for the Brady Bill: Tenth Amendment Challenges to a Controversial Unfunded Mandate": 843.
105. Ibid.: 840–41.
106. Finguerra, "The Tenth Amendment Shoots Down the Brady Act": 642.
107. Robert W. Lee, "Sheriffs versus the Brady Law," *The New American* (August 22, 1994): 15.
108. Duncan, "Looks Like a Waiting Period for the Brady Bill: Tenth Amendment Challenges to a Controversial Unfunded Mandate": 846.
109. Ibid.
110. Finguerra, "The Tenth Amendment Shoots Down the Brady Act": 661.
111. Tolley and Wallin, "Coercive Federalism and the Search for Constitutional Limits": 83.

112. *Printz v. United States*, 521 U.S. 898 (1997).
113. Robert W. Adler, "Unfunded Mandates and Fiscal Federalism: A Critique," *Vanderbilt Law Review* (Vol. 50, 1997): 1200.
114. Jaber, "Unfunded Federal Mandates: An Issue of Federalism or a 'Brilliant Sound Bite'?": 322.
115. "Revenue Sharing," *Encyclopedia Britannica*, www.britannica.com/EBchecked/topic/500387/revenue-sharing.
116. "State and Local Governments' Fiscal Conditions—Frequently Asked Questions," General Accounting Office, www.gao.gov/special.pubs/longterm/state/fiscalconditionsfaq.html.
117. Posner, *The Politics of Unfunded Mandates*, p. 41.
118. Ibid., pp. 43, 45.

I

Roads, Rum, and Restraints

3

Drinking, Driving, and *Dole*: How Washington Mandated a 21-Year-Old Drinking Age to the States

When, a century ago, prohibition fever swept across the United States, and those in its grip sought to purge the demon rum (and its sister demons beer and whiskey and wine and gin and so on) from the land, first at the municipal and state level, and then at the national level, at least the prohibitionists understood that they lacked the constitutional foundation from which to issue a national interdiction against alcohol. What they needed was a constitutional amendment.

That amendment, the eighteenth such alteration to our governing document, is commonly regarded as among the most egregious acts in American legislative history, right up (or down) there with the Fugitive Slave Act and the Alien and Sedition Acts. Upon the amendment's repeal, a kind of federalist equilibrium in the matter of alcohol laws seemed to be achieved. But the prohibition fever, while it may abate, never quite goes away. The urge to tell others how to live their lives is overwhelming for some. And when it returned, cloaked in sanctimony, in the early 1980s, its devotees had found a new instrument with which to wage their war: the unfunded federal mandate.

With the Twenty-first Amendment ending the "noble experiment" that was the apex of the nanny state, control over laws and regulations governing the purchase, possession, consumption, sale, and use while driving of alcoholic beverages reverted to the states. This was as the Founders had intended: the only mention of such laws in the Constitutional Convention came when Virginia delegate George Mason proposed on August 20, 1787, that Congress be enabled "to enact sumptuary laws" regulating eating and drinking and manners. There was very little debate on this motion, other than Elbridge Gerry of Massachusetts observing that "the law of necessity is the best sumptuary law." Mr. Mason's motion failed, eight states to three.[1]

Drinking by the young was widespread and socially acceptable in much of the colonies. Consumption of spirituous brews was subject to local regulation, although "youthful drinking was seldom a subject of specific regulation," according to James F. Mosher in "A History of Youth Drinking Laws." An exception was Massachusetts—always in the forefront of paternalistic legislation—which in 1786 enacted a law requiring minors (except travelers, who could drink to their heart's content) to get "special allowance" from parents to drink at taverns. "Outright prohibitions" of minors drinking "did not exist."[2]

In Colonial America, the drink flowed in a volume that would impress the denizens of John Belushi's Delta House. The concept of childhood as a time of innocence and sequestering from the sordidness of adulthood was in the future; the idea of the *teenager* had yet to hatch. Adults, as University of Texas Professor of Law Michael P. Rosenthal noted in the *Dickinson Law Review*, "encouraged adolescents to openly experiment with adult drinking behaviors."[3] Twelve- and thirteen-year-old boys accompanied their fathers into taverns, and their job was not to fetch schooners of beer for dad but to imbibe right beside him. In this way was the boy initiated into one of the rites and pleasures (or vices) of manhood.

Even "when laws concerning youthful drinking were passed, they explicitly recognized the family unit by respecting the rights of parents to be the ultimate deciders of their children's behavior."[4] Up through the nineteenth century, a young man answered to his family, not a faraway government.

It wasn't until after the Civil War that most states began setting a minimum age at which people could legally consume or purchase an alcoholic beverage, at least in public places.

In New York, for instance, whether or not children drank was considered a matter for parents to decide. In 1881, writes Mosher, "a law was passed prohibiting tavernkeepers from permitting children under 14 from entering the premises unless accompanied by a parent or guardian."[5] This was upped to sixteen in 1884 and eighteen in 1896. California banned selling or even giving alcohol to a person under sixteen in 1872; the age was raised to eighteen in 1891. Yet in no state, at that time, was it a crime for a minor to drink alcohol. And the right of parents to supervise the upbringing of their children remained beyond the interventionist powers of the child-savers. Not that the paternalists didn't dream.

As Mosher relates, "true drinking-age laws did not actually appear prior to Prohibition because there was never a ban on all youthful drinking. . . . No crime was committed if a youth drank on the streets or at home."[6] But "child-saving" was all the rage in the Progressive Era, and laws regulating minors and alcohol appeared as part of a raft of such "reform" measures including child labor laws, compulsory school attendance laws, and various hygienic and judicial laws relating to families and children.

Then came Prohibition. A movement that had begun in Maine in the 1850s and steadily spread across the country reached its apex—or nadir—during the First World War.

The Eighteenth Amendment to the Constitution was resolved by Congress on December 18, 1917. This was therefore a wartime amendment, and as Randolph Bourne said, war is the health of the state. The Prohibition amendment was ratified by the thirty-sixth state (the requisite three-fourths of the then forty-eight states) on January 16, 1919, and became operative on January 16, 1920. Section I of the amendment declared: "After one year from the ratification of this article the manufacture, sale, or transportation of intoxicating liquors within, the importation thereof into, or the exportation thereof from the United States and all territory subject to the jurisdiction thereof for beverage purposes is hereby prohibited."

More than a baker's dozen years later, a nation belatedly come to its senses ratified the Twenty-first Amendment, which with elegant if long-overdue succinctness said, "The eighteenth article of amendment to the Constitution of the United States is hereby repealed." A million toasts were raised in celebration. The states, as the most common interpretation of this amendment had it, were again granted control over the manufacture, sale, and transportation of intoxicants within their borders. This included, of course, control over at which age persons may or may not purchase such intoxicants.

Post-Prohibition, with the government now firmly entrenched as arbiter of matters once left to the family, drinking ages became a matter to be decided in the forty-eight, later fifty, state capitals.

The federal government mostly stayed out of this fray. After all, the Twenty-first Amendment was that rare constitutional amendment that fortified the rights of the states vis-à-vis the federal government.

Despite the jurisprudential revolution of the New Deal era, when FDR's failed court-packing plan scared the Supreme Court into permitting unprecedented congressional powers of economic intervention, "there would remain, even after the revolution of 1937, an area of commerce within the exclusive power of the states," as Richard A. Epstein wrote in *Bargaining with the State*.[7] That area was the regulation of commerce in intoxicating liquors within state borders. This included, of course, setting the minimum legal drinking age.

After the repeal of national Prohibition, states established their own minimum-drinking-age laws: Maine and Vermont at eighteen, Nebraska at twenty, and others at twenty-one (though New York lowered its to eighteen in 1934). Alabama retained a statewide prohibition on alcohol until 1937, while Colorado did not establish a minimum drinking age (of eighteen) until 1945. Some states set different minimum ages for different types of drinks (wine, beer, distilled spirits).[8] This was called—federalism.

The most common minimum legal age to purchase and consume alcohol was twenty-one: in 1969, 37 states forbade beer to anyone under twenty-one, and 48 states outlawed liquor to that same group. Responding to changing mores and the trite but true argument that those who were old enough to fight and die in Vietnam were old enough to drink a Budweiser—or finally accepting long-standing patterns of behavior—states liberalized their laws in the early 1970s. This was not a universal wave, however; Michael Dukakis, technocratic liberal governor of Massachusetts, "vetoed two bills to lower the drinking age," acts that "apparently contributed to his unexpected defeat" in 1978.[9]

While the political coloration of the youth movement of the 1960s can and has been vastly overstated—the conservative Young Americans for Freedom was likely as potent as the leftist Students for a Democratic Society—the greater political visibility of young people led to, among other reforms, the Twenty-sixth Amendment to the US Constitution, under which the federal government established a minimum voting age of eighteen for all federal, state, and local elections. (This was, in its own way, a federal mandate; theretofore, the states had set their voting ages.)

The Vietnam War had served, unintentionally, as a spur to the amendment. "If you're old enough to fight, you're old enough to vote," asserted the voting-age amendment's supporters. This idea, even the motto, slightly reworked, was easily transferred to the minimum drinking-age issue. "If you're old enough to fight, you're old enough to drink," went the slogan, and it had an undeniable appeal.

Twenty-nine states reduced their drinking ages between 1970 and 1975, and in the last half of that decade thirteen states raised their ages, while none reduced them. Twelve boosted their minimum drinking ages between 1981 and 1983, as the mass media—the chain newspapers, the *Time-Newsweek* axis, and the network news—discovered drunk driving as a national problem. Eventually, the media would be on to new scourges—missing children, crack babies—but the concentration of news coverage of teenage drinking and driving clearly drove much of the national minimum drinking-age momentum. The issue was hot.

There was a problem, however. The issue was largely beyond the reach of Washington. True, the National Highway Safety Act of 1966 provided for grants from the feds to state and local agencies and entities for the purpose of curtailing drunk driving. These grants were expanded over the years, as the size of the federal government itself expanded apace. But not until the advent of President Ronald Reagan— whose rhetoric had been more federalist and less centralist than any president since at least Dwight D. Eisenhower—did drunk driving become a hot topic for those who viewed the federal government as the scourge of all evils.

Congress, responding to perceived public (or at least interest-group) pressure to *do something*—a pressure Congress can *never* resist—held a series of hearings on raising the drinking age. The House Subcommittee on Commerce, Transportation, and Tourism kicked off the legislative dance with a pair of hearings in October 1983. Two Senate subcommittees, those on Surface Transportation and Drug and Alcohol Abuse, followed suit in June 1984. The word "hearings" may actually overstate the semi-farcical nature of these meetings. While the House subcommittee attracted real live members of Congress and witnesses, the two Senate hearings were barely worthy of the name. "No members besides the chair attended," noted economist Darren Grant of Sam Houston State University, and witnesses merely read statements into the record, answering only to the chair of the respective subcommittees.[10] The fix was in; the bill was going to pass; the US Senate, though on the verge of usurping a traditional state responsibility and altering, in a basic way, the social lives of millions of young Americans, could not be bothered to look into the details of what it was about to do.

President Reagan, who with his Hollywood background was tolerant of social drinking, had established by executive order a 32-member

Presidential Commission on Drunk Driving in April 1982. When in doubt, appoint a blue-ribbon commission to make anodyne recommendations. But this commission went with the flow, and that flow proved to be unstoppable.

It was amusing, if also dispiriting, to watch the allegedly federalist Reagan Administration weakly resist, then wholeheartedly embrace, this abandonment of federalist principles.

In December 1983, the Presidential Commission on Drunk Driving disgorged its report. Among its central pieces of counsel was withholding highway monies from states that refused to buckle under to the commission's key recommendation to "enact and/or maintain a law requiring 21 years as the minimum legal age for purchasing and possessing all alcoholic beverages."[11] As punishment for holdouts clinging to antediluvian notions of states' rights and limits on federal power, the Commission called for the imposition of sanctions in the form of reduced Department of Transportation grants. In other words: crossover sanctions. The call was for a federal mandate—unfunded—under which a state would be deprived of its share of federal highway monies unless it obeyed Washington's diktat as to where to peg its minimum drinking age.

Larry Speakes, Reagan's aptly named press secretary—actually, he was never officially press secretary, as that position was reserved for the wounded James Brady of Brady Bill fame; Speakes's position was assistant to the president and principal deputy press secretary—said that while the president favored states raising the age of consumption to twenty-one on their own initiative, "we do not think the federal government should impose this requirement."[12]

The public seemed to be behind the mandatory national drinking age, at least if Gallup polls are accurate. In January 1983, a whopping 77 percent of Americans polled—and 58 percent of eighteen- to twenty-year-olds polled—favored a national twenty-one-year-old drinking age.[13] But then the nuances of federalism tend to escape said public. Drunk driving is bad. Therefore any law with the ostensible purpose of curbing it must, by definition, be good.

The interest groups pitched in, too. These included the Insurance Institute for Highway Safety, Mothers Against Drunk Driving, the National Safety Council, the American Medical Association, and the PTA. In legislative weight and savvy, the pro-nationalized drinking age forces had it all over their weak opposition, which tended to be localized associations of tavernkeepers and restaurant owners and manufacturers and distributors of alcoholic beverages, as well as college student groups—whose members, as every politician understands, vote at much lower rates than do older cohorts. The advocates for this federal mandate were smooth and professional; those against "often lacked the appropriate professional background."[14] It's not that they were wrong, or stupid, or clumsy, or inarticulate: they just weren't, for the most part, professional lobbyists. (Which, in most other contexts, would be taken as high praise!)

On June 7, 1984, by voice vote—the cowards did not want to go on record!—the House of Representatives approved an amendment to the Surface Transportation and Uniform Relocation Assistance Act of 1984. The legislation would order the Secretary of Transportation to withhold 5 percent of a state's Federal highway construction monies if that state did not have in place a minimum drinking age of twenty-one by October 1, 1986. If that state did not have a minimum drinking age in place a year later, by October 1, 1987, 10 percent of the state's Federal highway construction aid would be withheld. Crossover sanctions met neo-prohibitionism.

The amount states stood to lose ranged from $8 million to $99 million.[15] (Among those standing to lose the most was New York, which had some serious states' rights advocates on its side.) If—when—states knuckled under, they would receive the monies withheld during their fits of principle.

"Minimum drinking age" needs further clarification. The language of the law required states to ban the "purchase or public possession" of alcoholic beverages by persons under the age of twenty-one years. This left the tiniest bit of wiggle room for the states, who responded with minor exemptions: for instance, permitting those eighteen to twenty years of age to consume alcohol in the presence of supervising adults, or older spouses ("Dear, may I please have a beer?" the twenty-year-old Marine asks his twenty-one-year-old wife.)

The Reagan administration's end-run around its own professed principles was announced on June 13 by Transportation Secretary Elizabeth Hanford Dole, wife of the Kansas Republican senator Robert Dole, a man never known for scrupulous adherence to constitutional principle. Secretary Dole spoke at a rally on the Capitol steps, accompanied by activists from the neo-prohibitionist organizers Mothers Against Drunk Driving (MADD) and Save Our Students (SOS). Alas, there were no officials present from Save Our Constitution. Doubly alas, there seems to be no constituency for such a lobby anyway.

Secretary Dole's persuasive powers must have been great—or perhaps President Reagan's fealty to constitutional principles was not quite as strong as his admirers claimed. For he converted to the Dole position without offering much resistance.

Reagan flack Marlin Fitzwater, given the job of explicating the administration's betrayal of federalist principles, said weakly that "we have taken a look at the evidence of the number of lives saved, and the record, and it is so overwhelming it is a case we feel deserves our support, despite our states' rights philosophy."[16]

President Reagan explained his about-face in a speech at River Dell High School in Oradell, New Jersey, on June 20. "Some may feel that my decision is at odds with my philosophical viewpoint that state problems should involve state solutions, and it isn't up to a big and overwhelming Government in Washington to tell the states what to do," he told the students. "And you're partly right." Actually, if one listened only to Reaganite rhetoric, one would be completely right in saying that a federally mandated drinking age for each of the fifty states was a gross violation of his oft-expressed viewpoint. But the president went on to call drunken driving "a national tragedy involving transit across state borders." This was, as we shall see, a very thin reed on which to hang his about-face. But when grasping at straws, any straw will do. The supposed epidemic of cross-state drinking binges and resultant accidents made this one of those "special cases in which overwhelming need can be dealt with by prudent and limited Federal action."

Prudent. Limited. Good words, though in the unfunded federal mandate that was the twenty-one-year-old drinking age one is hard-pressed to find anything prudent or limited. The president continued: "In a case like this, where the problem is so clear-cut and the benefits are so clear-cut, then I have no misgivings about a judicious use of Federal inducements to encourage the states to get moving, raise the drinking age, and save precious lives."[17]

"Judicious?" "Inducements"? Those are odd words to apply to a threat to take away highway money that comes from a trust fund into which the citizens of *all* states pay, including states with drinking ages below twenty-one. But this issue was one that seemed to call forth creative euphemisms. The proper word is "blackmail," but that was too harsh for the sensitive ears on Capitol Hill.

The Senate followed the lead of the House and on June 26, 1984, by a vote of 81–16 (ten Republicans and six Democrats voting no), adopted the twenty-one-year-old drinking age amendment. The measure "will save lives," promised Senator Frank Lautenberg (D-NJ). "The facts could not be clearer."[18]

Opponents, most vociferously Senator Max Baucus (D-MT), argued on primarily federalist grounds. As Senator Baucus explained, "The real issue is whether the Federal Government should intrude into an area that has traditionally and appropriately been left to the States and force them into accepting its solution to the problem of drunk driving."[19]

On the other side of the aisle, Senator Gordon Humphrey (R-NH) asked, "Who are we, the national legislature, who have done a perfectly abysmal job of managing the affairs which are legitimately our concern, to tell the State legislatures who, by and large, have done a far better job of managing their affairs, how to conduct their business? Where does it all end? Where do we stop enlarging the power of the Federal Government and attacking the sovereignty of the States?"[20]

Senator Humphrey is long gone from the Senate, but to answer his question, the enlargement of the Federal Government has no end in sight.

Senator Baucus denied that the punitive aspect of the law left the states with any true choice. "How can it be said realistically that the States are free to choose their own drinking age when they face the immediate cutoff of Federal funds if they make the wrong choice?" he asked. "How can it be said that the States are free to develop alternative programs if they must devote their resources to the enforcement of laws against a group of individuals whose actions are not now illegal?"[21]

The senator's questions were for naught. They were not answered, but then the side that has the votes and the lobbying power and the fawning coverage of the mass media doesn't need to answer questions.

Reagan signed the national drinking-age bill into law in a White House Rose Garden ceremony attended by Candy Lightner, president of Mothers Against Drunk Driving. Mrs. Lightner had lost her 13-year-old daughter to a drunk driving accident in 1980; the intensity of her emotions was completely understandable. Senator Lautenberg explained just how unassailable the position of Mrs. Lightner and the mothers was: "Those who support this bill are not high-paid lobbyists; they do not know all the tricks of the trade or the mysteries of the Senate rules. But they do know the pain of losing a child—a daughter or a son, or a niece or a nephew—to this senseless practice. They come to Washington, not asking us the impossible, not asking us to bring back their children, but to help another mother or father avoid the same tragedy. We owe them a hearing and we owe them a bill."[22]

In defense of the Reagan administration, it is difficult to say to a mother who has lost her child that the mother's proposed legislative remedy is contrary to the proper functioning of the American political system. It is tremendously hard to tell her that while you cannot begin to understand her grief, we must not lose sight of liberty, justice, and verifiable fact in the swirl of emotionalism. But that is what a statesman must do.

President Reagan, in his remarks upon signing the bill into law, made no concession to federalism. In fact, he denounced the "crazy quilt of different states' drinking laws," which is also known as, well, federalism. "The problem is bigger than the individual states," said President Reagan. But then this is *always* the excuse for overriding the Tenth Amendment.

The president went on to refer, indirectly, to the underlying principle he was trampling. "It's a grave national problem," he said of young people drinking and driving, "and it touches all our lives. With the problem so clear-cut and the proven solution at hand, we have no misgiving about this judicious use of Federal power."

There's that word again: Judicious. It's the open-sesame for the excessive use of federal power. And as for the "proven solution," as we shall see, the experience of the states after the imposition of the Reagan-Dole national drinking age did not bear this out. The president insisted that "Raising that drinking age is not a fad or an experiment. It's a proven success."[23] But this was simply not so.

****

The rush to legislate occurred even though "the facts about minimum-drinking-age laws remain unclear," as Henry Weschler and Edward S. Sands wrote in 1980 in *Minimum Drinking-Age Laws: An Evaluation.*[24]

"In the abstract," writes James F. Mosher in his informative history of minimum drinking age laws, "one would predict that increasingly stringent controls on availability and emphasis on enforcement would lessen the actual amount of alcohol consumed. Indeed, for all the problems associated with national Prohibition, use did decline during that period. Such is not the case with youthful drinking. Statistics show that underage persons increased their use of alcohol steadily from the

1930s to the 1960s, when legislation to curtail sales was most active."[25] So setting aside constitutional questions, perhaps the law isn't the right way to approach the matter of teenage drinking in the first place.

The data have never been as clear-cut as advocates of jacking up the drinking age have assumed. State legislatures were boosting their drinking ages by the end of the 1970s in the belief that teen drinking had increased, yet "Surveys of adolescent drinking behavior conducted by the Research Triangle Institute in 1974 and 1978 appear to show no changes in drinking patterns in a national sample of senior high school students."[26]

Writing in 1980, two researchers of the National Highway Traffic Safety Administration noted that "males aged 15 to 19" represent "the age group with the highest proportion (39 percent) of deaths resulting from motor-vehicle accidents."[27] These deaths have a "frequent" association with alcohol. However, studies of the ten states that reported the BAC (blood alcohol concentration) levels of traffic fatalities in at least 75 percent of cases showed that "half of all fatally injured [teen] drivers" in the age-twenty-one states "have alcohol in their bodies," which "suggests that much of the effect of lowering the legal minimum drinking age might already be discounted by the apparent availability of alcohol to teenagers."[28]

Summarizing the state of minimum legal drinking age (MLDA) research on the eve of the Reagan-Dole era, Paul C. Whitehead and Henry Wechsler noted that lowering the drinking age in recent years had resulted in "'statistically and socially significant' increases in all types of alcohol-related collisions among those affected by the modified law." But "On the other hand," they observed, there are states that lowered their drinking ages and yet their "teenage drinking-and-driving patterns were similar before and after" the liberalization. Similarly, studies of consumption patterns of those affected by the raising and lowering of the minimum drinking age have been "provocative"—in some cases no evidence of increased consumption by adolescents was found, where in others it was.[29] So the jury was out. But Congress and the president were in no mood to wait for the jury to return. There was a straw man to burn.

Nor did they want to hear a lot of philosophical guff about rights and liberties. The philosophical case for such laws is not exactly unimpeachable. Even Richard J. Bonnie, a self-described advocate of "the new paternalism," conceded "that minimum-drinking-age laws have the purpose and effect of curtailing free choice for an identifiable segment of the population in the name of the public health, safety, and welfare." Many paternalists support a uniform age-twenty-one MLDA regardless of the empirical evidence because of the "symbolic functions of the law."[30] These symbols, alas, crash right into legal rights of eighteen- to twenty-year-olds.

Beltway proponents of the uniform drinking age made much of the differing minimum drinking ages in the states ringing the Imperial City. The District of Columbia's drinking age was eighteen, Maryland's was twenty-one, and Virginia's was nineteen for beer and wine and twenty-one for the hard stuff. Secretary Dole, apparently unfamiliar with the concept of *federalism*, spoke of varying state laws as if the Devil himself was riding herd: "The resulting checkerboard of different state minimum drinking ages actually creates the 'blood borders,' where young people drive across state lines to drink."[31]

Blood borders. No cause—no unexamined fad—is complete without a ridiculously exaggerated catchphrase, preferably alliterative. Such was "blood borders," a chillingly evocative phrase describing the supposed epidemic of eighteen-, nineteen-, and twenty-year-old youths who drove across state borders in order to drink legally. This was the dubious peg upon which the Presidential Commission on Drunk Driving hung its support for a federal mandate. Only a uniform mandated drinking age, averred the Commission, could "adequately address the needless tragedies caused by young persons commuting to border states."[32] (Hawaiian legislators would ask just why the blood borders justification should force them to raise their drinking age. After all, a motorist who wished to drive beyond the Aloha State's borders would find her ardor for alcohol inevitably dampened in the Pacific Ocean. The feds had no response other than to wave the exemption-less mandate at them.)

The blood borders argument was also the constitutional bulwark, or thin reed, on which Congress based this wholesale violation of states' rights. The House Committee on Commerce and Energy, in its report on the minimum drinking age, observed first that Congress has the right to regulate interstate trade, and of course liquor (like almost every product) is traded across state lines. Drunk drivers, the committee observed, may sometimes use interstate highways. So far, so expansive: almost any federal mandate could be justified under these standards. But then came the blood borders' kicker: "prevention of the adverse effects of a lack of uniformity in state laws is a traditional situation for appropriate exercise of the commerce power."[33] These "adverse effects" are the (uncounted) young people who drive across state lines to purchase booze. The fact that a "lack of uniformity in state laws" is also a traditional feature of the American system of government seems not to have occurred to, or bothered, the James Madisons of the US House Committee on Commerce and Energy.

Estimates of the reduction in alcohol-related highway fatalities that would result from the adoption of the national minimum drinking-age law ranged from 15 percent all the way up to more than 30 percent. These were preposterous overstatements, as all but the most zealous advocates of such laws had to know, and they were "abandoned almost as soon as they had served their purpose," as economist Darren Grant observes.[34]

The centerpiece of the mandater's empirical evidence, as it were, was a 1981 study by the Insurance Institute for Highway Safety (IIHS) on the effect of raising the drinking age. The IIHS predicted confidently that a national twenty-one mandate would save up to 2,500 lives annually. This study was fodder for oft-quoted National Transportation Safety Board (NTSB) guestimates. Indeed, researcher Michael Males notes that the IIHS and NTSB reports "were cited in both House and Senate debates more than fifty times, almost to the exclusion of all other research on the question. The passage of the national-twenty-one legislation is to a large degree attributable to their influence."

Two years after the federal mandate came down, Males published his seminal "The Minimum Purchase Age for Alcohol and Young-Driver Fatal Crashes: A Long-Term View," in the *Journal of Legal Studies*. He subjected the Insurance Institute for Highway Safety and the NTSB publications to the scrutiny Congress never bothered to give them. And he concluded that they both "drastically overestimated the life-saving potential of a national MLPA [minimum legal purchase age] of twenty-one."[35]

The problem with the Insurance Institute for Highway Safety study, as Males explained, was that it focused on too brief a slice of time, so that it revealed only the short-term, and not the longer term, effect of raised drinking ages. Moreover, it ignored other possible causes of reductions in rates of fatal accidents involving young drivers: improved safety features in cars, greater seat-belt use, better training for young drivers—the list goes on.

Taking a longer-term view, Males demolished the quick and easy and too-convenient findings of the insurance lobby. Fatal automobile accidents had declined sharply across all states, no matter their minimum drinking ages, between 1978 and 1984, so a claim that, for instance,

Michigan had reduced its rate of fatal accidents involving young drivers by 31 percent after raising its drinking age could be met by the equally valid assertion that Vermont, which did not boost its drinking age, had also seen a 31 percent reduction in such accidents.[36] Clearly something was going on to make the roads safer—and it wasn't a change in the minimum legal drinking age.

Males found that (1) when a state raises its minimum drinking age, it experiences an average decrease in fatal accidents of 6 percent among drivers of the previous minimum age, but a 16 percent increase in fatal crashes among drivers of the new minimum age; and (2) in the period 1976–81, when states were boosting their drinking ages, those that did not raise them "experienced a slightly larger *decrease* [my italics] in fatal crashes among drivers under twenty-one years of age than did those states that did raise their MPLAs." The increased MPLA did not save lives, found Males. It simply redistributed fatalities from eighteen-year-olds to twenty-one-year olds.[37]

As for NTSB chairman James Burnett's 1983 assertion that a national drinking age of twenty-one would save 1,250 lives annually, an NTSB official admitted to Males that "no written documentation exists for the NTSB estimate."[38] It seems, instead, to be extrapolated from flimsy numbers that extended backward as well as into the future.

Males concluded that "increases in state drinking ages do not save lives," for there are "more lives lost among older drivers than are saved among younger drivers." Yes, jacking up the drinking age from eighteen to twenty-one "has slight beneficial effects on eighteen-year-old drivers," but that is more than offset by the negative effects on nineteen- to twenty-one-year-old drivers. Why is this so? Males speculates that the not-quite-old-enough-to-drink-legally drivers might consume alcohol clandestinely. Because they can't drink legally at bars, they may well over-consume *before* going out on the town. And while eighteen-year-olds tend to live with their parents, and are thus subject to a certain degree of parental control, those nineteen and above are more often *not* living with parents and "not subject to the same family controls."[39]

Economist Darren Grant of Sam Houston State University assayed the substance of the debate surrounding the National Minimum Drinking Age Act of 1984 (NMDAA—these acronyms never end) and found it thin. Advocates of the act misread or exaggerated the available empirical evidence. The relied on the handful of states that had recently raised their drinking ages to twenty-one. Proclaiming with certitude that these "laboratory states" offered rock-solid proof that the NMDAA would save lives, they were able to paint those federalists and mandate foes as hard-hearted enablers of drunk drivers.

The "judicious and discerning evaluation of the evidence" that such a sea change in federal-state policy required was utterly missing from the national drinking-age debate, according to Grant. He set out three reasons for this: First, the "relatively quiet voices" of those who actually knew something about the subject were drowned out by the din of microphone-chasers and neo-prohibitionists. Second, the pro-NMDAA side had substantially more political know-how. And third, the National Highway Traffic Safety Administration (NHTSA), which was "the key government agency" supplying advice to Congress, lacked independence, judiciousness, and technical skills. Add this all up and you get a landslide.

The NHTSA, which was born of the Highway Safety Act of 1970 and given a mission "to save lives, prevent injuries, and reduce traffic-related healthcare and other economic costs," is charged with administering federal highway safety programs, not taking sides on pending legislation. Yet it assumed a lead role in congressional hearings on the national minimum drinking-age legislation, even though it exists in "academic isolation" and failed to take into account those studies that cast doubt upon the effectiveness of a mandated rise in the drinking age.[40]

The NHTSA's sister agency within the Department of Transportation, the NTSB, which dates to 1926, is supposed to be "an independent federal agency charged with determining the probable cause of transportation accidents, promoting transportation safety, and assisting victims of transportation accidents and their families."[41] As Darren Grant points out, the involvement of the NTSB on the side of the national drinking age partisans was most unusual. In fact, the minimum national drinking age law was "the only such law it has forcefully advocated."

Lost in the self-congratulation of the NMDAA partisans was the "incompleteness of the evidence on how the drinking age affects traffic safety—the law's raison d'être." This fragmentary, sometimes contradictory evidence was "almost wholly excluded" from the hearings and speeches and rallies, writes Professor Grant.[42] It complicated the narrative—it just didn't fit the storyline.

Among the salient items ignored by Congress and the president in the rush to make twenty-one the law of the land was this paragraph from a 1984 NHTSA publication, *Alcohol and Highway Safety: A Review of the State of Knowledge*:

The results to date of studies increasing [*sic*] the drinking age have generally been favorable. However, these laws could have been in place for only a short time. During that time, other factors which could produce a reduction in accidents have been present. . . . The question of whether increasing the legal age of purchase will reduce accidents remains to be proven when longer experience with these higher age laws generates sufficient data for a more definitive analysis of impact, from which the effect of transient economic factors can be eliminated.[43]

In other words, *no one was really sure if the NMDAA would have the desired effect.* Even the National Highway Traffic Safety Administration wasn't sure. Yet this passage, and publication, was "wholly ignored," as Grant notes. Just a month before President Reagan signed the national minimum drinking age into law, Morris Chafetz of the Presidential Commission on Drunk Driving confessed that "the research is not as overwhelming as we would like it to be."[44] But that wasn't about to get in the way of crusading lawmakers who saw cameras and headlines and endorsements in their future.

The problem may be as simple as this, Grant speculates: policymakers, especially politicians, are so focused on the short-term that they neglect, or perhaps are unable to really comprehend, the long-term nature of research. In the case of the national drinking age, some very early studies of those states that had raised their minimum age to twenty-one in the early 1980s—and had done so *not* in response to federal coercion, it must be pointed out—seemed to suggest that raising the drinking age was associated with lower rates of drunk-driving-related fatalities. But that association fades as the years go by and the sample becomes larger and more reliable. Quite simply, as Professor Grant writes and as those who dominated the 1984 debate did not understand, "academic studies take years to complete and publish and many such studies may be needed to settle the question."[45] This may annoy the quick-fix activists and the smarmy lobbyists and the issue-hopping media, but it's a fact of academic life.

The studies relied on by the twenty-one crowd were for the most part drawn from the states that had raised their drinking ages from 1981–83—which was, from the researchers' vantage point of 1984, almost like yesterday. These researchers had only one or two years' worth of data to draw from. Moreover, the brevity of this post-law period meant that other factors likely to have influenced rates of drunk driving—changing attitudes, crackdowns on drinking and driving regardless of age, the media spotlight shining on the issue of the moment—were difficult to disentangle by the use of regression analysis. A widespread campaign was underway against drinking and driving among all ages—might not the deterrent effects of this campaign be the primary cause of any reduction in eighteen to twenty fatalities? "Activists," as is their wont, lacked the patience to wait for the answer. They plunged ahead with their panaceas.

Working with thirty years of state-level data since the hasty passage of the MLDA, Jeffrey A. Miron, an economist at Harvard University, and Elina Tetelbaum of Yale Law School concluded that the law's impact was driven by the states that boosted their drinking ages to twenty-one *before* the federal mandate came down—and even in those states, the "impact of the MLDA did not persist much past the year of adoption."[46]

Miron and Tetelbaum take the long view. Examining traffic fatality rates (TFRs) for 15–24 year olds and the whole population from 1913–2004, they find that TFRs increased in each group from 1913–1969 and then declined thereafter. The introduction of the national minimum drinking age was not reflected in these patterns. Similarly, the introduction of vehicle miles traveled (VMT) fails to reveal the impact of the minimum drinking age. Fatalities per VMT "exhibit a persistent downward trend over the entire sample period."[47]

Miron and Tetelbaum then plot the average minimum legal drinking age against the fifteen- to twenty-four-year-old traffic fatality rate. They find that the only large increase in the TFR for this cohort occurred from 1961 to 1967—when the average minimum legal drinking age in the fifty states "remained constant." "The aggregate data," write the researchers, "thus provide little confirmation that MLDAs reduce traffic fatalities." The reductions, instead, seem to be the result of improved safety technologies and car designs (manifested in such advances as seat belts, air bags, anti-lock brakes, safety glass) as well as better driver education and such voluntaristic anti-DWI programs as designated drivers and bar-supplied taxi services for bibulous patrons.[48]

Turning their attention to state-level data, Miron and Tetelbaum examined traffic fatality rates within states as well as such variables as the unemployment rate, per capita income, a state's blood alcohol concentration laws and mandatory seat-belt laws, beer taxes, and total vehicle miles traveled. They found that within the thirty-eight states that had increased their minimum legal drinking ages since 1975, fatalities in the eighteen-to-twenty age group had decreased by 5 percent in six states and by 10 percent in nine. Yet eighteen- to twenty-year-old traffic fatalities had *increased* by 5 percent in four of those states and by 10 percent in five states. Moreover, the most significant reductions had occurred in states that boosted their minimum legal drinking ages *before* the 1984 law. That is, the law had "virtually no effect" on those states that increased their drinking ages to twenty-one in compliance with the Reagan-Dole-Lautenberg "life-saving" law.[49]

Why did the 1984 law have so little impact on eighteen- to twenty-year-old traffic fatalities? Using data from an annual survey of high-school seniors called Monitoring the Future, the researchers found that boosting the minimum drinking age to twenty-one had some effect on both drinking participation and heavy drinking in those states that acted before the mandate kicked in, while it had a "weaker and insignificant effect on alcohol consumption" in the states acting under federal compulsion. Moreover, for all states, including early adopters, the twenty-one-year-old minimum drinking age had a "statistically insignificant" effect on reported alcohol-related traffic accidents among eighteen- to twenty-year-olds.[50] Miron and Tetelbaum conclude that the MLDA has been a failure, at least if its ostensible goal is to reduce alcohol-related traffic accidents and fatalities among those whom it bars from bars. Or bars from the purchase and consumption of alcohol.

Yet despite the dubious statistical evidence upon which the twenty-one crowd made its case, the increase in the drinking age passed easily. "The heart-wrenching narratives from the family members of drunk driving victims and the traffic-fatality statistics, limited though they might have been, ultimately held sway over federal lawmakers," explains Mary Pat Treuthart, professor of law at Gonzaga University School of Law, writing in the *New York University Journal of Legislation and Public Policy*.[51] Cold hard facts melt into insignificance when compared to the emotional heat of the bereaved.

****

Whether or not the whole concept of a minimum legal drinking age makes sense is a topic for another time. As Mike A. Males has written, "drinking age laws discourage rather than encourage a transition period between youthful abstinence and adult use of alcoholic beverages."[52] Nineteen-year-old college students drinking to excess in private and then loading into a car for a night's carousing cannot be anyone's idea of a desirable policy outcome. But for this to be the (unintentional, to be sure) result of a federally mandated and unfunded directive is a cruel twist.

The feds can mandate changes in state laws, but government edicts can't always change human behavior. In setting the national drinking age at twenty-one, the United States joined a select company of the world's countries: Fiji, Pakistan (for non-Muslims; Muslims are barred from consumption), Palau, and Sri Lanka are the others that have set twenty-one as the alcohol threshold. Far and away the most common minimum drinking age is eighteen, and more than twice as many countries set the minimum age at sixteen as at twenty-one. Clearly, Americans assess the maturity level of their young people much more harshly than do the people (or at least legislators) of other lands.

Numerous nations have no minimum drinking age at all: Albania, Armenia, Azerbaijan, Comoros, Equatorial Guinea, Gabon, Ghana, Guinea-Bissau, Jamaica, Kyrgyzstan, Morocco, Solomon Islands, Swaziland, Togo, Tonga, and Vietnam.[53] While that kind of laissez-faire is probably too potent for Americans ever to swallow again, many researchers into what is now called "substance abuse" have concluded that a gradual exposure to alcohol, especially within the family or at public places (including restaurants) where one's family is present, reduces its "forbidden fruit" appeal and eases the transition from abstemious youth into responsible adult drinker. "In countries where people start to drink at an early age," says Brown University Professor Dwight Heath, "alcohol is not a mystical, magical thing. . . . People are less likely to 'drink to get drunk' because they know that's a stupid thing to do."[54]

In the all-or-nothing world of the neo-prohibitionists and their congressional paladins, alas, drink does possess magical powers—the power of good publicity in a cause beloved by the media. And that carries a great deal more weight with most politicians than rusted old artifacts like the Tenth or Twenty-first Amendment.

****

The enforcement of the MLDA was assigned to the states and localities. Enforcement thereof was not, of course, subsidized by the federal government that handed down the order—thus the "unfunded mandate" label that attaches to the age-twenty-one law. As Professor Mary Pat Treuthart notes, the 1984 law never "addressed the critical issues of enforcement mechanisms, penalties, or sanctions" upon states that inadequately applied the law.[55] The feds had spoken: the provinces must listen, and pay.

A decade after the MLDA's passage, Alexander C. Wagenaar and Mark Wolfson, writing in the *Journal of Public Health Policy*, explained that state and local law enforcement of the law had been fairly lax. They estimated that only two of every thousand occasions of underage drinking resulted in arrest. The authors urged a massive crackdown on such drinking, with greatly enhanced enforcement of a law that many, especially in college towns, regard as largely unenforceable.[56]

Because enforcement is an unfunded mandate, there is neither means nor motive for such a crackdown. "Lax enforcement by police is typically the result of limited resources," writes Treuthart, but pressure by such groups as MADD has resulted in tougher enforcement of the law in selected jurisdictions.[57]

There are no good (or even so-so) estimates of the enforcement costs to states that had formerly set their legal drinking ages under twenty-one. But they surely exceed the paltry federal aid that has been offered toward enforcement of this mandate.

In 1998, the Enforcing the Underage Drinking Laws (EUDL) program was created by the federal government and placed under the administrative guidance of the Office of Juvenile Justice and Delinquency Prevention. Distributing both block grants and discretionary grants to the states at the rate of $25 million per year since its initial year, the EUDL was designed to enhance education about and enforcement of the federally mandated drinking-age law. But no matter how many alcohol awareness seminars these grants subsidize, eighteen- to twenty-year-olds will continue to resent a seemingly invidious law that deprives them of what many see as their legitimate right to purchase and consume alcoholic beverages. As University of Florida professors Lonn Lanza-Kaduce and Pamela Richards found in a study of the unintended effects of raising the drinking age, young people "developed a sense of injustice at their arbitrarily lost rights, an attitude . . . that often results in disrespect for the laws and increased deviance."[58]

****

Did the states rise up in resistance to this heavy-handed and unfunded (for even the meager EUDL program was enacted fourteen years after the Reagan-Dole law) federal mandate?

Not really, though seven states (Colorado, Iowa, Louisiana, Montana, South Dakota, Texas, and West Virginia) included in their twenty-one-drinking-age laws a mechanism of automatic repeal—commonly called "court of last resort" provisions—if the national law were overturned in the courts. (As of June 1984, twenty-two states had set the drinking age for wine, beer, and spirits at twenty-one. Only three—Louisiana, Hawaii, and Vermont—had an eighteen-year-old drinking age for all intoxicants.)

The general attitude at the state level was well, if pusillanimously, expressed by an unnamed state official whom federalism scholar Sarah F. Liebschutz of SUNY College at Brockport quoted: "We don't like it, but if it means federal money, we generally cave in."[59]

Now there's a profile in courage!

Not every state caved. A few exhibited the moxie and spirit that the Founders had hoped would sustain the federal system. From the prairies and the West came sounds of defiance: South Dakota, Wyoming, Montana . . . but the East, too, had its resisters.

New York, which stood to lose $99 million if it retained its legal drinking age of nineteen (it had been eighteen until December 1982), took a stand for states' rights. State senator John J. Marchi, long-time Republican tribune of Staten Island and chairman of the Senate Finance Committee, denounced the Reagan-Dole act as a "Little Prohibition."[60] Governor Mario Cuomo, who never met a paternalist law he didn't like (and smother in sanctimonious prose), was pushing to boost the age to twenty-one, but New York was lucky in that its political class still included men such as Senator Marchi, who were unintimidated by the neo-prohibitionists.

Senator Marchi, also chairman of New York's Joint Legislative Committee on Revision of the Alcoholic Beverage Control Law, said in 1982 that "federal legislative intrusion is completely unwarranted in this area and would be a dangerous precedent." Not only did he forthrightly oppose federal meddling in this traditional state matter, he even suggested—horrors!—that maybe government at *any level* was not the proper entity to deal with the matter of young people and alcohol. Instead, opined Senator Marchi, "the home and other social forces" should play the dominant role. Senator Marchi and President Reagan, in this case, might be taken to represent two antithetical "conservative" responses to social problems: one relies upon family, church, and other mediating institutions to ameliorate the problem, while the other depends upon the iron fist of centralized government.

(But putting it this way threatens the myth of Ronald Reagan, apostle of limited government.)[61]

Governor Mario Cuomo, though a Son of Italy and citizen of the City of New York like Senator Marchi, had a vastly different conception of the role of government in family and social life. After all, he famously compared his state government to the "family of New York"—with himself as father and boss, naturally. The governor prodded the state legislature in 1984 to increase the drinking age from nineteen (it had been eighteen from the repeal of Prohibition until 1982) to twenty-one; it rejected his proposal.

A 1984 New York State Assembly Committee on Transportation and its Subcommittee on Drunk Driving report credited a New York State program called STOP-DWI with a 14.5 percent reduction in alcohol-related accidents between 1980 and 1983, as federalism scholar Sarah F. Liebschutz noted in *Publius*. STOP-DWI was not age-specific: it increased penalties for drunk driving and it funded countywide anti-DWI projects. The authors of the report asserted that the unwise focus on raising the drinking age had "obscured" the accomplishments of STOP-DWI.

The New Yorkers cut through the fog of media hype and activist-generated myth. They asserted that "flawed evidence" was being used to promote a twenty-one-year-old drinking age, and noted that traffic fatality rates did not respond as predicted in those states that had recently boosted their minimum drinking ages to twenty-one. Against the cool reason of the skeptics, the activists had Governor Mario Cuomo, who seemingly had no interest in the hard evidence. "If it saves one life, we should do it," the governor stated, using a rationale that could be deployed to support virtually any totalitarian or police-state measure.[62]

The New York State Assembly said no to twenty-one on May 30, 1984, by a vote of 80–69. And as Sarah F. Liebschutz notes, proponents of a mandated national drinking age used the New York vote as ammunition. Instead of pointing to New York as a case study in federalism, or as a shining example of the states serving as the "laboratories of democracy" celebrated by Justice Brandeis, the mandaters lamented New York's intransigence and bad manners. How dare the state not fall in line! The nerve of those New Yorkers! Didn't they understand that when the media gave fawning hype to the cause of the day, every legislative head was supposed to bow in reverence? Laboratories of democracy? Hah! There was only to be one laboratory in this country, and it was located along the Potomac River, not the Hudson.

Even as the federal noose was tightening, and the submission of New York seemed inevitable, dissenting voices cut the air. State senator Martin Connor, a Brooklyn Democrat, roared, "Statistics, statistics, statistics. I'm sure that we can save a lot of lives by lowering the speed limit to twenty-one and raising the drinking age to 55. And I can prove it statistically. So what? We're not going to do it. Our system is one of fairness, that you don't let the majority take away the rights of the minority."[63]

The states, or at least those states that prized their historic rights, did not go down without a fight. In this case, a US Supreme Court fight. In *South Dakota v. Dole* (1987), the Supremes, by a vote of 7–2, permitted Congress and the president what Richard A. Epstein, in *Bargaining with the State*, called "a statutory end run around the Twenty-first Amendment."[64]

To set the stage, the Twenty-first Amendment, so widely and joyously toasted around the country in taverns and saloons and places where convivial imbibers meet, repealed the Noble Experiment in its Section 1 but in Section 2 stated that "The transportation or importation into any State, Territory, or possession of the United States for delivery or use therein of intoxicating liquors, in violation of the laws thereof, is hereby prohibited." The earliest cases heard by the courts subsequent to the amendment's ratification interpreted this section as "authorizing the states to exercise broad 'home rule' powers to regulate almost everything pertaining to alcoholic beverages," says Albert J. Rosenthal, but as the scope of the federal government swelled, the authority of the states shrunk.[65]

When President Reagan signed into law the national minimum drinking-age law, South Dakota was operating under a minimum age of nineteen for 3.2 beer purchase. The state had the unmitigated gall, the appalling effrontery, to think that it, and not the federal government in Washington, DC, should determine such policy. So South Dakota challenged the law via a suit against the US Department of Transportation. (Joining the great state of South Dakota in an amicus brief were Colorado, Hawaii, Louisiana, Montana, Ohio, South Carolina, Vermont, and Wyoming.) South Dakota argued that the national MLDA violated the Twenty-first Amendment to the Constitution, which granted the states the right to set drinking ages as among their "core powers"; and was an "invalid exercise" of the spending power granted Congress by Article 1, Section 8, of the Constitution.[66] The District Court and the US Court of Appeals for the Eight Circuit rejected the state's claims, which the Supreme Court then agreed to consider.

The article and section at question begins: "The Congress shall have the power to lay and collect taxes, duties, imposts and excises, to pay the debts and provide for the common defense and general welfare of the United States." It also authorizes Congress to perform such functions as the borrowing of money, the regulation of commerce with foreign nations and Indian tribes and among the states, the coining of money and fixing of standard weights and measurements, the establishment of post offices and post roads, the granting of patents and copyrights, the declaration of war and maintenance of a navy and army, and various other duties, among which is not, of course, the establishment of minimum drinking ages for the several states.

The court, however, noted that "incident to this power, Congress may attach conditions on the receipt of federal funds" in order to "further broad policy objectives." This means, in practice, that "objectives not thought to be within U.S. Const. art. I's enumerated legislative fields, may nevertheless be attained through the use of the spending power and the conditional grant of federal funds." So much for the enumerated powers.

The court did acknowledge that the spending power is not unlimited. It placed four conditions, as it were, on the conditions. First, the exercise of the spending power must be "in pursuit of the general welfare," though in making this determination the court should "defer substantially" to the Congress. In other words, this condition is virtually toothless. Second, Congress, in placing conditions on a state's receipt of federal funds, "must do so unambiguously, enabling the states to exercise their choice knowingly, cognizant of the consequences of their participation." This is easily met, too, by the use of clear language— though that is not always a given when lawyers put fingers to keyboard and compose legal prose.

Third, any conditions on federal grants to the states "might be illegitimate if they are unrelated to the federal interest in particular national projects or programs." The ends must somehow be related to the means, or at least to the federal interest, which is today as vast as the cosmos. They must be, in the argot of the 1960s, *relevant*. And fourth, and finally, "other constitutional provisions may provide an independent bar to the conditional grant of federal funds." This was the ground upon which South Dakota stood—mostly. This last condition on the conditions seemed to open the door for the voiding of the national MLDA on the grounds that the mandate violated the Twenty-first Amendment.[67] Alas.

The Supreme Court upheld the Reagan-Dole national MLDA. It found that, first, the law's "indirect imposition of a minimum drinking age was a valid exercise of Congress's spending power, reasonably calculated to advance the general welfare and national concern of safe interstate travel," and, second, "the Twenty-first Amendment was not violated as the statute did not induce petitioner to engage in unconstitutional activities."

Despite its strictures upon ambiguity, the court phrased its decision in somewhat equivocal language. "Even if Congress might lack the power to impose a national minimum drinking age directly"—that question, said the court, was "not decided here"—Congress's threat to withhold funds is still a "valid use of the Congress's spending power under U.S. Const. art. 1, S. 8."[68] (Chief Justice Rehnquist's opinion does not imply that directly setting a national drinking age is beyond the powers of Congress; one wonders if the neo-prohibitionists might at some point attempt to fill that ambiguous space with a direct order to the states regarding their laws regulating alcohol—and whether the court will permit the steamroller of federal power to crush whatever federalist principles lay in its path.)

The court emphasized the dubious "blood borders" argument, noting that Congress had "found that differing minimum drinking ages in the states created particular incentives for young persons to drink and drive while commuting to border states where the drinking age was lower." This alleged phenomenon was deemed by the court to be a "dangerous situation" that provided the "general welfare" rationale necessary to the measure's constitutionality. The difference in state minimum drinking ages, while a quintessentially federalist circumstance, "created particular incentives for young persons to combine their desire to drink with their ability to drive," declared the court, and "this interstate problem required a national solution." The "goal" of the Interstate Highway System—safe travel between states—had been "frustrated by varying drinking ages among the States."[69]

The majority opinion was written by Chief Justice Rehnquist and joined by Justices White, Marshall, Blackmun, Powell, Stevens, and Scalia. It affirmed the constitutionality of the national MLDA as a valid exercise of the spending power, meeting as it did the court's stated conditions for federal funding conditions, and also found it to be consistent with the Twenty-first Amendment. In regard to the latter finding, the court opined that "the percentage of highway funds that were to be withheld from a state with a drinking age below twenty-one was relatively small"—a judgment call open to question—and that the smallness of this penalty meant that the mandate "did not coerce the states."

Parsing the penalty in the manner of medieval monks arguing how many angels can dance on the head of a pin, the majority in its opinion asserted that the withholding of highway funds was "not so coercive as to pass the point at which pressure turns into compulsion." Just how they made that finely calibrated calculation the court did not see fit to inform the citizenry. The court allowed that it had, in *Steward Machine Co. v. Davis* (1937), which upheld the unemployment compensation provisions of the Social Security Act, been capable of judging the difference between pressure and compulsion. But the national MLDA was a mere slap on the wrist, according to the court: the feds were offering "relatively mild encouragement" to the states to boost their drinking ages. Why, the states would hardly even miss the millions ($99 million in the case of New York State) forfeited should they be so obtuse as to refuse to comply. And in any event, enacting or refusing to enact the twenty-one-year-old drinking age remained a "prerogative of the States not merely in theory but in fact."[70]

There were two dissents. Justice Brennan, in a single paragraph, opined that "regulation of the minimum age of purchasers of liquor falls squarely within the ambit of those powers reserved to the States by the Twenty-first Amendment," so that "Congress cannot condition a federal grant in a manner that abridges this right." Justice Brennan seemed to affirm South Dakota's argument that the law violated the Prohibition-repeal amendment.

More voluble was Justice Sandra Day O'Connor in her dissent. Justice O'Connor denied that the law was either a valid exercise of the spending power or consistent with the Twenty-first Amendment. While she had no disagreement with the conditions the court laid down that may attach to the receipt of federal funds, she argued that the national MLDA satisfied only two of them: it was aimed at the general welfare, and it was "entirely unambiguous." It was not, said Justice O'Connor, "reasonably related to the purpose for which the funds are expended." Pressuring the states to adopt drinking ages of twenty-one "is not sufficiently related to interstate highway construction to justify" placing such a condition upon funding. Under the court's reasoning in *South*

Dakota v. Dole, Justice O'Connor charged, Congress could "regulate almost any area of a State's social, political, or economic life."

Justice O'Connor also doubted the proclaimed life-saving effect of the law. It was, she said, "Far too over- and under-inclusive. It is over-inclusive because it stops teenagers from drinking even when they are not about to drive on interstate highways," and it is under-inclusive because "teenagers pose only a small part of the drunken driving problem in the Nation." For if one's sole goal was to reduce alcohol-related traffic fatalities, then why not, as Justice O'Connor quotes Senator James McClure (R-ID), raise the drinking age to thirty—or even higher? (Scholars generally agree that the twenty- to twenty-four-year-old age group is the most prone to alcohol-related automobile accidents, yet no one in the debate seriously suggested barring twenty-four-year-olds from bars.)

Finally, Justice O'Connor in her spirited dissent argues that the law is unconstitutional because "the regulation of the age of the purchasers of liquor, just as the regulation of the price at which liquor may be sold, falls squarely within the scope of those powers reserved to the States by the Twenty-first Amendment."[71] And no amount of blood-borders rhetoric or indictment of the liquor industry can change that.

Legal scholars were struck by the apparent nationalism of the "extremely generous"—generous, that is, to the federal government—decision in *South Dakota v. Dole.* The Rehnquist court had led a modest—very modest—"federalism revival," in the phrase of Lynn A. Baker and Mitchell N. Berman, writing in the *Indiana Law Journal,* and yet in *South Dakota v. Dole* that court set up a constitutional obstacle course so easy for a contested law to pass through that it would seem to enable almost any mandate, funded or not, by the federal government to the states.[72] And indeed, in the years since, "the lower courts, with few exceptions, have read . . . [the] most promising provisions of the *Dole* test to be toothless, even nonjusticiable, en route to sustaining a wide range of conditional federal spending legislation."[73] In *South Dakota v. Dole,* the allegedly "states' rights" bloc of the Supreme Court had the chance to advance the ball a considerable distance in the direction of federalism. But with the shining exception of Justice O'Connor, it reversed field and lit out for the nationalist goal line. (Curiously, Rehnquist's successor as Chief Justice, John G. Roberts, "assisted in the preparation of a 1986 amicus brief [in *South Dakota v. Dole*] on behalf of the National Beer Wholesalers' Association."[74])

The courts since *Dole* have been unable to determine that fine line between *compulsion* and *pressure.* The "lower courts have consistently failed to find impermissible coercion," write Professors Baker and Berman, and who can blame them?[75] If penalizing New York State $99 million for setting its own drinking age is permissible, what could fall on the other side of that line?

Baker and Berman go on to argue that the prevailing view of "'liberal' academics and judges" and liberal Democratic activists—that *South Dakota v. Dole* was a rare home run for the Rehnquist court—is seriously mistaken, for *Dole* was "intellectually suspect" and yields "normatively troublesome results." *Dole* was a significant step forward for uniformity, homogeneity, and intolerance. A judicial defense of states' rights, which the court failed to make in *Dole*, would give "'outlier' or 'minority' states protection from federal homogenization in areas in which they deviate from the national norm, *whether that deviation is to the left or right of the political center.*" Decentralized decision making ensures and protects diversity; in the formulation of Baker and Berman, "in the absence of a nationwide consensus, permitting state-by-state variation will almost always satisfy more people than would the imposition of a uniform national policy, and will almost always therefore increase aggregate social welfare."[76]

Unfortunately for diversity, and for aggregate social welfare as well, the temptations of centralized political power are such that when activists of any stripe are able to exercise that power, they almost always choose to enforce—to mandate—their preferred behavior upon as wide a range of subjects as possible. Yet as Baker and Berman assert, "*Dole* should strike its present-day supporters (who we assume are disproportionately liberal nationalists) as bad constitutional doctrine because it enables Congress to use the carrot of federal funds to induce states to adopt a raft of policies likely to be favored by conservative Republicans," among them law enforcement grants conditioned upon a state's willingness to adopt concealed-carry laws or the death penalty; social-welfare grants conditioned upon a state's willingness to jettison affirmative action; and child-welfare grants conditioned upon a state's willingness to prohibit homosexual couples from adopting children. These conditions would "pass muster under *Dole*."[77] But liberal nationalists seem willing to cross that bridge when they come to it—that is, to behave as situational decentralists whose view of the proper balance between national and state and local powers depends entirely upon whose ox is being gored and whose policy preferences are being enforced. This is not principled nor is it wise, which is to say it is politics as usual.

Professor Mary Pat Treuthart assesses the likelihood of a successful new challenge to the national MLDA. The chances of the court simply reversing the decision, thereby admitting that *South Dakota v. Dole* was wrongly decided, are meager, she opines. (Despite Chief Justice Roberts's past work-for-hire.) *Stare decisis* remains a formidable principle. The Twenty-first Amendment and the regnant interpretations of the spending clause are unlikely to serve as vehicles to overturn *Dole*. A revivified Tenth Amendment offers more hope, she says: the federal "commandeering" decried by the court in *New York v. United States* would seem to be a central feature of the national MLDA.[78] And the increasing use of sticks rather than carrots—the now routine threat to withhold funds if states don't bend to the federal will on numerous matters—could cumulatively come to be seen as coercion.

Yet as Ryan C. Squire concludes in the *Pepperdine Law Review*, "no type of federal expenditure under the spending power affords Congress greater influence over states than the practice of conditioning states' receipt of federal funds upon the implementation of federal regulations and guidelines."[79] It is a license—a license affirmed emphatically by the allegedly federalist Rehnquist court—to dictate the actions of the states, and to stick the states with the bill. It is a license to mandate away, without regard to whether or not the mandate is funded.

****

Having achieved the twenty-one mandate, Mothers Against Drunk Driving has since gone on to other issues. Most prominent—and controversial—is the push to establish a national BAC (blood alcohol concentration) standard of 0.08 to define drunk driving. That is, if BAC machines, which analyze the presence of alcohol in a subject's blood, saliva, urine, or—as with the famous Breathalyzer—breath, measure 0.08 grams of alcohol per deciliter of blood, one must be charged with driving under the influence of alcohol.

In the past, the most common BAC definition of per se driving under the influence was 0.10 or, in the earliest years of the technology, before prohibition fever flared, 0.15. States, of course, set these limits. So the push to nationalize a 0.08 BAC was, like the push for a nationwide mandated drinking age, a serious departure from constitutional practice. As the burden of enforcement would fall on state and local police departments, this, too, would be an unfunded federal mandate.

Outraged manufacturers, sellers, and consumers of beer, wine, and liquor objected that a 0.08 BAC would penalize socially responsible drinkers and do little if anything to get drunks off the road—but cool and clear-eyed analysis is not the norm when drinking and driving issues are on the tapis. (In general, a 120-pound woman reaches a 0.08 BAC if she consumes three beers in two hours. This is not, by most folks' lights, binge or irresponsible drinking.)

The National Highway Traffic Safety Administration, not having learned its lesson from its earlier advocacy of a nationwide mandated twenty-one-year drinking age despite the paucity of solid research on the subject, jumped into this debate, too. The NHTSA urged the states to adopt the 0.08 standards "when there was virtually no evidence on their effectiveness," as Darren Grant has written. The NHTSA produced a 1998 report, "Presidential Initiative for Making .08 BAC the National Legal Limit," which asserted at several points that mandating such a federally imposed law would reduce drunk-driving-related auto fatalities by double digits—even though, as Grant writes, "only 3% of all traffic fatalities involve drivers with BACs of .08 or .09." (The next year, a report of the General Accounting Office asserted that "the evidence does not conclusively establish that 0.08 BAC laws, by themselves, result in reductions in the number and severity of alcohol-related crashes," and even chastised the NHTSA for "overstat[ing]" such a connection.)[80]

The first state to go 0.08 was Utah, in August 1983. Oregon followed two months later. Maine adopted 0.08 in August 1988. By the time Congress poked its nose into this state matter, fifteen states had chosen, as is their right, to set the BAC for per se driving under the influence/driving while intoxicated at 0.08.[81]

A look at the concerted effort in 1998 to establish a federally mandated (and federally unfunded) national 0.08 BAC throws into stark relief the exaggerations, even truth-stretching, of the neo-prohibitionists, as well as their vast contempt for the Tenth Amendment and the by-now ghostly outlines of federalism. It also reveals the role played by a tendentious media in framing the narrative as pitting virtuous moralists against sleazy booze peddlers. (One wonders if the reporters who commit these offenses against fair play are teetotalers or just hypocrites who assume they'll never be stopped by a cop after downing three drinks, enough in many cases to blow a 0.08.)

In March 1998, the US Senate, by a vote of 62–32, approved an amendment to a transportation bill that would withhold up to 10 percent of a state's federal highway funding unless that state defined drunk driving as meeting or exceeding a blood-alcohol level of 0.08. The prime sponsors were the bipartisan team of uber-prohibitionist Senator Frank Lautenberg (D-NJ) and Senator Michael DeWine (R-OH). There was no hard evidence or detailed research behind this—it was yet another feel-good measure that solons, heedless of the consequences of their actions, could sell back home as a life-saving measure.

Fifteen states had already adopted a 0.08 BAC, but relying on the federalist system was not the preferred option of such groups as Mothers Against Drunk Driving—or, it seems, Mothers Against Driving After Having Any Drinks At All.

The Senate had passed its BAC mandate after very little debate, but when the action shifted to the House, both sides moved into high gear. It is, apparently, perfectly acceptable for neo-prohibitionists in the insurance industry and the nanny-state corner to lobby ferociously for their favored measures, but heaven forbid that those targeted by the nannies fight back. Consider the way the *Baltimore Sun* reported the debate: "The alcohol and restaurant industries have mounted a furious lobbying assault on Congress that could kill a tough drunken driving proposal. . . ." Is it possible to phrase a lead sentence any more tendentiously? These nasty (and entirely legal) industries are then said to have launched "a blitzkrieg of lobbying," a choice of words that calls to mind Nazi aggression. The National Restaurant Association, which in this analogy must be equivalent to the Wehermacht, if not the Panzer division, is said to have "flown in 150 restaurateurs from 40 states."

"The lobbying is unprecedented," mewled mandatory 0.08 sponsor Representative Nita Lowey (D-NY). This is so ridiculous an assertion—150 small businessmen lobbying is *unprecedented*?!—that it boggles the mind, yet the *Sun* reporter records it as gospel truth.

The reporter goes on to describe the advocates of the federal mandate—people who would toss the Tenth Amendment into the garbage bin of history—as "safety activists." That's sure a nice euphemism if you can get it! One such "safety activist," newly elected MADD president Karolyn Nunnallee, was said to be "disheartened" by the fact that the restaurant owners were actually fighting back to protect their livelihoods. "I am shocked," she said of the restaurateurs' defensive acts. "I didn't learn this in Civics 101."[82]

It is doubtful that she learned in Civics 101 how to use the federal government to shut down businesses she dislikes and dictate the social lives of eighteen- to twenty-year-olds, either, but then Civics class ain't what it used to be.

When a House-Senate conference committee scrapped the punitive Senate mandate and opted instead for the House-passed 0.08 measure, which authorized half a billion dollars over six years in additional aid for states that "voluntarily"—heh, heh—adopted the lower BAC standard, the media caterwauled.

Was this an example of negotiation, of compromise, of splitting the difference, or even of shying from a blatant violation of the Tenth Amendment to the US Constitution? No it was not. Rather, it was "a capitulation to the liquor lobby" that was done in order to not "delay essential road, bridge and mass transit" funding.[83] The transportation bill carried a hefty price tag of $200 billion: all for essential work, no doubt, and none of it a payoff to unions or contractors.

The *Washington Post* chose to cover the story by fitting Senator John Chafee (R-RI), a liberal Republican sponsor of the 0.08 mandate, for a halo. Senator Chafee, depicted as a man of integrity in a world of gritty politics, nobly supported a "tough new drunk driving standard" but was thwarted by "back-room pressure politics." He had on his side all the forces of righteousness: more than 60 of his Senate colleagues, Mothers Against Drunk Driving, "highway traffic safety groups" (as opposed to lobbies for reckless drivers), and even that paragon of restraint and virtue, President Bill Clinton.

Yet the "weary and stoop-shouldered Chafee [threw] in the towel" after a fierce battle against those evil liquor lobbyists. "There's only so long you can slug it out—duke it out—and maintain your position. Even for a veteran of two world wars like Chafee, eventually you have to give in," said an anonymous Chafee aide. The whole piece sounds as if it were penned by a Chafee press secretary: the gallant war hero who selflessly sought an unfunded federal mandate upon the states, and was tripped up by the wicked Senator Trent Lott (R-MS), who for some atavistic reason "shared House conservatives' antipathy toward new state mandates." What a troglodyte!

"We want incentives, not mandates," Senator Lott is reported to have said to Senator Chafee. The nerve! Lott explained himself to the *Post*: "I've never made any secret, I think that the blood alcohol level should be .08, but I'm opposed to punishing poor states if for some reason their legislators don't feel that they can do that." (Poor states were not the only ones to be punished: estimates were that California and Texas stood to "lose roughly a billion dollars over six years if . . . they failed to comply.")

The neo-prohibitionists were not appeased by the carrot approach. They live and legislate by the stick. "The money being offered today is a pitiful sum compared to what the liquor lobby can spend to keep this bottled up," sniffed the wealthy Senator Frank Lautenberg, formerly CEO of Automatic Data Processing, who could buy and sell members of that lobby if he wished to.[84] (He'd rather use his political power to order them around.)

The carrot, it seems, worked just fine this time. No need for the stick. By August 2005, every state had enacted a 0.08 BAC level to define DUI/DWI. Minnesota was the last to cave. Sometimes just the threat of a mandate does the trick.

The 0.08 BAC crusade throws into revealing relief a central truth of many such "moral" crusades: their purpose is not to actually erase or erode the disputed behavior, but rather to make the crusaders feel good about themselves. The panacea doesn't have to work—but it does have to make the peddlers of said panacea look good.

For evidence, one might examine the move in the 1990s to set BAC limits at 0.01 or 0.02 for drivers under twenty-one years of age. This was the vaunted "zero tolerance" strategy. In 1996, Congress enacted yet another law encroaching upon the traditional bailiwick of the states. It mandated that all states adopt a 0.02 BAC limit for drivers under twenty-one years of age. The penalties were to be revocation or suspension of the offender's driver's license. The coercive mechanism applied to the states was a virtual carbon copy of the national MLDA: the withholding of up to 10 percent of a state's federal highway funds. Every state complied. There were no South Dakotas this time around.

Yet zero tolerance does not mean zero drinking. As the ever-perceptive Darren Grant notes, zero tolerance laws "generate strong marginal disincentives against taking the first drink, but much smaller marginal disincentives thereafter." One drink or three—either course puts your BAC above 0.01. And as Grant found in a panel analysis of data from the 1988–2000 Fatality Analysis Reporting System, "zero tolerance laws have no material influence on the level of fatalities."[85] Do not, however, expect the states to rush to repeal these laws. For their purpose was not so much to eliminate drinking by nineteen-year-olds as to put a feather in certain legislative caps and to keep neo-prohibitionist organizations busy now that their entire agenda seems close to being enacted. Success, to a lobby, can be a terrible thing.

****

Prospects of a congressional repeal or modification of the twenty-one-drinking-age mandate are dim. Indeed, anyone bold enough to propose returning this matter to the states will be demonized as a pro-drunk-driving, pro-teenage carnage enabler of party animalism. If anything, as Professor Mary Pat Treuthart of Gonzaga University School of Law writes, "Since the NMDA's passage, Congress has not relented in its efforts to take control of drinking laws away from the states." And it is clear that "Congress has shown no inclination to alter its commitment to taking the necessary steps to maintain a twenty-one-year-old drinking age."[86]

By the dawn of the twenty-first century, college administrators and others whose professional lives lead them to engage with eighteen- to twenty-year olds were beginning to ask, sometimes even demand, a modification in the national drinking age law. The law was widely violated on college campuses and at college-area bars. In 2001, the First Daughters, nineteen-year-old twins Jenna and Barbara Bush, were busted for underage drinking in Austin, Texas. The news was greeted with yawns: the fact that nineteen-year-olds were buying and consuming alcohol, whether with fake IDs or because bar and liquor store owners looked the other way, surprised none but the terminally naïve. Surveys have consistently found that about three-quarters of American youths begin drinking before they turn twenty-one. Writing in the *New York University Journal of Legislation and Public Policy*, Professor Treuthart said of the MLDA that "Given the widespread lack of compliance with laws prohibiting underage drinking, it could be concluded that their initial adoption and continued retention is a colossal failure and a glaring example of misguided public policy."[87]

Some college presidents opened what they hoped—in vain, it turned out—to be a national dialogue on revising the drinking age. For as *Time* magazine reported, upping the drinking age to twenty-one had not banished booze from campus, it had merely moved it from out in the open, where campus security and RAs and other adults could monitor it, to places hidden from the public eye: frat houses, behind closed dorm room doors, and wherever the prying eyes of supervisors could not see. "We're dealing with real hypocrisy to say that kids under age twenty-one don't drink," said Roderic Park, ex-chancellor of the University of Colorado at Boulder. "What we are doing is teaching them to flout the law."[88]

"If there were an 18- or 19-year-old drinking age, we could address the issues more favorably," Dartmouth College president James Wright told *Time*. But "we can't go around sniffing students' breath or smelling their cups."[89]

Binge drinking seemed to be one undeniable fruit of the increased drinking age. Students would drink immoderately before going out on the town because a night on the town could not (legally, at least) include a pop or two at the local tavern. So they got good and drunk before going out. And that meant drunken eighteen-year-olds behind the wheel—just the kind of behavior the national minimum drinking-age law had been meant to curtail.

"The twenty-one-year drinking age has not reduced drinking on campuses," said Middlebury College President John McCardell, "it has probably increased it. Society expects us to graduate students who have been educated to drink responsibly. But society has severely circumscribed our ability to do that."

So convinced were President McCardell and Middlebury that the drinking age was too high that they looked into the prospect of paying the state of Vermont the money it would lose from disobeying the NMDAA on the condition that the state legislature lower the drinking age. The school determined that raising $12.5 million was beyond its capability, but the very fact that it seriously considered taking this extraordinary step showed just how serious Middlebury was about reintroducing common sense and federalism into the drinking age question.[90]

Vermont has also been one of the few states where state legislators still make noises about defying the feds on the minimum drinking age. Vermont state representative Richard Marron, a Stowe Republican, has proposed dropping the minimum age for purchase and possession of alcohol from twenty-one to eighteen, arguing, "It's very much a civil rights issue. At eighteen years old you have the right to vote, to marry, to join the military and die for your country. There's not much room for a double standard." (His bill did not pass, though it attracted bipartisan support and the then governor James Douglas offered philosophical backing but "was also very concerned about the loss of federal transportation funds."[91] When philosophy meets federal funds, the smart money is *always* on the money.)

Although the restaurant and beverage industries sometimes make noise about lowering the drinking age, the largest potential constituency for such a change—the eighteen- to twenty-year-old crowd—ages out of the proscribed category pretty quickly. And once they turn twenty-one, the issue loses its potency for most of them.

If change is to come, it will be because a gutsy state legislature—Vermont's seems a leading candidate—dares the risk of losing federal highway funds. Or, rather, it values its constitutional role over its role as obedient supplicant to the federal government. The MLDA is one unfunded federal mandate that seems unassailable at present—but so did the Eighteenth Amendment during the Roaring Twenties.

Notes

1. James Madison, *Notes of Debates in the Federal Convention of 1787*, with an introduction by Adrienne Koch (Athens, OH: Ohio University Press, 1984), pp. 488–89.
2. James F. Mosher, "The History of Youth-Drinking Laws: Implications for Current Policy," in *Minimum Drinking-Age Laws: An Evaluation*, edited by Henry Wechsler (Washington, DC: Lexington Books, 1980), p. 13.
3. Michael P. Rosenthal, "The Minimum Drinking Age for Young People: An Observation," *Dickinson Law Review* (Vol. 92, 1987–88): 650.
4. Mosher, "The History of Youth-Drinking Laws: Implications for Current Policy," p. 15.
5. Ibid., p. 18.
6. Ibid., p. 20.
7. Richard A. Epstein, *Bargaining with the State* (Princeton, NJ: Princeton University Press, 1993), p. 151.
8. Henry Wechsler and Edward S. Sands, "Minimum-Age Laws and Youthful Drinking: An Introduction," in *Minimum Drinking-Age Laws: An Evaluation*, p. 1.
9. Mosher, "The History of Youth-Drinking Laws: Implications for Current Policy," p. 11.
10. Darren Grant, "Politics, Policy Analysis, and the Passage of the National Minimum Drinking Age Act of 1984," as yet unpublished manuscript, unpaginated.
11. Presidential Commission on Drunk Driving Final Report, 1983, p. 10.
12. Douglas B. Feaver, "Reagan Now Wants 21 as Drinking Age," *Washington Post*, June 14, 1984.
13. Sarah F. Liebschutz, "The National Minimum Drinking-Age Law," *Publius* (Vol. 15, No. 3, Summer 1985): 42.
14. Grant, "Politics, Policy Analysis, and the Passage of the National Minimum Drinking Age Act of 1984."
15. Steven A. Weisman, "Reagan Signs Law Linking Federal Aid to Drinking Age," *New York Times*, July 18, 1984.
16. Feaver, "Reagan Now Wants 21 as Drinking Age."
17. Steven R. Weisman, "Reagan Calls for Drinking Age of 21," *New York Times*, June 21, 1984.
18. Mike A. Males, "The Minimum Purchase Age for Alcohol and Young-Driver Fatal Crashes: A Long-Term View," *Journal of Legal Studies* (Vol. 15, January 1986): 181.
19. Liebschutz, "The National Minimum Drinking-Age Law": 39.
20. Ibid.: 49.

21. Ibid.: 46.
22. Mary Pat Treuthart, "Lowering the Bar: Rethinking Underage Drinking," *NYU Journal of Legislation and Public Policy* (Vol. 9, No. 1, Fall 2005): 310.
23. Weisman, "Reagan Calls for Drinking Age of 21."
24. Wechsler and Sands, "Minimum-Age Laws and Youthful Drinking: An Introduction," p. 1.
25. Mosher, "The History of Youth-Drinking Laws: Implications for Current Policy," p. 25.
26. Wechsler and Sands, "Minimum-Age Laws and Youthful Drinking: An Introduction," p. 8.
27. Robert B. Voas and John Moulden, "Historical Trends in Alcohol Use and Driving by Young Americans," in *Minimum Drinking-Age Laws: An Evaluation*, p. 59.
28. Ibid., p. 69.
29. Paul C. Whitehead and Henry Wechsler, "Implications for Future Research and Public Policy," in *Minimum Drinking-Age Laws: An Evaluation*, p. 178.
30. Richard J. Bonnie, "Discouraging Unhealthy Personal Choices through Government Regulation: Some Thoughts about the Minimum Drinking Age," in *Minimum Drinking-Age Laws: An Evaluation*, pp. 39–40, 48.
31. Feaver, "Reagan Now Wants 21 as Drinking Age."
32. Presidential Commission on Drunk Driving Final Report, 1983, p. 11.
33. Liebschutz, "The National Minimum Drinking-Age Law": 45.
34. Darren Grant, "Politics, Policy Analysis, and the Passage of the National Minimum Drinking Age Act of 1984."
35. Males, "The Minimum Purchase Age for Alcohol and Young-Driver Fatal Crashes: A Long-Term View": 182.
36. Ibid.: 187.
37. Ibid.: 183.
38. Ibid.: 192.
39. Ibid.: 203–204.
40. Darren Grant, "Politics, Policy Analysis, and the Passage of the National Minimum Drinking Age Act of 1984."
41. www.ntsb.gov/about.
42. Darren Grant, "Politics, Policy Analysis, and the Passage of the National Minimum Drinking Age Act of 1984."
43. Ibid.
44. Ibid.
45. Ibid.
46. Jeffrey A. Miron and Elina Tetelbaum, "Does the Minimum Drinking Age Save Lives?" National Bureau of Economic Research, Working Paper 13257, p. 3.
47. Ibid., p. 6.
48. Ibid., p. 7.
49. Ibid., pp. 10–11.
50. Ibid., p. 15.
51. Treuthart, "Lowering the Bar: Rethinking Underage Drinking": 311–12.
52. Males, "The Minimum Purchase Age for Alcohol and Young-Driver Fatal Crashes: A Long-Term View": 207.
53. www2.potsdam.edu/hansondj.LegalDrinkingAge.html.

54. Treuthart, "Lowering the Bar: Rethinking Underage Drinking": 366.
55. Ibid.: 340.
56. Alexander C. Wagenaar and Mark Wolfson, "Enforcement of the Legal Minimum Drinking Age in the United States," *Journal of Public Health Policy* (Vol. 15, No. 1, 1994): 37–53.
57. Treuthart, "Lowering the Bar: Rethinking Underage Drinking": 340.
58. Ibid.: 363.
59. Liebschutz, "The National Minimum Drinking-Age Law": 50.
60. "Marchi Sees 'Little Prohibition,'" United Press International, July 17, 1984.
61. "Solution to Alcohol Problems Must Come from the Home," Associated Press, Amsterdam (NY) *Evening Recorder*, May 18, 1982.
62. Liebschutz, "The National Minimum Drinking-Age Law": 48.
63. Treuthart, "Lowering the Bar: Rethinking Underage Drinking": 351.
64. Epstein, *Bargaining with the State*, p. 151.
65. Rosenthal, "Conditional Federal Spending and the Constitution": 1137. In 1978, plaintiffs brought suit after Michigan, by popular vote, approved a state constitutional amendment raising its drinking age to twenty-one. The plaintiffs, according to Professor Treuthart, "alleged numerous constitutional infirmities, including violations of religious free exercise and the right of parents to control their children's upbringing." In *Felix v. Milliken*, the Michigan Supreme Court upheld the law, asserting that the right to purchase and consume alcohol was not "fundamental." But this, of course, was a state-level law, and it has been generally agreed that states do have the right to regulate such behavior. Treuthart, "Lowering the Bar: Rethinking Underage Drinking": 313.
66. *South Dakota v. Dole*, 483 U.S. 203 (1987).
67. Ibid.
68. Ibid.
69. Ibid.
70. Ibid.
71. Ibid.
72. Lynn A. Baker and Mitchell N. Berman, "Getting off the Dole: Why the Court Should Abandon Its Spending Doctrine, and How a Too-Clever Congress Could Provoke It to Do So," *Indiana Law Journal* (Vol. 78, 2003): 460.
73. Ibid.: 466.
74. Treuthart, "Lowering the Bar: Rethinking Underage Drinking": 328.
75. Baker and Berman, "Getting Off the Dole: Why the Court Should Abandon Its Spending Doctrine, and How a Too-Clever Congress Could Provoke It to Do So": 468.
76. Ibid.: 470–71.
77. Ibid.: 483.
78. Treuthart, "Lowering the Bar: Rethinking Underage Drinking": 326.
79. Ryan C. Squire, "Effectuating Principles of Federalism: Reevaluating the Federal Spending Power as the Great Tenth Amendment Loophole," *Pepperdine Law Review* (Vol. 25, 1998): 903.
80. Darren Grant, "Politics, Policy Analysis, and the Passage of the National Minimum Drinking Age Act of 1984."
81. Thomas S. Dee, "Does Setting Limits Save Lives? The Case of 0.08 BAC Laws," *Journal of Policy Analysis and Management* (Vol. 20, No. 1, 2001): 113.

82. Jonathan Weisman, "Industry may kill alcohol measure: Drunken-driving bill could fall victim to furious lobbying," *Baltimore Sun*, March 30, 1998.

83. James Dao, "Highway Bill Accord Rejects Tougher Standard on Alcohol," *New York Times*, May 19, 1998.

84. Eric Pianin, "How Pressure Politics Bottled Up a Tougher Drunk-Driving Rule," *Washington Post*, May 22, 1998.

85. Darren Grant, "Dead on Arrival: Zero Tolerance Laws Don't Work," *Economic Inquiry* (Vol. 48, No. 3, July 2010): 756.

86. Treuthart, "Lowering the Bar: Rethinking Underage Drinking": 331, 346.

87. Ibid.: 305.

88. Ibid.: 306.

89. Jeffrey Kluger et al., "How to Manage Teen Drinking (the Smart Way)," *Time*, June 18, 2001.

90. Ibid.

91. Treuthart, "Lowering the Bar: Rethinking Underage Drinking": 341, 342. For a contemporary instance of states defying the federal government by trying to encroach on territory that has traditionally been the realm of the feds—immigration policy—see Matthew Parlow, "A Localist's Case for Decentralizing Immigration Policy," *Denver University Law Review* (Vol. 84, 2007): 1061–1073; and Lina Newton and Brian E. Adams, "State Immigration Policies: Innovation, Cooperation or Conflict?" *Publius* (Vol. 39, No.3, 2009): 408–31. Writes Parlow, "calls for requiring local governments to enforce federal immigration laws are . . . untenable for a localist because this would constitute an unfunded mandate that undermines local autonomy and violates the Tenth Amendment." Parlow: 1071.

4

"I Can't Drive 55"?
Oh Yes You Can!

Before there was a nationwide mandated minimum drinking age, there was the nationwide mandated speed limit. It was set at 55 miles per hour, which seemed even at the time an absurdly low number and gave rise to a popular rock song by Sammy Hagar that declared, simply if with gusto, "I Can't Drive 55."

As in other areas traditionally left to the states, the federal government had breached the field of traffic enforcement during the Great Society. Under the Highway Safety Act of 1966, Washington began distributing monies to the states for programs, subject to approval by the US Secretary of Transportation, "designed to reduce traffic accidents and deaths, injuries, and property damage resulting therefrom." A range of activities was subsumed under the rubric of highway safety, and these measures included "an effective record system of accidents (including injuries and deaths resulting therefrom), accident investigations to determine the probable causes of accidents, injuries, and deaths, vehicle registration, operation, and inspection, highway design and maintenance (including lighting, markings, and surface treatment), traffic control, vehicle codes and laws, surveillance of traffic for detection and correction of high or potentially high accident locations, enforcement of light transmission standards of window glazing for passenger motor vehicles and light trucks as necessary to improve highway safety, and emergency services."[1]

So while federal subsidies were directed to the improvement of methods of detecting and ticketing speeders on the highways, they were hardly the centerpiece of the 1966 act. But a warning shot had been fired. Or perhaps it would be more accurate to call it the gunning of an engine as a foreboding roar. For the US Department of Transportation had been created in that very same year of 1966 at the request of President Lyndon B. Johnson, who saw no limit to the volume of guns and butter and alms and napalm and grants to the states that the federal government was capable of administering. The Highway Safety Act of 1966 should have come with an epilogue printed in enormous font and reading "MORE TO COME."

The 55 mph speed limit, this early experiment in unfunded federal mandates, transportation division, had its genesis in the 1973 Arab oil embargo and the resultant long lines at the gasoline pump. In October 1973, the members of the Organization of Arab Petroleum Exporting Countries (OAPEC) instituted an embargo on oil to the "hostile" United States, in retaliation for US support of Israel in the Yom Kippur War.

Reduced supplies of gasoline translated into price increases (from an average of 38 cents a gallon in summer 1973 to 55 cents per gallon by spring 1974), which in turn spurred the Nixon administration to impose a counterproductive regimen of price controls and gasoline rationing. This led to localized gasoline shortages, manifested most visibly by stations closing due to lack of supplies or by ridiculously long lines at the pump. These lines were due in large part to government rules that required gasoline to be allocated equally to all service stations. When price increases and the fear of shortages spurred urban drivers to hoard gas, those urban stations soon ran dry—while in rural areas the stations were abundant with gasoline. Yet the regulatory state prevented oil companies from transferring the rural surplus to the desperate-for-gas cities. It was the recipe for chaos—and that recipe was cooked up in Washington.

All hell seemed to break loose in the period 1973–75. Truckers struck, year-round Daylight Saving Time was adopted, and bizarre rationing schemes based on license plate numbers were taken up and just as quickly dropped. Federal government policymakers seemed to grasp at every conceivable straw and nostrum and panacea to contend with the "energy crisis," save the one policy that would have worked best: permitting the market to work without political or bureaucratic interference.

Corking the speed limit was among the policies hit upon by those in search of solutions, and though it was sold as a temporary expedient, it enjoyed a considerably longer life than license-plate-number-based rationing or year-round Daylight Saving Time. As is often the case, the national speed limit began as a voluntary—if strongly urged by the federal government—policy. In May 1973, the US Secretary of Transportation, Claude Brinegar—surely one of the most obscure holders of this obscure Cabinet post; ID'ing his name could probably win a bar bet even at the DOT's rathskeller—encouraged the fifty state governors to impose their own limits. The US Senate followed with a resolution along the same lines two weeks later. Then President Nixon, on June 29, 1973, added his voice to those urging a reduction of speed limits throughout the Union.

The implied threat, of course, was that if the state governors didn't take the advice of Washington, the feds would apply more and more pressure, until the states saw the light. A few knuckled under right away. By the end of November 1973, seventeen states had reduced their maximum speed limits, including several (Maryland, Massachusetts, New Jersey, New York, Rhode Island, Vermont, Washington) that established a thrifty, if not nifty, limit of fifty.

But it wasn't enough. When Washington urges "voluntary" action, it is as certain as death and taxes that the failure of the states to act "voluntarily" will bring coercive legislation to bear. Which is just what happened. After all, if left to their own devices the states might— gasp!—enact speed limits that best reflected traffic density and safety conditions in their bailiwicks. Why, some states—Montana and Nevada—didn't even have speed limits on some roads, and that kind of anarchy could lead to God knows what kind of chaos. (Actually, Montana and Nevada relied upon an older concept than numerical limits: that is, drivers were required to pilot their automobiles in conformity with the "basic rule," which translates to a "reasonable speed" with respect to road conditions.)

Pre-1974, speed limits of 70 or 75 mph were common on interstate highways. After all, they were built with such speeds in mind. As Robert O. Yowell of Stephen F. Austin State University explains, the interstate system's "focus on separated lanes, controlled access, long straight-aways, and gentle slopes precipitated speeds that were significantly higher than those safely traveled on the more dangerous two-lane state and United States highways."[2] The interstates were faster and safer highways: and these were exactly the roads the feds targeted in their rash reaction to the oil embargo and gas "shortage."

But something had to be done! And who better to do it than the federal government? President Nixon signed the Emergency Highway Energy Conservation Act, which included the National Maximum Speed Law (NMSL—it wouldn't be a government program if it didn't carry a mush-mouthed acronym), on January 2, 1974. The inclusion of

"Emergency" in the title was supposed to give it a special urgency. The states were given sixty days to submit. That is, to reduce their maximum speed limits on public highways to 55 miles per hour. The penalty for not doing so? The US Secretary of Transportation would withhold all federal highway construction money from the recalcitrant state. The responsibility for enforcing this federal mandate fell entirely upon state and local law enforcement agencies. Despite some grumbling, all fifty states obeyed. None wanted to forfeit that federal highway construction money. As for the magic number of 55—it was, for all intents and purposes, an arbitrary number, not tied to any particular body of research. It just sounded right.

****

There was a truth in Sammy Hagar's "I Can't Drive 55" that went beyond the typical young male's bravado. Speed limits have not typically been plucked out of thin air or set arbitrarily by bureaucrats or panicked politicians who know nothing of local conditions. Rather, they have usually been gauged, according to the Institute of Transportation Engineers, according to the 85th percentile formula. That is, the limit is set "at or below the speed at which 85 percent or below of the traffic is moving."[3] Thus the "speeders" are limited to the fastest 15 percent of drivers. In practice, police generally give drivers a 5–10 miles per hour cushion as well. Using the 85th percentile formula, the drivers themselves, in a sense, establish the limit. Enforcement of these limits is widely accepted by drivers as scofflaws consist of only the very fastest motorists. Most accidents are not caused by excessive speed but poor drivers of the sort who weave in and out of traffic, change lanes without signaling, tailgate, and fail to watch out for the other guy. You know—the jerks of the road.

Drivers seem to understand instinctively the truth spoken by Tom Hicks, an engineer with the Maryland State Highway Administration: "People who drive at the 85th percentile speed are the least likely to be in motor vehicle crashes. It's the people who drive much slower or faster who are most at risk."[4] Charles Lave, professor of economics at the University of California–Irvine, was a pioneer in studies linking rates of speed with traffic safety. He found that the problem was not speed per se but the relative speed of cars on a given stretch of road. Because "highway fatality rates are strongly related to the variation in speed between cars," Lave denied the truism that Speed Kills.

Rather, he said, "Variance kills. What matters most in setting a speed limit is choosing one that people will obey, hence reducing variance between cars."[5]

The 85th percentile speed at the time of the national 55 mph mandate differed from road to road and from state to state, but it was generally in excess of 60 mph, and as high as 68 mph. Even a student in Traffic Engineering 101 could have told the Congress that most drivers, to borrow a lyric, can't drive 55.

An Automobile Association of America study found, as *Consumers' Research Magazine* reported, that speed variance was positively related to highway accident rates, and that the higher the average speed on a highway, the lower the variance. The lowest accident rates occurred when drivers piloted their vehicles at between six and twelve mph over the "mean" speed—that is, at the 85th percentile.[6] Unfortunately, those who dominated the public debate over 55 seldom bothered to read research. They were too busy trumpeting their own righteousness.

****

The National Maximum Speed Limit instructed the US Secretary of Transportation to "withhold approval of all Federal-aid highway construction projects if a State fails to establish a maximum 55-mile-per-hour speed limit or to certify that it is enforcing the limit."[7] This was a serious punishment, but perhaps it was overdone. No state was ever thus punished, and in fact the states seemed to regard this as a draconian threat that was unlikely to be carried out. The feds would have been wiser to have set a more realistic penalty—say, the forfeiture of 10 percent of a state's federal highway construction monies—for that would have seemed the more plausible threat. But they would learn this lesson soon, in the matter of the national drinking age.

(Nevada challenged the mandatory speed limit. In *Nevada v. Skinner* (1989), the Ninth Circuit Court of Appeals rejected the state's contention that its "choice" to drop the limit to 55 mph was involuntary, given the threat of withheld federal highway funds. Congress, said the court of appeals, had the authority under the commerce clause to order the states to adopt speed limits, whether directly or indirectly.)

The states were required to submit to the US Department of Transportation data regarding their monitoring and enforcement of the mandated speed limit. To meet the monitoring requirement, the states had to provide the feds data regarding "average speed, median speed, the 85th percentile speed, and the percent of motorists exceeding 55, 60, and 65 miles per hour" compiled while state and local agents monitored the various highway types, ranging from rural and urban interstates to nondivided rural highways.[8] To satisfy the enforcement requirement, the states were compelled to submit to US DOT details of their enforcement policies, the number of speed citations issued, highway mileage patrolled, and other information indicating the extent of their compliance with the 55 mph mandate.

The information thus supplied was, in the assessment of all relevant parties, desultory, incomplete, and inadequate. How could it not be? The burden of enforcement fell upon state and local governments, which had better things to do than prove to the US DOT that they were ticketing hapless motorists who drove 58 mph on an interstate.

The Comptroller General averred that thirty-six states had failed to meet the certification requirements as of January 1, 1976. Not that it mattered: the threatened punishment (forfeiture of all federal highway funds) was so over the top that it failed to frighten the states into supine obedience. It was a bit like a $5,000 fine for littering in the park: potential litterers understand that there is almost zero chance of such a fine being levied, so the deterrent effect is limited. A $50 fine, which seems plausible, would be more effective.

Moreover, the feds vacillated on just what constituted an acceptable level of enforcement by the states. In its first batch of proposed rules, the US Department of Transportation suggested—and it was only a suggestion, not a dictate—that the states shoot for 55 mph compliance rates of "70 percent in 1975, 80 percent in 1976, and 90 percent in 1977 and subsequent years."[9] These goals were as fanciful and unachievable as the goals later set out in the G.W. Bush administration's No Child Left Behind Act. *Ambitious* doesn't even begin to capture its nature; *quixotic* would be far too generous. *Hopeless* would be a better description.

One flaw in the original law was that DOT did not define "enforcement" for the states. The details of 55 mph enforcement, from fines to police man hours to the design of No Speeding signs, was left to the states. This was not so much a case of a federal bureaucracy opting for leniency as it was a baffled bureaucracy unable to divine any believable way of making a pie-in-the-sky mandate effective. It just couldn't be done. It wasn't enforced because it couldn't be enforced.

So there was very little carrot and a strange sort of stick to the 55 mph speed limit mandate: the stick was big enough, but no one really thought it would ever be swung. It did succeed in irritating state officials, who resented the federal bullying, and who argued that such a sanction would be counterproductive, for it would "have an adverse impact on highway safety because safety is enhanced by the construction of new limited access roads and adequate maintenance of existing roads."[10] But even the most timorously obedient state officials doubted that the hammer of the sanction would ever come down: the states, the construction unions, and the states' representatives in Washington would cry so harshly, so shrilly, that the US DOT would back off. Remember that this was the mid-1970s, when "cooperative federalism" was in the saddle, and "coercive federalism" was not even a gleam in the young George W. Bush's eyes. The national 55 mandate seemed to many an outrageous and, once the ostensible fuel shortage passed, unnecessary intrusion into what had always been a concern of the states, not the national government. There was still residual federalist sentiment in the United States, and the tenor of the times—the country having just passed through Vietnam, Watergate, the Nixon resignation, and countless revelations of government officials' malfeasance and skullduggery—was skeptical of big government, of centralized authority, and of the Cold War era's deference to the wisdom of Washington wise men.

The Comptroller General concluded in 1977: "The lack of enforcement criteria and the severity of the sanction provided by law lead us to conclude that the sanction is virtually an empty threat."[11] But still, this unenforceable mandate mulcted state taxpayers for two decades. The Comptroller General, in his report on the achievability of the 55 mph mandate, noted that some state officials cited "additional paperwork and increased monitoring efforts and costs" due to 55.[12] These spelled out another feature of the problem: the National Maximum Speed Limit was an unfunded federal mandate.

There were no additional monies coming from the federal government that had forced upon the states the much-despised 55. The states were in something of a quandary: they were required, upon threat of withdrawal of federal highway funds, to ticket those who violated this federal edict, and yet enforcing this speed limit encouraged disrespect for those uniformed agents of the state whose job it was to hand out tickets to drivers who had broken what seemed to many a picayune and silly law. As Tom Hicks of the Maryland State Highway Administration observed, "There are many traffic engineers, myself included, who think that the 55 mph speed limit caused a degradation of respect for traffic laws and contributed to what we call aggressive driving. . . . [Since the law came in], everybody has been going 15 to 20 mph over the speed limit, including the police. It's terribly harmful to have a law and not enforce it."[13]

Yet enforcing it carried its own cost. Policing funds were shifted to traffic-law enforcement, which meant less money for more traditional activities of state and local police. Fewer resources were available for enforcing laws against theft, assault, murder, and so on, not to mention the plethora of non-speeding-related duties incumbent upon local and state police forces, for example, assisting at accident scenes, rescuing (or at least calling AAA for) stranded motorists, or arresting drunk or drug-addled drivers.

Economists Charles Lave and Patrick Elias write that the national 55 mandate led to what most law-enforcement officials regarded as a misallocation of resources. Indeed, the International Association of Chiefs of Police testified before Congress about the effects of this misallocation. The national law, combined with the threat of the forfeiture of highway funds, forced highway patrols to shift manpower and other resources away from such safety-oriented tasks as patrolling for drunk drivers and enforcing truck safety regulations and toward ticketing drivers on the interstates (the safest roads) for traveling at perfectly safe speeds above 55 mph. Lave and Elias note that by 1983, "29% of patrol hours were devoted to rural interstate highways, though these were already the safest highways and produced only 9% of fatalities."[14]

As Bill Jackman of the American Automobile Association told reporter Tyce Palmaffy, "People move off and onto interstates depending on the speed; if the speed limit is only 55 or 65, they will move onto a country road that will get them there just as fast. The problem there is that the fatality rate is three times higher when you get off the interstates. Interstates are the safest highways we have."[15]

So the 55 mph mandate had the perverse consequence of routing drivers away from the very safest roads and onto more dangerous thoroughfares. And yet the last-ditch defenders of 55 had the nerve, the unmitigated gall, to prattle on sanctimoniously about how they were all about safety, and saving lives, and how those who would return speed limit decisions to the states were speed freaks who were indifferent to the human cost of their policy advocacy. Incredible!

The National Highway Traffic Safety Administration estimated in 1977 that the states were using about 25 percent of their federal highway safety monies to enforce the 55 mph limit—a piddling amount, given that such federal funds added up to "less than 1 percent" of the approximately $2.5 billion that states and localities spent annually on traffic-law enforcement.[16] The overwhelming burden of enforcement fell upon state, county, and municipal taxpayers.

Ticketing was up: four million American motorists were cited for exceeding the speed limit in 1973, six million in 1974, and seven million-plus in 1975. But as the Comptroller General pointed out, the distortions introduced by the demands of the national 55 mph mandate actually made traffic-law enforcement *less effective*. In Oregon, for instance, the state police had to devote one-third of their traffic man-hours to policing interstates, yet only 6 percent of the state's highway fatalities occurred on those roads. The more dangerous roads—on which drivers typically operated at lower speeds—went under-monitored. In fact, a mere 5 percent of Oregon's traffic fatalities were ascribed to speeds exceeding 55 mph, while 20 percent of those fatalities were caused by someone driving on the wrong side of the road.[17] If ever there were a perverse traffic safety law that actually undermined safety, it was the mandated national 55 mph speed limit.

****

The NMSL was advertised as a one-year emergency measure. But emergency measures have a way of blending into the background and becoming permanent. In 1975 the temporary nature of the 55 mph law was exchanged for an indefinite lifetime.

The stated purpose of the law was energy conservation. Safety was a distant second consideration, if even that. The first years of the nationwide 55 mph mandate did see a decline in highway fatalities, though as a foremost researcher in the field has written, "the causes are difficult to disentangle," and include a sharp reduction in travel due to the recession and hassles at the gas pump, as well as "patriotic compliance with the new speed limit."[18] But that compliance, even if motivated by patriotism, had its own limits.

In the first year of the mandated nationwide limit, average speeds on primary roads fell by five miles per hour, to a national average of 55.6 mph. On interstates, the average speed fell almost seven miles per hour, to 58 mph. Yet those numbers hid vast rates of noncompliance. For instance, the Comptroller General reported that in 1975, when the law was relatively new and motorists were most likely to heed it and the associated propaganda, 80 percent of California drivers broke the 55 mph speed limit on that state's rural interstates. Comparable figures in the other four states the CG visited for his study were 85 percent in New York, 72 percent in New Mexico, 68 percent in Texas, and a curiously low 37 percent in Louisiana.[19] (No one has ever suggested, before or since, that Louisianans are more prone than most to obey laws.)

The majority of states reported in 1975 that a majority of motorists exceeded 55 mph on the relevant roads. Under such conditions, enforcement becomes at best a crapshoot, at worst an impossibility. The clear delineations of the 85th percentile formula are blurred; when most of those behind the wheel are breaking the law, how does an officer decide whom to arrest? A law broken by a majority of subjects, or drivers, is unenforceable, and efforts to enforce it will seem arbitrary, capricious, and illegitimate.

The oil embargo was lifted by the oil cartel on April 29, 1974, but the 55 mph speed limit kept on truckin'. The rationale for this mandate shifted from energy conservation to safety. Proponents of the mandate pointed to the sharp drop in highway fatalities between 1973 (55,096) and 1974 (46,049), but skeptics and researchers countered that several non-speed-related changes played significant roles in accident reduction; to wit, a decrease in the number of miles traveled by automobile due to fuel shortages and price increases; such safety innovations as seat belts and, later, anti-lock brakes and air bags; stepped-up enforcement (at least at first) of speeding laws; and declines in automobile travel at night and on weekends, times that feature more accidents than weekday daylight travel.

As with highway fatalities, fuel consumption also fell in the wake of the national 55 mph law, though numerous factors other than speed limits played a role. These included improvements in tire design (radial ply tires), fuel economy, automobile design (smaller, more efficient cars), and highway engineering. Putting an exclamation point on the basic inutility of the law, even for its ostensible purpose, the comptroller general noted a September 27, 1974, National Science Foundation–sponsored study by Braddock, Dunn, and McDonald that "calculated that if there was strict compliance with the 55 mph speed limit, the theoretical fuel savings would be 200,000 barrels a day. However, after examining motor vehicle gasoline consumption trends and traffic volume trends during the winter of 1973 and the spring of 1974, the study concluded that there was no actual improvement."[20]

The Comptroller General of the United States, in a Valentine's Day 1977 report to the Congress, conceded that in trying to force the states to enforce the uniform speed limit, "provisions of the law . . . have generated State resentment" and "a lack of voluntary observance of the speed limit by many people."[21] That was an understatement.

State police and county sheriffs were overwhelmed by the magnitude of the general disregard of the new speed limit. Ticketing those exceeding 55 miles per hour was like trying to catch droplets in a rainstorm. You can catch as many as you like, but they are vastly outnumbered by the ones that get away. As the Comptroller General put it, "Limited money and staff and more pressing problems preclude any more emphasis on speed enforcement."[22]

In time, some states in the Mountain West—where opposition to 55 was fiercest—weakened penalties for violating the federal mandate to the point of near-ridiculousness. Arizona, Idaho, Montana, Nevada, and Utah instituted "energy wastage" or "energy conservation" fines, which replaced speeding tickets for those nabbed while exceeding 55 mph but still driving below the pre-national minimum speed limit state limit, which in Montana, for example, was infinity. The "energy conservation violation" fee for those caught speeding in Montana during the reign of federally mandated speed limits? Five bucks.[23] Pay the nice officer and be on your way. As we shall see when considering the REAL ID mandate, Montana is not a state that knuckles under to federal nannies.

Other states saw in the new law the potential for revenue—but at a cost of misapplication of police manpower.

The feds cast about for just the right mix of carrot and stick to make 55 work. Again, the Comptroller General summarized the problem: "Federal involvement in state traffic enforcement is a delicate issue." It sure is! The law asserted federal control in this previously state-centered area by forcing states "to certify to the Secretary of Transportation that they are enforcing the speed limits," but this blatant subjugation of states to feds in the matter of traffic law enforcement irritated the states and their transportation and law-enforcement officials.[24] The indignity of it all. Not only did Washington tell Topeka and Helena and Jackson how fast the drivers of those states could travel on roads within those states, but it compelled police within those states to issue tickets and enforce these laws—at the expense of the states, not the mandate-issuing national government. The nerve!

In 1978, the law was "strengthened." In strengthening it—by stepping up enforcement and reporting requirements—Congress weakened true highway safety. For the effect of this mandate was to shift traffic-enforcement officers away from the more dangerous roads and those roads with higher accident and fatality rates and toward the interstates—mile for mile, the safest roads we have. Mandate madness, indeed.

When appeals to good sense and conscience don't work—perhaps because the law is congruent with neither—Washington calls in the public relations people for some Madison Avenue-style persuasion. "Fifty is thrifty," went the first slogan on behalf of slowing down, but this predated the mandatory 55 mph limit and in its use of the term "thrifty" sounded, well, old-fashioned and even spinsterish.

"It's the law," went the P.R. doctors' early pitch for 55, but when the nation's motorists responded with a collective shrug and a big "So what?" the advertising men were sent back to the drawing board. For as one state traffic official remarked, "It is not sufficient merely to say that 'It's the law.' We all recall that Prohibition also was once a law."

There were minor variations on this theme, the most publicized being "Speed Limit 55. It's not just a good idea. It's the law." But this motto wasn't such a good idea. Next up from the creative pen: "Speed Limit 55. It's a law we can live with." This registered every bit as feebly on the message meter. Americans in fact could not live with it, and by forcing the misallocation of police resources it was probably costing lives.

The US DOT even birthed a character called "Mr. 55"—think of an even less hip version of Mr. Peanut, and one whose job it was to lecture around the country on the virtue of traveling at or under the speed limit. Now there's a fictive figure we can all get behind! (Or, rather, we can all be trapped behind on the expressway as he insists on driving at a ridiculously low rate of speed.)

The states, too, launched their own mini-55 "public information" (a polite way of saying *propaganda*) campaigns, and with no greater success than the feds' image-meisters had achieved.

In the despairing words of the Comptroller General, "In spite of these Federal and State efforts, many people still appear unwilling to drive 55 mph or slower."[25]

The states, lacking the means to carry out this unfunded federal mandate and, in most cases, the will to do so as well, pled for mandate relief. Calls for repeal of 55 echoed from the provinces.

The most visible manifestation of the alleged "energy crisis" that engendered the 55 mph limit—the long lines at the gasoline pumps—was long gone by the late 1970s. Traffic analysts scored the mandate as inefficient to boot: as early as January 1976, in the pages of *Traffic Engineering*, Gilbert H. Castle III weighed the costs and benefits of the new law and found that these costs, which included the effect of longer travel times on producer goods, including agriculture, and on personal income, significantly outweighed alleged benefits, including fuel conservation. Castle concluded from his cost/benefit calculations that "the U.S. Congress should not have made 55 mph the nation's official speed limit."[26] (His reckoning, of course, does not even include such considerations as the benefits of adhering to a federalist political system. Nor did he estimate the additional costs of traffic enforcement.)

Noncompliance sped up. For instance, from April to June 1982, the Federal Highway Administration monitored the New York State Thruway, one of the key pieces of the Interstate Highway System. A whopping 83 percent of drivers exceeded 55 miles per hour—a rate of traffic disobedience that made the Empire State's drivers sound like a road army of A. J. Foyts. A 1990 National Research Council report found that over 70 percent of motorists observed driving on 55 mph roads exceeded 55 mph—but then one could have learned that simply by turning on the radio and listening to Sammy Hagar wail, "I Can't Drive 55!"[27]

Disrespect for the law the flourished, and it soon begat disrespect for those charged with enforcing the law. Morale among those officers working the traffic detail declined, for who but a sadomasochist would want to arrest people for laws that pretty much everyone this side of the most fanatical safety Nazis holds in contempt? Police officers patrolling the highways had become, to many Americans, "*de facto* tax collectors."[28] Their assignments, though more or less mandated by the federal government, seemed designed to harass otherwise law-abiding citizens. In the words of one analyst, "officers and insurance groups" were the prime beneficiaries of the 55 mph law, as it generated "revenue for both groups, through tickets and higher rates, respectively."[29] But the insurance groups didn't have to face the furious ticketed drivers.

In retrospect, the 1974 law would be condemned, in one typical denunciation (by *U.S. News & World Report*), as "a panicky response to a gasoline shortage that never should have happened."[30] The long lines at the pump were the result less of the Arab oil embargo than they were of counterproductive federal regulations such as price controls and allocation rules. But this misfire scored one direct hit: it enabled the federal government to see just how far states could be pushed into ceding their grounds. Quite far, it turned out.

****

The national speed limit mandate was amended in 1987 and then further in 1991. But the federal government did not relinquish the whip. The 1987 reform permitted states to bump the limit on certain highways (four-or-more-lane, controlled access highways in rural or low-population density areas) to 65 mph, though an enhanced threat of federal penalties endured. Forty states responded to the 1987 amendment by raising speed limits on those select portions of rural interstates.

Charles Lave, the aforementioned economist at the University of California-Irvine, and his colleague Patrick Elias assessed for *Economic Inquiry* the effects of the 1987 reform. Referencing an early study that found an increase of fatalities on those roads with increased limits, they were quick to remark on its constricted scope: "Instead of measuring the local effect of a speed limit change, we should measure the statewide effect because a reallocation of traffic and patrol activities will have systemwide consequences."[31]

Viewed from this more sophisticated "resource allocation perspective," the speed limit increase actually corresponded with a *decline* in traffic fatalities. Raising the limit freed up resources better directed toward other safety purposes and programs. Encouraging drivers to shift from more dangerous secondary roads to the safer interstates ought to have the effect of reducing fatalities when one looks at *all* roads, not just the interstates involved.

The numbers endorsed these hypotheses. Dividing the 50 states into two groups—those that post-1987 bumped their rural interstate speed limits up to 65 and those that stayed at 55—and reckoning their total vehicular fatalities and vehicle miles traveled, Lave and Elias found that in 1987, the first year of the increased limit, the overall vehicle fatality rate dropped by 4.68 percent in the 65 mph states but remained unchanged in the 55 mph states. In 1988, rates fell in both categories. In its first two years of operation, the increased speed limit, they extrapolate, "reduced the fatality rate by 3.62%."[32]

The scholars go on to apply regression analysis to the data. Factoring in such other variables as the presence of mandatory seat-belt laws, economic conditions (which often affect driving habits), and long-term safety trends, Lave and Elias "obtained consistent results": in states that had raised the speed limit to 65 mph on the eligible highways, statewide fatality rates declined anywhere from 3.4 to 5.1 percent in the first year of the increase.[33] Speed, it is apparent, does not kill—variance does.

The US DOT's own figures showed that highway deaths per 100 million vehicle miles travelled (MVMT) decreased from 3.6 in 1974 to 2.3 in 1988—the first year after the 55 mph mandate was partially amended—and then to 1.7 in 1995.[34] (For perspective, the figure had been 25 in 1920.)

Lave and Elias were not alone in denying that Speed Kills. Writing in the *American Economic Review*, Ron Michener of the University of Virginia Department of Economics and Carla Tighe of the Center for Naval Analyses concluded in their study of the effect on highway fatalities of changes in highway safety laws of the 1980s that the new 65-mile-per-hour speed limit on rural interstates and the coerced rise in the drinking age had a "small and difficult to discern" impact on such fatalities. Boosting the speed limit was *not* a killer; and boosting the drinking age did *not* save lives. Wearing seatbelts, they said, was a far more promising method of reducing highway deaths.[35]

Robert O. Yowell of Stephen F. Austin State University concurred. His study of speed limit laws concluded that "there is no widespread positive relationship between raising the speed limit and the fatality rate."[36]

Indeed, many traffic analysts and engineers argued that an unreasonably low speed limit actually *increased* the likelihood of accidents. Oklahoma Department of Transportation chief traffic engineer Alan Soltani remarked in 1996, "When the 85th percentile speed was at 75 and the speed limit was set at 55, drivers weren't comfortable—some drove at 55, some at 65, some at 75. There was so much variance that accidents increased."[37]

But safety fanatics, seemingly immune to such tools of the devil as statistical analysis and fact, decried any lessening of the federal mandate as, in the ridiculous words of Joan Claybrook, who ran the National Highway Traffic Safety Administration during the Carter administration and headed the interest-group Public Citizen, "nothing short of a death sentence, particularly for a lot of young people."[38] Nonsense.

The full and final repeal of the NMSL in 1995 came by what Tyce Palmaffy in *Policy Review* called "chasmic margins": a voice vote in the Senate, and 419–7 in the House on September 20, 1995.[39] (Who were those seven hard-core holdouts against even the mildest federalism? Democratic representatives Beilenson, Dellums, and Waters of

California; Gibbons and Johnston of Florida; Jacobs of Indiana; and Orton of Utah). Repeal of the national 55 mph mandate was a central feature of the 1995 National Highway System Designation Act, which among other things also repealed the penalties imposed upon states that lacked mandatory motorcycle helmet laws (a subject taken up in the next chapter) and—running directly contrary to any states' rights or federalist themes present elsewhere in the 1995 act—imposed a federal mandate upon states to lower the blood alcohol concentration limit for drivers under the age of twenty-one to a minuscule 0.02.

This is not to say that repeal of 55 mph had smooth sailing: Republican committee chairmen Bud Shuster (House Committee on Transportation and Infrastructure) and John Chaffee (Senate Committee on Environment and Public Works) were less than enthusiastic, but the brief wave of Contract with America reform swept even those dinosaurs along. President Bill Clinton called himself "deeply disturbed" by the speed limit increase—but then he always was a moralist, wasn't he?[40]

The US DOT, safety-siren Joan Claybrook's former employer, was hardly less dire than Claybrook in its prediction of the post-55 world. The DOT forecast that in 1996, the year after the repeal of federally mandated speed limits, up to 6,400 more people would die on highways as a result. In fact, the increase in deaths was statistically insignificant. And as Robert O. Yowell points out, Montana, cynosure of much hysteria because of its lack of a speed limit, actually saw highway fatalities *fall* from 215 in 1995 to 200 in 1996.[41] Joan Claybrook seems to have had nothing to say in reaction to that little statistic. Facts can sure be inconvenient things.

The word *safety* had acquired the status of a talisman; it protected the sayer thereof against any amount of research, any accumulation of facts, any volume of truth. *Safety* was more important than liberty, it was more important than federalism, it was more important than the US Constitution, and it was more important even than common sense. It didn't matter that a speed limit of 55 mph on rural interstate highways was actually less safe than a speed limit of 65 or 70 mph: the *safety* card, once played, trumped all. But not in 1995. Or not now.

Quite predictably, those unregenerate supporters of any and all limitations on human activity, insurance lobbyists, resisted reform. When Tyce Palmaffy adduced the mountain of evidence that the national 55 mph mandate had had a deleterious effect on traffic safety, Judie Stone, president of the insurance-industry-funded Advocates for Highway and

Auto Safety, replied simply, "Well, they're wrong. I am not an engineer, but it is just common sense. . . . It doesn't take a rocket scientist to see that if you raise speed limits, speeds go up."[42]

Well, yes, but once again, researchers have established by now that speed alone does not determine the likelihood of an accident; wide variations in the speed at which motorists are traveling is a greater factor. As Charles Lave and Patrick Elias say, "Variance kills." And as they note, just as was the case in 1987, when states were permitted to raise the limit on certain highways, in 1996, the first year after the complete repeal of a national speed limit mandate, nationwide traffic fatalities decreased by 0.7 percent—quite a contrast to the prediction of pro-mandate advocates that fatality rates would jump by 10–14 percent.[43]

Seven states boosted their limits within a week of the repeal; Montana junked any limit whatsoever, returning to its "reasonable and prudent speed" standard (later amended in 1999 to 75 mph). Other states at first rejected higher limits, but as Palmaffy noted, "That's the beauty of a federal system. States can now set their own speed limits after assessing local conditions; some will increase their limits and some will not."[44] By 1993, 42 states had raised the speed limit on at least one highway above 55 mph.

America's highways hardly turned into stock-car tracks the day after the repeal of the national speed limit mandate. Average speeds increased by only modest amounts, and highway fatalities in many states actually declined. In their study of the link between state traffic law policies and motor vehicle fatality rates, David J. Houston, Lilliard E. Richardson Jr., and Grant W. Neeley of the University of Tennessee found, contrary to their hypothesis that increasing the speed limit will lead to an increase in fatalities, that "raising the maximum speed limit on rural interstate highways from 55 mph to 65 mph has reduced fatal and serious injury rates." Consistent with the earlier studies by Charles Lave and others, these researchers, writing in the scholarly journal *Evaluation Review*, explain that repeal of the federal speed mandate permitted states to redeploy police patrols from the safest roads (the interstates) to less safe roads, and it encouraged the faster drivers to use those roads that were built for speed.[45]

At this writing, the lowest speed limit in the fifty states is Hawaii's 60 mph on major highways. Fourteen states have set their maximum speed at 65 mph, nineteen have selected 70 mph, fourteen states have opted for

75 mph, and two states (Texas and Utah) have limits of 85 and 80 mph, respectively, on selected roads. The word for this variety? Federalism.

P.D. Kiser, the Nevada Department of Transportation's chief traffic engineer, pronounced a fittingly harsh eulogy upon the late unlamented law: "The repeal was way overdue; the 55 mph speed limit was an experiment that failed miserably."[46]

It was among the very few federal mandates to have suffered repeal. We turn next to a pair of transportation mandates sedulously pushed by the safety lobby—with somewhat less success than the ill-fated 55 mph law.

Notes

1. Highway Safety Act of 1966, 23 U.S.C. Chapter 4.
2. Robert O. Yowell, "The Evolution and Devolution of Speed Limit Law and the Effect on Fatality Rates," *Review of Policy Research* (Vol. 22, No. 4, 2005): 501.
3. "Speed Zoning Information," www.ite.org.
4. Tyce Palmaffy, "Don't Brake for Big Government," *Policy Review*, September/ October 1996, p. 11.
5. Charles Lave and Patrick Elias, "Resource Allocation in Public Policy: The Effects of the 65-mph Speed Limit," *Economic Inquiry* (Vol. 35, July 1997): 614.
6. Eric Peters, "Why Must Motorists Drive Only 55?" *Consumers' Research Magazine*, November 1995, p. 15.
7. "Speed Limit 55: Is It Achievable?" Report to the Congress by the Comptroller General of the United States, February 14, 1977, p. ii.
8. Ibid., p. 19.
9. Ibid., p. 21.
10. Ibid., p. 15.
11. Ibid., p. 24.
12. Ibid., p. 19.
13. Palmaffy, "Don't Brake for Big Government," p. 12.
14. Lave and Elias, "Resource Allocation in Public Policy: The Effects of the 65-mph Speed Limit": 615.
15. Palmaffy, "Don't Brake for Big Government," p. 12.
16. "Speed Limit 55: Is It Achievable?" p. 12.
17. Ibid., pp. 12–13.
18. Lave and Elias, "Resource Allocation in Public Policy: The Effects of the 65-mph Speed Limit": 620.
19. "Speed Limit 55: Is It Achievable?" pp. 5–6.
20. Ibid., p. 9.
21. Ibid., p. 24.
22. Ibid., p. i.
23. Yowell, "The Evolution and Devolution of Speed Limit Law and the Effect on Fatality Rates": 508.
24. "Speed Limit 55: Is It Achievable?" p. ii.

25. Ibid., pp. 15–17.
26. Gilbert H. Castle, III, "The 55 mph Speed Limit: A Cost/Benefit Analysis," *Traffic Engineering* (Vol. 46, No. 1, January 1976): 14.
27. Paul Grimes, "Practical Traveler: The 55 m.p.h. Speed Limit," *New York Times*, December 26, 1982.
28. Peters, "Why Must Motorists Drive Only 55?" p. 13.
29. Yowell, "The Evolution and Devolution of Speed Limit Law and the Effect on Fatality Rates": 507.
30. William J. Cook, "Why Did We Have to Slow Down in the First Place?" *U.S. News & World Report*, December 18, 1995, p. 22.
31. Lave and Elias, "Resource Allocation in Public Policy: The Effects of the 65-mph Speed Limit": 614.
32. Ibid.: 615.
33. Ibid.: 620.
34. "Traffic Safety Facts," www.dot.gov.
35. Ron Michener and Carla Tighe, "A Poisson Regression Model of Highway Fatalities," *American Economic Review* (Vol. 82, No. 2, May 1992): 456.
36. Yowell, "The Evolution and Devolution of Speed Limit Law and the Effect on Fatality Rates": 516.
37. Palmaffy, "Don't Brake for Big Government," pp. 11–12.
38. Peters, "Why Must Motorists Drive Only 55?" p. 13.
39. Palmaffy, "Don't Brake for Big Government," p. 11.
40. Yowell, "The Evolution and Devolution of Speed Limit Law and the Effect on Fatality Rates": 504.
41. Ibid.: 513.
42. Palmaffy, "Don't Brake for Big Government," p. 12.
43. Lave and Elias, "Resource Allocation in Public Policy: The Effects of the 65-mph Speed Limit": 620. It is the case, according to the National Highway Transportation Safety Administration via Robert O. Yowell, that for every increase of 10 mph for a vehicle traveling above 50 mph, "the force of impact the vehicle exerts doubles when involved in a collision." A driver also has less time to react to an unexpected challenge when traveling at a higher rate of speed. Yet again, it is variance in speed, and not speed alone, that is the greatest factor in highway fatalities. Yowell, "The Evolution and Devolution of Speed Limit Law and the Effect on Fatality Rates": 506.
44. Palmaffy, "Don't Brake for Big Government," p. 11.
45. David J. Houston, Lilliard E. Richardson Jr., and Grant W. Neeley, "Mandatory Seat Belt Laws in the States," *Evaluation Review* (Vol. 20, No. 2, April 1996): 153.
46. Palmaffy, "Don't Brake for Big Government," p. 11.

5

Motorcycle Helmets and Seat Belts: The Mandates That Weren't

Something about highways and roads and the persons and vehicles that travel on them attract the mandaters. The very idea that the fifty American states might have different rules of the road, laws of the open highway, drives those who prefer uniformity and regimentation mad. Speed limits, drinking ages, acceptable BAC limits: one size fits all, in the view of the nationalizers.

Yet not all transportation law has been nationalized, or channeled into the realm of unfunded federal mandates. In this chapter we will consider a pair of failed—though not completely failed—federal mandates: the first requiring that all the states pass mandatory helmet laws for those riding motorcycles, and the second forcing the states to adopt mandatory seat-belt laws for drivers and passengers in automobiles. Why and how did Harley riders avoid the chains of federal mandate—especially as the empirical evidence for the efficacy of motorcycle helmets is far stronger than what links a lower speed limit on interstate highways to reduced fatalities? And why is there no federal seat-belt mandate: was this a triumph for federalism, or was it simply unnecessary given the widespread adoption of such laws in the mid-1980s?

Certainly the considerable number of fatalities and serious injuries (crashes produce "more paraplegics and quadriplegics each year in the United States than all other causes combined"[1]) on the road justifiably focus our attention on ways to enhance auto safety. Yet those fatalities have declined, despite the dire predictions of the safety industry. For instance, in 1985, the National Highway Traffic Safety Administration, a branch of the US Department of Transportation, predicted that the number of US traffic fatalities would rise from 44,250 in 1984 to 70,000 by 1990.[2] There was absolutely no basis for predicting such a spike. In fact, the number of traffic fatalities held steady until the 1990s and declined significantly thereafter.

In late 2011, Transportation Secretary Ray LaHood announced that traffic fatalities hit their lowest level since 1949, as in 2010 a total of 32,885 persons died as a result of accidents on US highways.[3] And this without federal motorcycle helmet and seat-belt mandates!

The most recent data available at the time of this writing showed that motorcycle fatalities nationwide remained stable in 2011 at about 4,500, or approximately the same number as in 2010. This was a decrease from the 5,000-plus totals of 2008 and 2009.[4]

Yet motor vehicle accidents remain, according to the National Safety Council, far and away the leading cause of accidental death in the United States, accounting for upwards of 40 percent of such fatalities.[5] The primary cause of those accidents: distracted driving. In other words, drivers (often inexperienced) who text or chatter or daydream their way into a crash.

****

The motorcycle as a mode of transportation, a statement of one's free spirit, even a *way of life* reached an apex of sorts in the 1960s, capped by the classic youth on the road movie, *Easy Rider*, wherein two hippies took off for a ride across the country in search of sex, drugs, and freedom. Between 1964 and 1976, the number of registered motorcycles in America grew from slightly less than one million to five million.

Riding a motorcycle at 60 mph down the open road, wind blowing in one's hair, was rather more dangerous than steering a station wagon from the grocery store parking lot to one's driveway. Though the numbers vary from year to year, in general, motorcycle fatalities total about 10 percent of motor vehicle fatalities.

Lack of a helmet was judged to be a factor in some of these fatalities, so the safety lobby went into action. By 1966, New York, Michigan, and Massachusetts required motorcyclists to don helmets. Kick-starting a national campaign, the federal government, via the National Highway Safety Act of 1966, conditioned federal highway funding on a state's adoption of a mandatory helmet law for motorcyclists. Those states not measuring up would forfeit 100 percent of their federal highway safety funds and 10 percent of their federal highway construction funds. This rule was promulgated by the US DOT in 1967.

A federal mandate—unfunded, of course: enforcement was up to the states and local law enforcement officials—rode to the rescue. The tool was crossover sanctions.

By 1975, forty-seven of the fifty states had fallen in line. Cyclists from Maine to Arizona had their heads encased in bubble-like capsules. The three exceptions were California; Illinois, whose state supreme court threw out a state legislature-enacted helmet law, ruling that even the "laudable purpose" of protecting a rider or passenger from injury "cannot justify the regulation of what is essentially a matter of personal safety"[6]; and Utah, which required helmets only when one was driving on a road with a posted speed limit of 35 mph or greater. California in particular drove the safety nannies crazy, as it had more registered motorcyclists than any other state in the union.

Motorcyclists, speaking through the American Motorcycle Association (the *other* AMA) and the more forceful A Brotherhood Against Totalitarian Enactments (ABATE), protested the imposition of the national mandate. They drove *en masse* into the nation's capital in June and September 1975, an army of easy riders lobbying on choppers for the repeal of the national helmet-law mandate. In this they found unexpected support in Congress from, among others, Connecticut Republican and cyclist Stewart McKinney, who said, "My personal philosophy concerning helmets can be summed up in three words: It's my head. Personally, I would not get on a 55-mile-per-hour highway without my helmet. But the fact of the matter is that if I did, I wouldn't be jeopardizing anyone but myself, and I feel that being required to wear a helmet is an infringement on my personal liberties."[7]

The motorcyclists, by taking direct action, and taking the fight right to the mandaters, demonstrated the potential of anti-mandate protest. Unlike the K Street lobbying crowd, they wore neither Gucci shoes nor tailored shirts. But they spoke with passion and forcefulness using an American language of liberty—and they succeeded beyond the expectations of cynical observers.

This federal mandate may not have been funded, but it was also hollow. The threat to remove federal highway funding from the non-compliant states turned out to be so much hot air. The US DOT did not begin to punish the trio of holdout states until 1975, and no sooner did the sanction proceedings begin than Senator Alan Cranston, a California Democrat who never met a federal mandate or program or expenditure he didn't like, offered a successful amendment to repeal the law that mandated—by way of threatening cutoff of federal funds—the adoption of motorcycle helmet laws by the states. It seems that the Golden State was in danger of losing $50 million in federal aid—and when alms from Washington were at stake, Cranston's usual objections to "states' rights" and local control flew out the window.

Cranston's cosponsors included Senators Jesse Helms (R-NC) and James Abourezk (D-SD), who were generally regarded as, respectively, the most right-wing and left-wing members of the body.[8] Here, it seems, was an issue that principled men (and, in the case of Senator Cranston, the less-than-principled) could agree on. The amendment, approved by a vote of 52–37 on December 12, 1975, stated that "a highway safety program shall not include any requirement that a state implement such a program relative to requiring motorcycle operators to wear a safety helmet when operating or riding a motorcycle."

This was one of the rare instances when the Congress expressly repealed an unfunded federal mandate. Majorities of both Democrats (31–26) and Republicans (19–11; there was also one Independent and one Conservative) supported the repeal of the mandate. Their ranks included such liberals as Senators George McGovern (D-SD), Gary Hart (D-CO), and Gaylord Nelson (D-WI) and such conservatives as James Buckley (R-NY) and Strom Thurmond (R-SC). Among the defenders of the doomed federal mandate were Senators Bob Dole (R-KS), Ted Kennedy (D-MA), Howard Baker (R-TN), and Joseph Biden (D-DE).[9]

Congress repealed the motorcycle-helmet law mandate with the Highway Safety Act of 1976, signed into law by President Ford on May 5 of that year. What a difference a decade had made. Then came the repeals, state by state. They came in droves. Nine states repealed their mandatory helmet laws in 1976: Alaska, Arizona, Connecticut, Iowa, Kansas, Louisiana, Oklahoma, Rhode Island, and South Dakota. Fourteen followed in 1977. Four more repealed in 1978. Repeal did not necessarily mean that compulsion had completely left the bike. Typically, Arizona repealed its mandatory helmet law in May 1976, yet riders under the age of eighteen were still required to don headgear.

As of this writing, nineteen states and the District of Columbia require helmets on all motorcycle riders, twenty-eight states require at least some riders—usually those 17 and under—to wear helmets, and three states (Illinois, Iowa, and New Hampshire) do not require helmet use.[10]

****

Riding helmetless is undeniably a risky activity. As Denise A. Atwood writes in her history of helmet laws in the *Phoenix Law*

Review, "Healthcare providers have coined a term for people who ride motorcycles without helmets: 'organ donors.' They have nicknames for the motorcycles as well: 'donor cycles' or 'murder cycles.'"[11] Atwood points out the disproportionate number of motorcycle-related deaths compared to those related to automobiles. Depending upon the year studied, bike riders are twenty, thirty, even forty times more likely to die in a vehicular crash than are occupants of automobiles.

Yet many riders dislike helmets, despite their salutary qualities. They can be uncomfortable, sweaty, and confining, especially on hot summer days. Motorcycle enthusiasts rhapsodize over the feel, the ambiance, of the great outdoors, of breeze blowing back your hair while you zoom at 60 miles per hour down a back road or a great American highway. Of course this closeness to the elements that is so much a part of motorcycling's appeal is also a factor in its dangerousness: other than the clothes on one's back, the rider has no real protection should the rider lose control of the bike.

It is important to note that the vast majority of those on the "ride free" side do not disparage—indeed, they often wear—motorcycle helmets. In 1976, as the mandate-repeal campaign revved into high gear, Gary Winn, legislative analyst for the American Motorcyclist Association, emphasized that "the AMA has always urged the use of good quality safety gear.... Helmets are the most important and crucial part of that gear.... So we urge the voluntary use of helmets while we oppose laws governing their use."[12]

Repeal of the federal mandate drove the nanny lobby crazy. The NHTSA, forsaking any pretense of neutrality, was long a partisan for mandatory helmet laws. Its publications declare that the "passage of helmet use laws governing all motorcycle riders is the most effective method of increasing helmet use," and, admittedly, the benefits thereof are considerable. Helmets reduce the incidence of head injury in accident victims, and such injuries are "the leading cause of death in motorcycle crashes." Studies of fatality rates in various states—Kentucky, Arkansas, Texas—reveal sharp increases after the repeal of mandatory helmet laws.[13] (Critics point out that repeal often encourages more people to ride, so before-and-after death statistics are only meaningful if vehicle miles traveled is factored in.)

One study of the first twenty-six states to repeal their helmet laws after the success of the Cranston-Abourezk-Helms federal mandate repeal found that in twenty-three of those states, motorcycle fatality rates were higher than would have been predicted in the absence of repeal.[14]

Somewhat cold-bloodedly, mandatory-helmet advocates often pursued the economic rather than philosophical line of argument. Helmet laws saved money, they said, and wasn't money more important than some airy abstract principles of freedom?

In 1980, Professor Andreas Muller of Penn State, writing in the *American Journal of Public Health*, noted that the number of motorcycle fatalities increased by 23 percent in 1977, the first year after the DOT scrapped its federal mandate. Endeavoring to measure the increased medical care due to the repeal of helmet laws, Muller estimated the annual cost of helmet-law repeal to be $16–$18 million. Muller did not factor in the cost of the enforcement of this mandate—indeed, no researchers ever do. He instead observed merely that "Although the cost of law enforcement activities is unknown, it is not expected to consume a large amount of police resources." He notes the high percentage of compliance in states with helmet laws and seems to assume that such compliance translates into low enforcement costs, though it may well be that *vigorous enforcement is a primary reason for the high rate of compliance.*[15]

Expanding upon the economic argument for compulsion, in 1983 Nelson S. Hartunian, Charles N. Smart, Thomas R. Willemain, and Paul L. Zador wrote in the *Journal of Health Politics, Policy and Law* that the post-mandate repeal or weakening of mandatory helmet laws in twenty-eight states between 1976 and 1980 had been responsible for 516 extra deaths, a disproportionate number of which were young riders and women. Estimating the costs associated with these deaths in both direct (legal, medical, and funeral) and indirect (lost productivity) forms, they peg the price "society" paid for these 516 dead bodies at $176.6 million. It should be pointed out that the "direct" costs are a very small portion of this estimate—$5.4 million—and are dwarfed by the speculative "indirect" costs. As with the Muller study, the authors insist, though they do not put up numbers to back their claim, that reductions in enforcement costs associated with repeal are "insignificant."[16]

This paper by Professors Hartunian et al. was sponsored by the Insurance Institute for Highway Safety, which is ever and always an advocate of curtailing personal liberties in favor of mandated safety. From nationalizing the drinking age to mandating helmets to forcing automobile passengers to strap themselves in with seatbelts, the uber-nannies of the Insurance Institute for Highway Safety are always on the (anti-liberty) case.

The authors of the Hartunian et al. study quote P.A. Ruschmann that "When a person neglects his own health, safety or welfare, all of society suffers" in the form of "lost productivity, high welfare costs, [and] increased insurance rates" (ah, now we get to the *real* hub of the matter!).[17] This rationale would justify limitless government interventions in a person's private life and choices, from what he eats to his sexual behavior to how often he exercises.

And that's all right with crusaders for a nanny state. Time and again in the scholarly literature, one finds the authors grousing about "the extent to which concerns about individual liberties have shaped the public health debate," in the phrase of Marian Moser Jones and Ronald Bayer in the *American Journal of Public Health*.[18]

Lamenting the failure of legislators at state and federal levels to engage in "justified paternalism" and mandate helmet use, Jones and Bayer (of the Mailman School of Public Health at Columbia University) sighed that this lack of success was due to the "profound impact of individualism on American culture." Public health, in this view, has no greater enemy than the vestigial commitment to liberty of many—if, perhaps, a decreasing number—of Americans.[19]

No matter how voluminous the evidence that motorcyclists and their passengers should don helmets, some atavistic libertarian urge in the American people and, sometimes, their legislators keeps states and, even better, the national government from forcing everyone to cover their heads. The many rollbacks of state laws that followed the 1975–76 repeal of the federal motorcycle helmet-law unfunded mandate enrage these public-health writers. Jones and Bayer, for instance, fume over the "uneven patchwork of state regulations," which is also called federalism, and which is a combination of words that invariably precedes a call for nationalizing and mandating the authors' policy preferences. The topper, almost always, is the assertion that enlightened governments around the globe are enacting similar laws, and so the "United States contradicts a global movement."[20] Heaven forbid!

****

The ink was barely dry on the original federal helmet-law mandate when the first court challenges were filed to the new state helmet laws. So there is considerable case law on the subject of such laws.

119

They have, as Jeffery L. Thomas writes in the *Creighton Law Review*, "been upheld in almost every case in which their constitutionality has been challenged."[21]

Constitutional challenges to mandatory helmet—or seat-belt—laws have been launched from several legal and philosophical bases, usually without success. The lines of attack have been these: First and foremost, are such laws legitimate applications of the state's police powers, or do they violate the liberties of those forced to don protective wear? In other words, do these laws protect "the health, safety, and welfare" of the public, in which case they are deemed a proper subject for the state to exercise its police powers, or do they protect only the health, safety, and welfare of an individual, in which case they are (or so argue the anti-helmet law lawyers) "an unwarranted infringement on a motor-cyclist's personal liberty," in the formulation of Clay P. Graham in the *Ohio State Law Journal*.[22]

Other lines of attack include: Do such laws burden interstate commerce to an unconstitutional degree? Do they impede the right to travel or trespass upon the right to privacy of an individual? Are they ineffective and thus unreasonable exercises of the state's power?

In general, liberty has fared poorly in the courts. For instance, in *Love v. Bell* (1970), the Colorado Supreme Court sneeringly disposed of the individual liberty argument against mandatory helmets, overriding it with the welfare-state trump card: "It is, of course, part of a romantic tradition that an individual ought to be able to lead an adventurous and swash-buckling existence without regard to his own safety and without interference from the king. [Was Robin Hood the plaintiff here?] But when that individual as a result of this free-wheeling activity seriously injures or kills himself, the ultimate result is unfortunately not always borne by him alone. Today our society humanely accepts as one of its functions the responsibility for relieving the economic suffering of its members. . . . Persons often become public charges because of their prolonged hospitalization for serious injury, and families are often required to be supported by public welfare as a result of the death of their breadwinner."[23]

That this rationale could with equal justice be used to ban sky-diving or mountain-climbing or the consumption of Big Macs or cheese- and bacon-lathered French fries seems not to have troubled the sleep of the Colorado Supreme Court (or Mayor Bloomberg of New York City, for that matter). This is the slippery slope to end all slippery slopes. If the state reserves the right to ban any activity by any individual that may cause not only physical harm but also "economic suffering," where does one draw the line? As one Nebraska state senator argued during the debate in the Cornhusker State over mandatory seat belts: "If we're going to go ahead and mandate using seat belts, then I think it behooves us to come in with legislation to mandate that we outlaw smoking. . . . [S]moking kills seven times more people than automobile accidents. . . . We can state that on booze too. . . . I just wonder when Big Brother is going to come into our bathrooms and check and see whether we brushed our teeth three times a day."[24]

In *State v. Beeman* (1975), the Arizona Court of Appeals upheld a state mandatory helmet law. Its rationale verged on the totalitarian:

> From the moment of the injury, society picks the person up off the highway; delivers him to a municipal hospital and municipal doctors; provides him with unemployment compensation if, after recovery, he cannot replace his lost job, and, if the injury causes permanent disability, may assume the responsibility for his and his family's continued subsistence. We do not understand a state of mind that permits plaintiff to think that only he himself is concerned.[25]

An exception to the general rule of paternalism was *State of Ohio v. Betts*, a 1969 case in which the Municipal Court of Franklin, Ohio, sided with a motorcyclist who had challenged the Buckeye State's helmet law on Fourteenth Amendment grounds. The court held that "Included in man's 'liberty' is the freedom to be foolish . . . as he may wish, so long as others are not endangered thereby. The State of Ohio has no legitimate concern with whether or not an individual cracks his skull while motorcycling; that is his personal risk."[26]

The court ruled that compelling a motorcyclist to wear a helmet went beyond the police power of the state.

The libertarian language of *State of Ohio v. Betts* sounds so extraordinary in these days of the nanny state rampant; indeed, it sounds almost as if from another country, in another era. The notion that government, up to and including that based in the nation's capital, has no "legitimate concern" with how a person lives his or her life sounds downright revolutionary.

Similarly, the Illinois Supreme Court nullified a mandatory motorcycle helmet law in 1969 in *People v. Fries*. (The year 1969 seems to have been a good year for liberty, at least for motorcyclists.) The command to wear a helmet, ruled the Illinois high court, was an abuse of the state's police powers.

But if courts were by and large approving of such compulsion, legislatures, after the repeal of the federal mandate, were not. The trend was toward a reaffirmation of personal responsibility.

Yes, fatality rates did rise in those states that repealed their mandatory helmet laws. Freedom, as even its most ardent advocates must admit, comes at a price. As Florida governor Jeb Bush said when he signed a bill restricting the Sunshine State's mandatory helmet law to those under age twenty-one or without at least $10,000 in medical insurance, "we could significantly reduce deaths, injuries, or health risks . . . through a mandate that all individuals exercise, wear sunscreen, stop smoking and learn to swim; yet we impose no such requirements."[27] (And when was the last time a Bush was quoted in defense of personal liberties?)

As fatalities from automobile accidents dropped, those from motorcycle accidents rose. And yet even here there were anomalies that suggested the matter was not quite black and white. *Congressional Quarterly Weekly* noted that while motorcycle-related deaths rose sharply in mandatory-helmet law Mississippi from 2000–2003, fatalities in live (and ride) free New Hampshire fell during those years.[28]

Helmets were found in one Washington State study to reduce the likelihood of head injuries by a factor of three and serious head injuries by a factor of four. A Colorado study found that "individuals not wearing helmets were 2.4 times more likely as those wearing helmets to suffer a head injury in a crash." The National Highway Transportation Safety Administration asserts that of every 100 fatalities of helmet-less motorcycle riders, 37 would have been prevented by the use of a helmet.[29] And using cross-sectional, time-series data from all fifty states and the District of Columbia, David J. Houston and Lilliard E. Richardson Jr., writing in the *American Journal of Public Health*, found that from 1975 through 2004, mandatory universal helmet laws were associated with an 11.1 percent fatality reduction rate.[30]

That's not all. A 2009 study of 122,578 motorcycle-related injuries, drawn from the National Trauma Data Bank, found that helmet use is "strongly associated with survival" and reduces the likelihood of death by 16 percent. Translating this into cold hard cash for readers of the *Annals of Surgery*, four physician-authors from the University of Tennessee Health Science Center estimated that "the health care system would save $1,750 in ICU [Intensive Care Unit] per diems if all motorcyclists wore helmets."[31]

So on this there is no debate: helmet use is increasing, which even foes of mandatory laws hail as a good thing. According to the NHTSA's National Occupant Protection Use Survey, which carries the goofy acronym NOPUS and is based on random observations at highways and roadways across the country, in 2011 helmet use reached 66 percent, which was up 12 percentage points from the previous year.

Compulsion does make a difference, as one would expect it to. The rate of helmet usage in states with mandatory helmet laws was 84 percent, while the rate in states that leave the decision with the individual was 50 percent.[32] To which advocates of a federal mandate reply: make the law universal, and usage will zoom in the erstwhile free states. And that is where, controversy-wise, the rubber really meets the road.

****

It can be amusing to watch the insurance and safety lobbies sputter over the incredible power of the motorcycle riders' lobby—the only lobby whose activists typically wear sleeveless T-shirts when they go trudging from office to office on Capitol Hill. *Congressional Quarterly Weekly*, in a 2005 article about the surprisingly effective lobbying by the cyclists' lobby, marvels at its success given that its political action committee contributions are "small potatoes in national politics" and "a pittance" when compared with free-spending business and trade organizations, including the pro-mandate insurance industry.

The key, ventured *CQ Weekly*, was that the motorcyclists had "framed the helmet issue as a question of free choice rather than safety."[33] Instead of arguing on the turf of the public-health and safety industries, which have the studies and have the money, they choose to fight it out on the philosophical plane, where many Americans still respond to libertarian themes.

The leading pro-freedom (as they style it) cyclists' organization is the American Brotherhood Aimed Toward Education, or ABATE. (The acronym replaced the aforementioned and more aggressively named A Brotherhood Against Totalitarian Enactments, its birth name.)

"Let those who ride decide," declares ABATE. Or as ABATE's California director says, "Helmet laws go against the grain of everything this country stands for."[34] And those laws are not an unmitigated blessing. The National Highway Traffic Safety Administration, which since 1998 has been barred from lobbying for mandatory helmet laws, concedes that "Helmets cannot protect the rider from most types of injuries." And even the strongest advocates of a federal mandate admit that they decrease peripheral vision by approximately 10 percent out of each eye and diminish the wearer's hearing.

The vigor and force and energy of ABATE and the ordinary motorcyclists who protest mandatory helmet laws makes for a remarkable contrast with strapped-in motorists. For as Jacob Sullum writes in *Reason*, the puzzle is this: "While almost every state requires adults to wear seat belts, most do not require them to wear motorcycle helmets, even though riding a motorcycle is much more dangerous than driving a car." Moreover, there are about 8 million registered motorcycles in the United States as opposed to approximately 200 million registered automobiles. Yet cyclists were able to resist what Sullum calls "traffic safety paternalism," while motorists were not.[35]

But nannies never sleep.

The issue is far from dead. The mandaters never give up. Rhode Island Republican senator John Chafee, who, you will recall, was the media darling who pushed for national drunk driving standards, introduced in May 1989 the (who-could-possibly-oppose-this?) National Highway Fatality and Injury Act of 1989, which threatened to cut a state's federal highway aid by up to 10 percent if it did not commit the safety daily double of mandating motorcycle helmets and, for front-seat passengers in automobiles, seat belts. Senator Chafee was bidding to make himself the king of the unfunded federal mandate.

Senate hearings delineated a sharp contrast between advocates of the federal mandate, who emphasized safety and the costliness of messy motorcycle accidents, and opponents, such as Vermont senator James Jeffords (a Republican who later left his party), who asked, "Why don't we have motorcycle riders wear armored suits? Where do you draw the line? It is my understanding that the largest percentage of injuries are not by head, but are injuries to the chest and the abdominal areas and things like that. So where do you stop?"

In 1991, Senator Chafee and his allies inserted the punitive language into the surface transportation act of that year, though the penalty to a state for noncompliance with the mandate was reduced to 3 percent of its highway monies. Still, the feds were yanking the leash to show the states who's boss. And the states were to pay the price, both in lost federal monies and increased enforcement costs.[36]

Come the Republican "revolution" that swept Newt Gingrich into the House Speaker's chair, the motorcycle helmet/automobile seat belt federal mandate was repealed in 1995. Interestingly, a spate of new state-level laws followed in which states permitted helmetless riders—as long as the cyclist carried medical insurance with a certain minimum coverage, for instance Florida's floor of $10,000.

Three years after the 1995 repeal came a ban on the National Highway Traffic Safety Administration taking sides on state-level helmet-law debates. The sponsor of that amendment was Senator Carol Mosely-Braun (D-IL), who explained that she was trying to shift the agency "away from the misguided promotion of mandatory helmet laws."[37] (The NHTSA was still permitted to disburse grants to states that sponsored various motorcycle safety programs.)

Mandate foe Mosely-Braun was a Democrat, while advocate Chafee was Republican, but Jenny Homer and Michael French, sociologists at the University of Miami, have found that states with a Republican governor and Republican control of the state legislature are significantly less likely to have helmet laws.[38] So on this issue, party ID is a good predictor of the willingness to coerce. (For weather buffs, states with higher temperatures were less likely than others to have such laws, and states with high rates of precipitation were more likely to compel headgear.)

****

Why have Harley riders succeeded in defying the combined might of the insurance and traffic safety complex while Chevy drivers have not—especially as public-opinion polls report overwhelming public support for forcing cyclists to wear helmets?

For one thing, says Jacob Sullum of *Reason*, "legislators worry about provoking single-issue voters with long memories." Long snaking lines of motorcyclists wending their way through the streets leading to the national Capitol or the state capitols can be an impressive, not to mention intimidating, sight. Anti-mandatory helmet motorcyclists are also vocal single-issue voters: they show up at the doorsteps of legislators, they make their case, and they pledge to vote for "pro-freedom" legislators and against those who think they know best what riders should do.

As for seat belts, James Baxter, president of the National Motorists Association, told Sullum that although there was early and fitful grumbling, "there was no strong opposition. The legislators did not feel they would be affected by the consequences of their vote. There was no downside."

Or as Sullum sums up, "not enough people took seat belt laws personally."[39]

The wave of mandatory seat-belt-laws washed over the United States in the 1980s, that decade when Reaganism was supposedly in the saddle and liberty was making its comeback. It came, as with so many coercive schemes, from beyond the seas.

The Brits beat the Americans to the mandatory seat-belt post. Parliament approved such a law in 1981, though the law had first been formally proposed in 1973. The Tory-majority House of Commons—this was the Thatcher era, recall—approved requiring drivers and front-seat passengers to buckle up by a vote of 221–144.

As Howard Leichter notes in his account of the British seat-belt debate in the *International Journal of Health Services*, the "practical" objections to the law had a certain tenuity. The primary foe of the proposed law in the House of Commons was quick to say that "we are not anti-seat belts. We are, on the contrary, overwhelmingly in favour of them. We agree with the medical profession's powerful lobby [a quick jab to the body there, then a retreat] that the wearing of seat belts is far more likely than not to save the life of the driver or passenger in a car, and to avoid serious injuries." As would be the case in the States, anecdotal evidence was presented that in particular instances and settings a seat belt might hamper one's escape from a burning or sinking vehicle, but these were hard to quantify. (Indeed, the other side brought forth a study of the British Transport and Road Research Laboratory that only one in a thousand automobile accidents involved fire or submersion.)

Some claimed that mandatory buckling up might encourage reckless driving. In the words of Lord Monson in the debate in Britain's House of Lords, "the sense of security conferred by the wearing of seat belts unconsciously encourages motorists to take more risks and to drive with less care and attention."

Others worried that enforcing such a picayune law would embitter police-citizen relations, or that the alternative—not enforcing this picayune law—would breed disrespect for authority. But as Leichter writes, the most basic objection was philosophical. In the words of one opponent: "If we start legislating to prevent people from injuring themselves, there is no limit to the burden that we shall take on and no limit to the number of criminal offences that we shall create."[40]

Such libertarian objections were not enough to stop the public-safety juggernaut. Seat belts saved lives, and if citizens were too stupid or ornery to use them, the British state was perfectly willing to force them to do so. Besides, argued proponents of the law, mandating seat-belt use would ultimately save the national health service money.

These arguments made a seamless transition into the American vernacular. Safety was being privileged; liberty demoted. Talk of a federal mandate even spiced the air.

Anti-mandatory seat-belt writers and activists might argue that, at their base, such laws are awash in paternalistic tyranny. They subordinate the right of an automobile driver to use or not use a health-safety device—the seat belt—to the dictates of the state or federal government. Seen within a health-safety paradigm, the right to refuse to wear a seat-belt is akin to the right to refuse medical treatment.

The arrival on these shores of such obviously paternalistic schemes heralded, in the view of some, a paradigm shift, or "new perspective," in the words of a British observer, Albert Weale of the University of York, who described nanny-state measures as representing "an abandonment of the liberal [as in classical nineteenth-century liberal, or libertarian] doctrines that each person is the best judge of his or her own welfare, and that social welfare will be maximized when individuals obey certain general rules intended to prevent them from interfering with the pursuit by others of their own ends. In place of these principles, the New Perspective appears to substitute the collectivist principle that public officials are in a better position than are citizens themselves to stipulate those courses of action which best promote individual health and thereby all-around social good."[41]

Just as the "highly paternalistic"[42] New Perspective was replacing the old paradigm of liberty and free choice, it was explicated with revealing frankness by Professor Susan P. Baker of the Johns Hopkins School of Hygiene and Public Health. Dr. Baker, writing in the pages of the *American Journal of Public Health*, derided those "special-interest lobbies" that, in "making a pitch for individual freedom," actually "*reduce the freedom* of many individuals."[43]

How is the seeming paradox possible? It isn't. Or, rather, it is possible only by redefining *individual freedom*. Out with the old definition of individual freedom as the liberty to act as one pleases, free from governmental restraints, as long as one does not violate the selfsame rights of others. In Baker's world, one person's freedom—in this case the freedom to ride a motorcycle without a helmet—entails the loss of liberty by many others, who must pay for an injured cyclist's care, rehabilitation, and emotional needs. The possibility that such a cyclist has insurance is not considered. But then Professor Baker is also exorcised over what she regards as sham freedoms to carry guns and drink unpasteurized milk.[44] (She does not add the freedom to have an abortion in this list of bogus freedoms. That would be deviating from the party line, after all.)

Taking aim at Baker was Richard Perkins of the New Mexico Health and Environment Department, who rebuked the safety-above-all-other-values crowd and urged a new respect for "such intangible consequences [of helmet laws] as potential loss of opportunity for individual fulfillment and loss of social vitality."[45] Perkins added that rodeo riders were not compelled to don headgear, nor were rock climbers. One can almost see the light bulbs switch on above the heads of his public-health administrator readers. Eureka! We've found our next cause! Mandatory rodeo helmets! States will be penalized 10 percent of their, er, bull budgets if they fail to adopt these common-sense reforms.

The gathering storm of debate over seat-belt laws both mirrored and deviated from the ongoing controversy over mandatory motorcycle-helmet laws. As Daniel Compton points out in the *John Marshall Law Review*, the public-safety argument upon which motorcycle helmet laws sometimes rested—that is, that helmets enhanced public safety because they "kept debris from striking the cyclist's head and, therefore, prevented accidents involving other vehicles"—is inoperative with respect to seat belts.[46] Shoulder or belt straps come into play only after an accident has occurred, and they protect only the driver or passengers within a vehicle. They do not contribute to "public safety" by way of discouraging accidents.

A driver or passenger who refuses to buckle up is only endangering himself or herself. Yet defenders of the law argue that failing to buckle up leads to a drain on the public treasury, as state funds must be expended to care for those accident victims without insurance. Again, this argument can be used to defend the proscription of any number of activities, from skydiving to eating bacon cheeseburgers.

Constitutionally, seat-belt laws are harder to challenge than are helmet laws. Yvette Benguerel writes in the *Syracuse Law Review* that because buckling a seat belt takes only a few seconds, the beneficial effects of doing such might—arguably—aid interstate commerce, and because no state bans such seat belts, a driver is not faced with any cost to dismantle or modify them when crossing state lines.

As for privacy, if forcing a motorcyclist to sheathe his head isn't a violation of that rider's privacy, requiring an automobile driver or passenger to buckle a belt across his torso is ever so much less likely to be found a violation of privacy.

Like the wearing of motorcycle helmets, the fastening of seat belts lessens one's likelihood of perishing if one's vehicle crashes. As Yvette Benguerel noted at the time of the 1980s debate, research had found that "[r]estrained occupants experience approximately 50% fewer fatalities than unrestrained occupants."[47] Because ejection or impact with a windshield or other segment of the vehicle are primary causes of fatalities in auto accidents, especially for those sitting in the front seats, restraints such as seat belts and air bags are almost universally regarded as salutary safety devices.

There was one problem, though: Americans hated seat belts. They were too confining, too imprisoning, too damned uncomfortable. There was also, as Yvette Benguerel notes, "the well-documented fact that individuals have great psychological difficulty imagining themselves as accident victims." Whatever the reason for this reluctance to strap themselves into a car, in 1984, just as the campaign to force Americans to buckle up was kicking into high gear, seat-belt usage was pegged at a pathetic 15 percent.[48] Despite "buckle up" campaigns, this number had not grown all that much over the previous decade. For instance, a study of 1973 North Carolina accident victims found that 14.5 percent had been strapped in.[49]

Public relations campaigns just weren't going to do it. Most Americans regarded seat belts as at best a necessary nuisance and at worst—and more often—a pain in the neck that they were not going to assume voluntarily. It would take the power of the state to change their minds—or at least their actions.

A would-be federal seat-belt mandate advanced in the shadows of state actions.

New York was the first state to enact a mandatory seat-belt law (for occupants of the front seat). Debate—hotly, for there were in New York some legislators who took personal freedoms seriously, and who viewed this law as an affront thereto—swirled around the issue in the appropriate year of 1984. The measure, having been passed by both houses of the New York State Legislature and signed into law on July 12, 1984, by its ardent backer, Governor Mario Cuomo, became effective on January 1, 1985.

One New York legislator said that "this measure, like George Orwell's *1984*, is a warning. It is a warning about the future of human freedom and respect for individual dignity."[50] But what do freedom and dignity matter when *safety* is the topic of the day?

Governor Cuomo snobbishly called foes of the seat-belt law "NRA hunters . . . who drink beer, don't vote, and lie to their wives about where they were all weekend."[51] High wit from the nation's premier political moralist.

New York had the example of its Canadian neighbor to the North, Ontario, Canada. Before its mandatory seat-belt law took effect in January 1976, surveys found that just 17 percent of Ontario's drivers availed themselves of seat belts. Incredibly, just two months into the law, a whopping 76.8 percent were wearing their lap belts. Talk about the power of compulsion! (Or is this more a testimony to the obedient nature of the people of Ontario?)

Ontario held a lesson in the relative power of suasion and force. As E. Scott Geller, John G. Casali, and Richard P. Johnson explained in a 1980 article in the *Journal of Applied Behavior Analysis*, the Ontario government had engaged in a "comprehensive public education campaign to encourage safety belt wearing" prior to the enactment of the 1976 law. This campaign featured billboards, radio and television ads, propaganda in the schools, widely distributed pamphlets, and other manifestations of a full-court public relations press. After six months, however, surveys of Ontario motorists and passengers discovered that "the educational/prompting program had no effect on seat belt usage."[52] The lesson: Force works.

New York's action set off a chain reaction in which forty-seven states (all but Idaho, Nevada, and Kentucky) debated seat-belt laws in 1985. At first, the public was largely opposed to what seemed an unprecedented intrusion into one's front seat. Opinion polls found upwards of three-quarters of Americans against mandatory seat-belt laws. Voters actually repealed seat-belt laws by referendum in Massachusetts, Nebraska, and North Dakota.[53]

An Illinois assemblyman cautioned, "If there's ever a bill that said that Big Brother is here, if there's ever a Bill that said that 1984 is the appropriate year for acting on this legislation, this is it."[54]

But the resistance faded.

The cost to liberties, it was said, was dwarfed by the cost to taxpayers of highway carnage. The Highway Users Federation & Automotive Safety Foundation pegged the annual national cost of traffic deaths and injuries at exactly $31.418 billion, and estimated—*speculated* would be the better verb, as these projections were not borne out by events—that universal seat-belt use "could have saved 15,000 to 18,000 lives [in 1983 and] . . . would result in an *estimated savings of billions of dollars due to lives saved and injuries avoided or reduced.*"[55]

As with motorcycle helmet laws, there was zero discussion of the cost of enforcing such laws. This cost was not only monetary but also measured in terms of a misallocation of resources: "click it or ticket" campaigns pulled police officers away from the detection or prevention of real crimes and made them musclemen for the nanny state. Ticketing the unbuckled is an act that only a sadist could enjoy.

The form such laws took differed with respect to (1) whether or not all passengers or only front-seat passengers were covered (if seat belts save lives and if public safety overrides any concerns about personal liberty, then why did some states exempt backseat passengers from the law? Are their lives less valuable?); (2) the size of the fines (Mississippi, Rhode Island, and Wyoming omitted financial penalties for the infraction); and (3) whether a seat-belt violation was a matter of primary enforcement—that is, whether police could stop a car because and only because the driver or a passenger was observed unbuckled— or secondary enforcement, in which case drivers can only be ticketed for not wearing a seat belt if they have been stopped for some other offense.

The inconsistencies did not seem to trouble proponents of the laws, although Daniel Compton remarked that "Requiring only front seat passengers to wear seat belts is like inoculating only certain members of the public from an infectious disease, and leaving other members unprotected."[56]

To take a typical example, on June 5, 1985, Nebraska became the eighteenth state to force, under penalty of law, drivers of automobiles (and front-seat passengers, in this case) to buckle up. The fine for violating this law was twenty-five dollars, though no "points" were added to the scofflaw's driving record. Exempted from the law were those with written excuses from a physician (shades of elementary school!) and rural letter carriers for the US Postal Service.[57]

The year 1984 was symbolically apt as the birth year of mandatory seat belts in America, but the scheme really had its origin in an activity rather less lofty than saving lives: lobbying.

The US Department of Transportation, under that ubiquitous queen of meddlesomeness, Secretary Elizabeth Dole, promulgated on July 17, 1984 (Orwell's year), a final rule on the Federal Motor Vehicle Safety Standard No. 208: Occupant Protection Systems.

This bureaucratic mouthful contained a whopper. For within it, US DOT announced that by the end of the decade and starting with the 1990 model year, all new automobiles sold within the United States would have to include passive restraints—that is, airbags or automatic seat belts. (Seat belts themselves had been required in cars sold in the United States since 1968.)

This order for passive restraints, claimed the car companies, would be a costly burden for them to bear. Air bags are an expensive proposition, and the companies feared that in passing the cost of installation along to consumers, the price increase would discourage purchases of new automobiles.

Yet there was an out. The DOT's dictate would be rescinded "if states representing two-thirds of the US population enact mandatory seat-belt usage laws" prior to April 1, 1989.

This was a *federal mandate by indirection*. And it presented the auto industry with a political strategy: lobby heavily at the state level in order to prevent the costly passive restraint regulation from taking effect. William J. Holdorf, writing in *The Freeman*, explains, "Dole's promise amounted to an invitation to the automakers to use their financial resources to lobby states for seat-belt laws, something the Department of Transportation (DOT) was forbidden to do by law, in exchange for the government's not forcing them to install air bags. In effect, the DOT surreptitiously used the financial resources of the private sector to further the political agenda of the federal government through blackmail."

Immediately a lobby was formed: Traffic Safety Now. (That urgent "Now" was a nice touch.) Automobile manufacturers and insurance companies (reliable supporters of any "safety" measures, no matter the cost to liberties or treasuries) are formidable partners, especially when their opponents are rag-tag bands of libertarians and Americans who cling to certain old-fashioned verities about personal liberties and the limits of government. You know: NRA hunters who lie to their wives, drink too much beer, and yammer on about government conspiracies. Or at least that's how Governor Cuomo saw them.

The lobby would spend almost $100 million across the Union in a desperate effort to avoid mandatory air bags—er, to promote safety by requiring seat-belt usage.[58]

In one sense, the joke was on the auto manufacturers. The DOT went back on its word—surprise!—and required passive restraints anyway. This is what the insurance industry had desired all along. Mandated air bags, mandated seat belts—insurers have never met a safety measure they didn't like, or a liberty that they did.

The pro-mandatory seat-belt lobby was populated by the usual suspects: the Alliance of American Insurers, the American Association for Automotive Medicine ("automotive medicine"? take two quarts of STP and call me in the morning?), the Highway Users Federation, the Automotive Safety Foundation, and the Insurance Institute for Highway Safety. As Holdorf notes, "there is no record of any insurance company ever reducing its rates because a seat-belt law was passed."[59]

****

So seat-belt laws blanketed America by the mid-1980s due to a federal mandate of a different kind: rulemaking by the US Department of Transportation that spurred intensive lobbying for universal seat-belt laws at the state level.

Even that wasn't enough for those disposed to central control. Senator Hillary Clinton (D-NY) introduced, with Virginia Republican John Warner, a flat-out mandate bill in 2003. It would have withheld federal highway funds from any state that did not both enact a mandatory seat-belt law and achieve 90 percent compliance within three years.[60]

The Clinton-Warner bill did not pass, but then it was by 2003 almost a redundancy. Seat-belt laws covered the land.

As of this writing, New Hampshire, the Live Free or Die State, is the sole holdout from mandatory seat-belt laws. Thirty-two states permit primary enforcement of the laws: that is, one can be stopped and ticketed for not buckling up even if one has committed no other offense. The other seventeen states have secondary enforcement laws: in these states, drivers can only be ticketed for spurning a seat belt if they have also committed another traffic infraction.[61]

The laws have been successful, if one measures success by compliance. Those 15 percent usage rates of the pre-New York law are ancient history; recent surveys have found seat-belt usage at 85 percent. As the US DOT reports, in 2011, primary-law states saw 87 percent usage, while in secondary-and-other-law states 76 percent of motorists were buckled up.[62]

As for the life-saving effects of these laws, the record is mixed. Most researchers have concluded that mandatory seat-belt laws, by significantly increasing seat-belt usage, have decreased motor-vehicle accident fatalities. But there have been exceptions to these studies; a minority of researchers have found "no correlation between the implementation of a seat belt law and traffic fatalities."[63] There is, however, a correlation between the implementation of a seat belt law and a decline of liberty.

There have been instances of seat-belt restraints hampering the rescue or escape of accident victims. Yet the belts undeniably saved lives as well.

The efficacy of seat belts has never really been the question. The question is to what extent government may compel motorists to buckle up. The answer, it seems, is to a very great extent. A frank and plain federal mandate, funded or not, was not even necessary to force Americans to buckle up. The states, under lobbying pressure induced by the feds, did it to themselves. And it may be a sign of the dwindling spirit of liberty in America that very few people complain about the *1984*-ness of mandatory seat-belt laws anymore.

Notes

1. Jeffery L. Thomas, "Freedom to Be Foolish? L.B. 496: The Mandatory Seat Belt Law," *Creighton Law Review* (Vol. 19, 1986): 747.
2. Yvette Benguerel, "Mandatory Seat Belt Legislation: Panacea for Highway Traffic Fatalities?" *Syracuse Law Review* (Vol. 36, 1986): 1344.
3. "U.S. Transportation Secretary LaHood Announces Lowest Level of Annual Traffic Fatalities in More Than Six Decades," NHTSA press release, December 8, 2011.
4. Dr. James Hedlund, "Motorcyclist Traffic Fatalities by State," Governors Highway Safety Association, May 8, 2012.
5. www.nsc.org.
6. Marian Moser Jones and Ronald Bayer, "Paternalism and Its Discontents," *American Journal of Public Health* (Vol. 97, No. 2, February 2007): 4.
7. Ibid.: 7.
8. Ibid.
9. www.govtrack.us/congress/votes/94-1975/s583.
10. www.iihs.org/laws/HelmetUseCurrent.aspx.
11. Denise A. Atwood, "Riding Helmetless: Personal Freedom or Societal Burden?" *Phoenix Law Review* (Vol. 1, 2008): 270.
12. Clay P. Graham, "Helmetless Motorcyclists—Easy Riders Facing Hard Facts: The Rise of the 'Motorcycle Helmet Defense," *Ohio State Law Journal* (Vol. 41, 1980): 238.
13. Atwood, "Riding Helmetless: Personal Freedom or Societal Burden?": 274–76.

14. Geoffrey S. Watson, Paul L. Zador, and Alan Wilks, "The Repeal of Helmet Use Laws and Increased Motorcyclist Mortality in the United States, 1975–1978," *American Journal of Public Health* (Vol. 70, No. 6, June 1980): 579.

15. Andreas Muller, "Evaluation of the Costs and Benefits of Motorcycle Helmet Laws," *American Journal of Public Health* (Vol. 70, No. 6, June 1980): 586, 590.

16. Nelson S. Hartunian, Charles N. Smart, Thomas R. Willemain, and Paul L. Zador, "The Economics of Safety Deregulation: Lives and Dollars Lost due to Repeal of Motorcycle Helmet Laws," *Journal of Health Politics, Policy and Law* (Vol. 8, No. 1, Spring 1983): 84–85, 91.

17. Ibid.: 77.

18. Jones and Bayer, "Paternalism and Its Discontents": 2.

19. Ibid.: 9.

20. Ibid.: 2.

21. Thomas, "Freedom to Be Foolish? L.B. 496: The Mandatory Seat Belt Law": 751.

22. Graham, "Helmetless Motorcyclists—Easy Riders Facing Hard Facts: The Rise of the 'Motorcycle Helmet Defense'": 236.

23. Thomas, "Freedom to Be Foolish? L.B. 496: The Mandatory Seat Belt Law": 752.

24. Ibid.: 756.

25. Atwood, "Riding Helmetless: Personal Freedom or Societal Burden?": 291.

26. Thomas, "Freedom to Be Foolish? L.B. 496: The Mandatory Seat Belt Law": 753.

27. Jenny Homer and Michael French, "Motorcycle Helmet Laws in the United States from 1990 to 2005: Politics and Public Health," *American Journal of Public Health* (Vol. 99, No. 3, March 2009): 417.

28. Isaiah J. Poole, "Bikers a Surprising Force in Grass-Roots Lobbying," *CQ Weekly*, May 16, 2005, pp. 1287–89.

29. David J. Houston and Lilliard E. Richardson Jr., "Motorcycle Safety and the Repeal of Universal Helmet Laws," *American Journal of Public Health* (Vol. 97, No. 11, November 2007): 2063.

30. Ibid.: 2066.

31. Martin A. Croce, Ben L. Zarzaur, Louis J. Magnotti, and Timothy C. Fabian, "Impact of Motorcycle Helmets and State Laws on Society's Burden," *Annals of Surgery* (Vol. 250, No. 3, September 2009): 392–93.

32. "Motorcycle Helmet Use in 2011—Overall Results," *Traffic Safety Facts*, National Highway Traffic Safety Administration, April 2012.

33. Poole, "Bikers a Surprising Force in Grass-Roots Lobbying," *CQ Weekly*.

34. Jacob Sullum, "Freedom Riders," *Reason*, November 2005.

35. Ibid.

36. Jones and Bayer, "Paternalism and Its Discontents": 8.

37. Poole, "Bikers a Surprising Force in Grass-Roots Lobbying," *CQ Weekly*.

38. Homer and French, "Motorcycle Helmet Laws in the United States from 1990 to 2005: Politics and Public Health": 418.

39. Sullum, "Freedom Riders."

40. Howard Leichter, "Lives, Liberty, and Seat Belts in Britain: Lessons for the United States," *International Journal of Health Services* (Vol. 16, No. 2, 1986): 219–21.

41. Albert Weale, "Invisible Hand or Fatherly Hand? Problems of Paternalism in the New Perspective on Health," *Journal of Health Politics, Policy and Law* (Vol. 7, No. 4, Winter 1983): 785.

42. Ibid.: 787.

43. Susan P. Baker, "On Lobbies, Liberty, and the Public Good," *American Journal of Public Health* (Vol. 70, No. 6, June 1980): 573.

44. Ibid.: 574.

45. Quoted in Jones and Bayer, "Paternalism and Its Discontents": 7.

46. Daniel Compton, "The Illinois Seat Belt Law: Should Those Who Ride Decide?" *John Marshall Law Review* (Vol. 19, No. 1, Fall 1985): 194.

47. Benguerel, "Mandatory Seat Belt Legislation: Panacea for Highway Traffic Fatalities?": 1343.

48. Ibid.: 1345.

49. E. Scott Geller, John G. Casali, and Richard P. Johnson, "Seat Belt Usage: A Potential Target for Applied Behavior Analysis," *Journal of Applied Behavior Analysis* (Vol. 13, No. 4, Winter 1980): 669.

50. Leichter, "Lives, Liberty, and Seat Belts in Britain: Lessons for the United States": 223.

51. David E. Petzal, "Bad Bullets, Mario's Message, and a Mess in Montana," *Field & Stream*, August 1985, p. 34.

52. Geller, Casali, and Johnson, "Seat Belt Usage: A Potential Target for Applied Behavior Analysis": 670.

53. Sullum, "Freedom Riders."

54. Leichter, "Lives, Liberty, and Seat Belts in Britain: Lessons for the United States": 223.

55. Thomas, "Freedom to Be Foolish? L.B. 496: The Mandatory Seat Belt Law": 748.

56. Compton, "The Illinois Seat Belt Law: Should Those Who Ride Decide?": 198.

57. Thomas, "Freedom to Be Foolish? L.B. 496: The Mandatory Seat Belt Law": 745.

58. William J. Holdorf, "The Fraud of Seat-Belt Laws," *The Freeman*, September 2002, www.thefreemanonline.org.

59. Ibid.

60. Jon Dougherty, "States Should Oppose Seatbelt Mandate," wnd.com, December 19, 2003.

61. "Seat Belt Laws," www.ghsa.org/html/stateinfo/laws/seatbelt_laws.html.

62. "Traffic Safety Facts," www-nrd.nhtsa.dot.gov/Pubs/811544.pdf.

63. Houston, Richardson, and Neeley, "Mandatory Seat Belt Laws in the States": 148.

II

ABCs, IDs, and Voting: Mandates for the Twenty-First Century

6

No Child Left Behind: When George W. Bush Decided to Teach Your Children Well (or Otherwise)

Diversity, that word so beloved of college administrators, was once the hallmark of American education. Today, with about 15,000 school districts and almost 100,000 public schools throughout the United States, the sheer multiplicity of schools ought to guarantee various approaches to learning.[1] Yet there are those who would paint all these schoolhouses in a single color. The standardized test and the uniform curriculum are their lodestars. And their weapon is one of the most controversial unfunded federal mandates in our history: No Child Left Behind.

No Child Left Behind, or NCLB, ranks with the Iraq War as the weightiest legacy of the George W. Bush administration. Assessing the situation during the middle of the second President Bush's reign, Patrick J. McGuinn wrote in *No Child Left Behind and the Transformation of Federal Education Policy, 1965–2005*, that "the politics of education has been nationalized to a degree unprecedented in the country's history, and the federal government's influence over education policy has never been greater."[2] And the bulwark of that transformation was an unfunded federal mandate.

The US Constitution does not grant the federal government the power to make laws concerning the education of children. Indeed, education is nowhere mentioned in the Constitution. Not that the lack of such an authorization matters terribly much in our era, when most actions of the federal government also seem to lack such sanction. The Founders clearly did not regard the teaching of young people as a concern, even an ancillary concern, of the national government.

139

But they lacked the percipient understanding of such men as Lyndon B. Johnson and George W. Bush.

Since the middle of the twentieth century, advocates of greater federal spending and involvement in areas of life that had been generally regarded as the province of family, church, or local community found that the magic words to unlocking the public treasury are "child," "children," or "defense."

No appropriation, no usurpation, no violation of the Constitution or the erstwhile rights of parents is too egregious if the name of the proposal contains one of those words. As I have discussed at length in a previous book, *The Doomsday Lobby*, the federal government first poked its nose into public education in a big way under cover of the National Defense Education Act (NDEA) of 1958, which was sold to the public in the panic following the Soviet Union's successful launch of the *Sputnik* satellite. The National Defense Education Act—you will notice which word comes first, defense or education—was a product of the Cold War. It was sold as a weapon, and those who expressed doubt that the federal government possessed the wisdom to intervene in what had always been a local matter were scorned as sentimental fools who did not understand the nature of the communist threat.

"We no longer have the freedom of choice that used to be an important feature of our way of life," thundered Admiral Hyman Rickover, one of the loudest supporters of the NDEA. "[E]ducation," argued Admiral Rickover, "is now our first line of defense, and we neglect it at our peril."[3]

The newspapers and magazines that guided public opinion were filled with hysterical accounts of Soviet advances in science. The failure of Americans to beat the Soviets in the satellite-launching game was blamed upon the decentralized nature of American schooling. Local school officials and parents were at best hapless, at worst stupid and irresponsible. "We cannot be modern, streamlined, atom-powered in our industrial and defense structures and remain bucolic and archaic in our educational system," declared Max Ascoli, editor of the influential liberal magazine *The Reporter*.[4]

The public education lobby, which had for years vainly argued for increased federal aid (if not control—but then that would follow naturally, for he who takes the king's shilling becomes the king's man), piggybacked onto the Cold War/defense argument for a massive federal education program. The National Education Association, responding to the launch of two *Sputnik* satellites, expressed the hope that the "advances made by the Soviet Union, as shown by the two satellites, may awaken our nation to the importance of stronger school programs." An NEA lobbyist, assessing the NDEA's legislative chances, remarked, "The bill's best hope is that the Russians will shoot something off."[5]

He needn't have worried. The $1 billion NDEA (back when $1 billion was real money), justified as an expenditure under the incredibly and increasingly broad spending clause, passed both houses easily. President Dwight D. Eisenhower, who had steadfastly refused to panic in the face of *Sputnik*, dismissing it as "one small ball in the air," signed the measure, though he assured those who had misgivings that it was to be temporary.[6] *Fat chance of that happening.* Eisenhower's statement upon signing the NDEA into law on September 2, 1958, was a classic in wishful thinking. The act, he emphasized, was "an emergency undertaking to be terminated after four years." He would be out of office in four years, but the federal government was just getting started in the public-schooling business. Yet Eisenhower pressed on, as if saying the words would make them permanent, even binding. "The federal government having done its share," he said, "the people of the country, working through their local and State governments and through private agencies, must now redouble their efforts toward" the improvement of public education.[7] Washington, DC, it turns out, would more than redouble *its* effort.

As Robert A. Divine wrote in *The Sputnik Challenge* (1993), "Eisenhower was beginning a process of federal involvement that set important precedents for the much more extensive educational programs that Congress would enact in the 1960s."[8]

Building upon the National Defense Education Act, the 1965 Elementary and Secondary Education Act (ESEA) expanded federal involvement in education based on a new rationale: ameliorating poverty and its ill effects through more spending on education. The ESEA was a Great Society program. While LBJ was waging war on communism in Vietnam and Southeast Asia, he was waging war on poverty at home. The fact that both Vietnamese communism and poverty endured after LBJ left office offers a hint as to the ultimate efficacy of the Great Society.

The ESEA was sold as a temporary program. Surely, those Americans who worried about federal encroachments into local matters were told, the problems associated with poverty would be resolved by the Great Society, and just as the Marxists promised that the state would wither away in due time, so were Americans assured that federal aid to education would become less necessary once certain tractable social and economic difficulties were resolved.

LBJ signed the ESEA into law "in Johnson City, Texas, on the site of the one-room schoolhouse he attended as a boy."[9] This was a very sentimental staging for a law that would serve, over the years, as a primary legal means by which little schools in places like Johnson City were stripped of any semblance of self-governance and instead took orders—meekly or under pressure—from central authorities. In fact, No Child Left Behind was the most prominent in a series of ESEA reauthorizations.

LBJ aide Samuel Halperin told Paul Manna, "The people who you could call the Kennedy and Johnson elites—I don't use the term negatively—didn't think that we could get educational justice from the states. Some of them said that the states were actually the problem." Or as US Commissioner of Education Francis Keppel, of LBJ's 1964 task force on education, told an interviewer, many task force members "felt that the state departments of education were the feeblest bunch of second-rate, or fifth-rate, educators who combined educational incompetence with bureaucratic immovability."[10] The feds would be so much better! With the government involved, what could possibly go wrong? Who wouldn't want Lyndon B. Johnson's cronies designing their children's history and science lessons? The task force, chaired by long-time bureaucrat John Gardner, recommended the creation of a US Department of Education, a dream that would take fifteen years to realize.

The Elementary and Secondary Education Act provided "categorical" aid—aimed at disadvantaged students—rather than general aid to benefit all. This was channeled through ESEA's Title I, the major federal conduit for aid to schools that served disadvantaged students. Money was doled out under Title I proportionate to a district's disadvantaged students. The federal oversight was not exactly panoptical; the districts were largely trusted to see that the monies got to their intended beneficiaries. Title I was therefore a "funding stream," the course of which was largely determined locally. And once the federal government carves out the wending path of a funding stream, not even an act of God can stop the flow.

There were solons who saw beyond the next election. Senator John Williams (R-DE) said of the ESEA that it was "merely the beginning. It contains within it the seeds of the first federal education system which will be nurtured by its supporters in the years to come long after the current excuse of aiding the poverty stricken is forgotten. . . .

The needy are being used as a wedge to open the floodgates, and you may be absolutely certain that the flood of federal control is ready to sweep the land."[11]

Senator Williams, it seems, had foresight. The somewhat narrow scope of the ESEA would broaden considerably in the coming decades. Between 1958 and 1968, the federal share of education funding went from 3 to 10 percent. A federal education administration bulked up, as the "ESEA facilitated the centralization, bureaucratization, and judicialization of education policymaking."[12] ESEA rapidly became what reformers regarded as a bureaucratic rat hole.

There would be no retrenchment or retreat by the feds. Other national interventions into the erstwhile local field of education followed under the administrations of Presidents Richard Nixon and Gerald Ford. Just as President Eisenhower, a putatively parsimonious Republican, was at the helm for the first major incursion by the federal government into education policy, so were later Republican presidents intimately entangled in the federal takeover—or makeover—of American education. These laws bore names such as the Education Amendments Act of 1972, the Rehabilitation Act of 1973, the Equal Educational Opportunities Act of 1974, and the Education for all Handicapped Children Act of 1975.

Democratic President Jimmy Carter pushed through the creation of the US Department of Education in 1979 as a payoff to his loyal supporters in the National Education Association, though it is interesting to note that the other major teachers' union of the time, the American Federation of Teachers, dominated by New York City-area social democrats, opposed the DoED, not out of any philosophical objection to bureaucracy but rather because the AFT understood that an NEA-dominated DoED could render the AFT DOA. (The rather unusual acronym for the Department of Education is due to the fact that "DOE" was already assigned to the US Department of Energy. Sometimes the Department of Education is referred to as "ED," but as that abbreviation evokes the notion of "erectile dysfunction" and the many medicinal cures for it, DoED is used herein.)

The begetters of this bureaucracy tried to assure skeptics of their benign intentions with this language: "[T]he establishment of the Department of Education shall not increase the authority of the federal government over education or diminish the responsibility for education which is reserved to the states."[13]

Wanna bet?

Ronald Reagan came to the White House having pledged to abolish the Department of Education, but he did just the opposite. Reagan created a National Commission on Excellence in Education, which produced the alarmist publication *A Nation at Risk: The Imperative for Education Reform* (1983), whose bellicose rhetoric and calls to action made clear that Washington was wielding the whip hand in education policy and would do so for the foreseeable future. Manna writes, "*A Nation at Risk* may have saved the Department of Education from Reagan's ax."[14]

President Ronald Reagan's Department of Education oversaw the publication and massive publicity blitz for *A Nation at Risk*, one of those documents concocted by a blue-ribbon panel with an obvious agenda: in this case, a Reagan-led, top-down reform of American education, with an emphasis on more testing and a greater nationalization of the curriculum.

A Nation at Risk echoed the militarized language associated with the National Defense Education Act. The most famous passage of the 1983 clarion call read,

> If an unfriendly foreign power had attempted to impose on America the mediocre educational performance that exists today, we might well have viewed it as an act of war. As it stands, we have allowed this to happen to ourselves. We have even squandered the gains in student achievement made in the wake of the *Sputnik* challenge. Moreover, we have dismantled essential support systems which helped make those gains possible. We have, in effect, been committing an act of unthinking, unilateral educational disarmament.[15]

To hear our children referred to as victims of an act of war, and to read their education compared to the arming (or disarming) of a nation's military, is jarring. But this was the intent of *A Nation at Risk*. The authors understood that Americans in the Reagan years had tired of social-welfare programs, and grown (rightly) skeptical of their effectiveness. Military readiness seemed to be a stronger selling point than ending poverty.

As Paul Manna writes, "it is curious to note that during the 1980s, state governors became increasingly enthusiastic about the federal government's presence in education and even called for more federal monitoring of state educational progress."[16] Some would later have cause to regret this early enthusiasm for an interventionist federal government.

Accountability and standards and testing-testing-testing became the new mantra, which *A Nation at Risk* proclaimed. With the ascent of President George H.W. Bush, Reagan's vice president and successor, the era of Republican hostility to the DoED was over. Bush had no apparent philosophical problem with the federal government assuming a larger role in this traditionally state and local matter.

Bush, who pledged a "kinder, gentler" conservatism, convened a 1989 education summit of the nation's governors at Charlottesville, Virginia, where in the cradle of Thomas Jefferson they repudiated the Jeffersonian belief that government is best which governs least and instead endorsed "clear, national performance goals" as a "first step in a long-term commitment to re-orient the education system."[17] Bush's National Education Goals Panel would monitor state progress in meeting a range of education goals.

The Charlottesville summit at least implicitly supported lading Washington with greater responsibilities in education. The symbolism of its setting in the historic home of Thomas Jefferson, who narrowly defined the essential duties of the national government—duties that decidedly did *not* include directing the education of the nation's young—was painful for those of Jeffersonian disposition.

The governors at Charlottesville had latched onto education as the next big policy issue of the fin de siècle. Across the union, states were imposing their own standardized tests, expanding after-school programs, and in some cases strengthening the hand of the governor as opposed to the state legislature and local school boards. As Kentucky governor Paul Patton would later put it, "Educating each and every one of America's young people is the paramount responsibility of governors."[18]

Patton's bombast, his policy megalomania, his almost farcically overblown notion of what a governor is responsible for, suggests just how expansive a view politicians had developed of their powers to cure society's ills and to supervise the training of the next generation.

President George H.W. Bush included in his 1990 State of the Union Address an endorsement of "national goals for education." The feds were more than happy to provide guidance and set goals, even if the funding provided was not commensurate with the amount of advice. As Patrick McGuinn writes in his account of increasing federal involvement in education policy, "Bush embraced a federal role in education reform and helped to legitimize the idea that the country's historically decentralized public schools needed national leadership to help them improve."[19]

Accountability became the new buzzword in education policy. This denoted the seemingly uncontroversial idea that schools should be in some way accountable to parents and the community, and that there should be clear and understandable methods of measuring a school's performance and transmitting that measurement to parents and the broader community. The 1980s and '90s saw most states adopt new testing programs as a means of achieving that accountability. The problem—aside from the inexact science of testing, and the frequent failure of the various players to agree on what constitutes satisfactory progress by the students—is that this marked a transfer of responsibility from local districts to the states. Power was flowing upward, away from the grass roots and toward technocrats in the various state education offices. To an unprecedented extent, states were seizing control of education, reducing localities to mere executors of state demands.

Democrats liked the emphasis on increased government spending on education; Republicans liked the supposed accountability that increased federal oversight was said to bring. Opinion polls, those lodestars by which politicians set their courses, revealed that Americans responded favorably to the idea of greater federal spending on education. The old Reaganite GOP platform pledge to abolish the US Department of Education was quietly dropped. (Not that Reagan had ever really acted upon that pledge anyway: his administration's sponsorship of *A Nation at Risk* was a significant step down the road of activist federal education policy.)

President Bill Clinton certainly had no philosophical objection to a greater national role in education, but he was hamstrung, at least fitfully, by Republican opposition from undertaking any ambitious initiatives in the field. (Though as Patrick McGuinn points out, the ostensibly penny-pinching congressional Republicans actually appropriated *more* on education than Clinton proposed during his second term.)

The 1994 ESEA reauthorization required any state receiving Title I funds—that is, every state—to devise and submit to the federal government standards to which they would hold students and measure their performance. The age of standardized testing was upon us. And while the 1994 law did not explicitly provide penalties for states or districts that failed to meet goals, it "suggested" such penalties—and any observer of government understands that what begins as a suggestion very quickly matures into a dictate.

When in his 1999 State of the Union speech Clinton called for increased federal funding for school districts that adopted various of his pet education causes, from forcing children to wear uniforms to enhanced training for teachers to the distribution of school "report cards" to parents, the Republicans in his audience refrained from standing and cheering. Senator Lamar Alexander (R-TN), who had served as secretary of education under the first President Bush, sneered, "The President has proposed a national school board. But we should go exactly in the opposite direction—liberating the schools, not regulating them. We should send the money to the parents and let them choose where their children attend school." Senator Alexander's interest in "liberating the schools" did not extend beyond the end of the Democrat Clinton's term; he supported George W. Bush's No Child Left Behind, a measure so intrusive and centralizing it made Clinton's education proposals look like something suggested by Henry David Thoreau.

Not all Republicans looked askance at Clinton's initiatives. Neoconservative apparatchik Linda Chavez, for instance, told the *New York Times*, "I don't see any point in being overly ideological on this question of local control. I would urge Republicans to do what they did with welfare control—seize on it and take it further."[20]

That they did. As Patrick McGuinn wrote in *Publius*, while the Clinton-era educational reforms, such as Goals 2000, "*encouraged* states to create standards, testing, and accountability systems," No Child Left Behind "*requires* it."[21] This was not so much educational reformism of the Clinton-New Democrat variety as it was educational activism of the sort formerly associated with the most interventionist liberals. The operating philosophy seemed to be: if the other party has control of government, decentralize, but if we control it, *centralize like hell*.

Clinton's "Goals 2000" proposed voluntary national standards for the states to meet—though the states would have to submit these standards to the Department of Education for approval and the money that would follow. The 1994 ESEA reauthorization foreshadowed No Child Left Behind in its focus on federally approved standards and assessments. But, writes Patrick J. McGuinn, "the lingering conservative opposition to a strong federal role in education and the continuing liberal reservations about testing and accountability meant that Goals 2000 and the ESEA reauthorization contained little in the way of mandatory reforms for the states."[22] That would be corrected under Clinton's successor, George W. Bush.

As Elizabeth DeBray of Brown University wrote in *Voices in Urban Education*, the Clinton administration's enforcement of the 1994 law was "relatively weak."[23] States were routinely granted waivers. But the advent of George W. Bush, combined with a rising technocratic trend among "New Democrats," who sought to distinguish themselves from the paleo variety—the Ted Kennedys who never could throw enough money at a problem—created a welcoming milieu for what became No Child Left Behind.

Bipartisanship was about to rear its ominous head!

Consider the great leaps forward in the nationalization of American education policy: NDEA-ESEA-*A Nation at Risk*-NCLB. Three of the four were signed into law by Republican presidents! And the Democratic initiative, ESEA, was at least targeted at disadvantaged youth. The three GOP initiatives were more sweeping in their reach. Republicans, it appears, only dislike Big Government when the Democrats are in charge.

For instance, John Boehner (R-OH), later Speaker of the House, was among those who in the 1990s, the Clinton years, advocated abolition of the DoED, but once a Republican was in the White House he led the legislative charge to enact No Child Left Behind. He said, "I think we realized in 1996 that our message was sending the wrong signal to the American people about the direction we wanted to go in education."[24] Thus guided by poll numbers and focus groups, and in pursuit of the votes of the fabled soccer moms, Boehner and his party shifted gears, foisting upon the American people the largest and most intrusive federal education program yet—what Clinton education advisor Andy Rotherham called "the high water mark of federal intrusion in education."[25]

****

Passage of No Child Left Behind was a breeze. On May 23, 2001, the House approved the landmark No Child Left Behind Act by a vote of 384–45. Three weeks later, on June 14, the Senate passed it by 91–8; conference reports were subsequently approved by House (381–41) and Senate (87–10) by easy margins. The eight senators who braved the bipartisan storm and voted nay on NCLB deserve to have their names recorded: they were Republicans Bennett (UT), Helms (NC), Inhofe (OK), Kyl (AZ), Nickles (OK), and Voinovich (OH), and Democrats Feingold (WI) and Hollings (SC).

So this was hardly a nail-biter or barnburner. Republicans and Democrats alike enshrined No Child Left Behind into law. Federalism may have been left behind in the act, but that didn't overly bother the vast majority of House and Senate members. Despite the occasional gusts of anti-Washington wind issuing from candidates for Congress every two years, few of those who serve in the body have a realistic sense of the limits of national policy.

The only real congressional opposition to NCLB came from the handful of authentic fiscal conservatives on the Right and anti-testing liberals on the Left; for the most part, passage of the act was a widely bipartisan effort uniting, in the admiring words of one observer, "New Democrats and Compassionate conservatives."[26] Bush Republicans were ecstatic: Senator Judd Gregg (R-NH) called NCLB "an exceptional piece of legislation," and the president hailed "a new era" of public education.[27]

In a meaningless nod to past American practices, the president said, as he signed the bill into law in front of students in Hamilton, Ohio, that "the federal government will not micromanage how schools are run. We believe strongly . . . the best path to education is to trust the local people."[28] As long as the local people act in ways that please the federal government, that is.

In just twenty years, or a single generation, "federal education policy had shifted from minimal federal involvement [Reagan pledging to abolish the Department of Education—though by overseeing *A Nation at Risk*, his administration actually strengthened the department] to the development of voluntary national standards (under President Clinton) to the new law mandating testing of all students in Grades 3–8," writes Lance D. Fusarelli in the *Peabody Journal of Education*.[29] This was more than a sea change; it was a revolution through which the historically local function of education was effectively nationalized. And it was nationalized by, more than anything else, an unfunded federal mandate.

No Child Left Behind was George W. Bush's first major domestic initiative, and it would be his most lasting. Technically, it was a reauthorization of the ESEA of 1965, but it took that cornerstone piece of federal education legislation and constructed upon it an unprecedented edifice.

Supporters of No Child Left Behind sold it as a long-overdue introduction of accountability and standards into federal education funding. At 1,100 pages in length, it was, almost literally, unreadable.

Its purpose, according to its architects, was "to ensure that all children have a fair, equal, and significant opportunity to obtain a high-quality education and reach, at a minimum, proficiency on challenging State academic achievement standards and state academic assessments."[30] To ensure this, states were required to administer annual standardized tests in math and reading to all children in grades three through eight, and a high school grade as well. Science tests were to begin in 2007–2008. These scores were broken down by school, school district, and state by race, income, and various disabilities or special needs. To scratch the "accountability" itch, schools were then directed to issue "report cards" in which the performance of their students was revealed.

States were required to file plans for compliance with NCLB's mandates with the US Department of Education. This, you may recall, was the federal department that the Republican Party platform had pledged to abolish in the bad old days. But in the George W. Bush GOP, abolition of DoED had turned to adoration. And the method of choice for this invasion of state and local education policy was the conditional spending power of Congress, the club with which federal mandates may be carelessly wielded.

Exhibiting a seemingly boundless faith in American public education, the authors of No Child Left Behind gave that educational system a dozen years to raise every student in every racial or ethnic category, as well as students who are migrants, disabled, or speak English as a second language, to a level of "proficient" in mathematics and reading. Seemingly oblivious to real life as it is actually lived, the authors of NCLB dictated that "not later than 12 years after the end of the 2001–2002 school year, all students in each group [economically disadvantaged students, major racial and ethnic groups, students with disabilities, and students with limited English proficiency] . . . will meet or exceed the State's proficient level of academic achievement on the State assessments."[31]

Sure they will. It envisioned the Lake Woebegone world in which all the students would be above average.

So to recap: To measure the progress of their young charges, states were mandated to test all students in grades three through eight in math, reading, and science. Test scores were broken down by subgroup: those with disabilities, the economically disadvantaged, various racial and ethnic groups, and those with limited facility in English. District-wide report cards were issued for the entire student population and each subgroup.

If the percentage of "proficient" students did not show sufficient annual increase, penalties could be levied upon the schools. The charge? Failure to make "adequate yearly progress" (AYP—the NCLB crowd loved acronyms) toward "universal proficiency" by the target date of 2014. Never mind that, as Yale University professor of psychology and education Robert J. Sternberg avers, probably the best predictor "of achievement in a school is the socioeconomic status of the parents," and that schools in which a substantial percentage of students come from single-parent backgrounds and poverty will, almost invariably, fare worse than others in their collective scores on standardized tests.[32] These truisms of social science are thrown out the window when Washington politicians smell an easy (if not cheap) cause.

If a school fails to meet its AYP goals for two years running, it is hung with a "school improvement" tag. Students may transfer out of such delinquent schools to a school that is meeting its goals. If a school fails three years running, "corrective action" will be taken. Students in such schools may use Title I monies to purchase tutoring—even from private sources. If a school fails to measure up for four consecutive years, staff and curriculum will be replaced or at least all shook up. And by year number five of failure, the school will be remade, at least in theory, and approach its next lustrum with a brand new bureaucratic structure.

Each state defined "proficient" in its own way, subject to Washington's scrutiny. Drawing up, administering, and evaluating the mandated tests, reporting the data, and rendering the prescribed assistance to schools that fall short of the mark are the prime unfunded mandates within NCLB. Now, a state could refuse to comply with the act's directives, but it would lose its Title I funding, which, in FY 2012, amounted to approximately $14 billion nationally.

Furthermore, NCLB requires the states, as a condition of Title I financing, to ensure that all teachers of academic subjects are "highly qualified," which in practical terms means they have a bachelor's degree, the necessary complement of certifications and licenses, and demonstrate a mastery of their subject matter.

And in an odd and perhaps portentous bit of phrasing, NCLB declared that school curricula must be verified by "scientifically based research." Henceforth, curricular selections were to be overseen by the federal government, which has announced itself the arbiter of what is and what is not scientifically valid. This means a thudding affirmation of conventional wisdom in every field, and the virtual outlawing of unconventional or experimental curricula, not to mention curricula that challenge the status quo or carry outré or radical political baggage. Washington, DC, is in the saddle, and it intends to ride hard, even roughshod, over any little school district or nonconformist state that dares to dissent from the feds' preferred brand of science.

Demonstrating the same commitment to meaningless paper guarantees as did the late and unlamented Soviet Union, with its model—and seldom obeyed—constitution, the authors of NCLB assured one and all that no monies appropriated through NCLB to the US Department of Education could be spent to "endorse, approve, or sanction any curriculum designed to be used in an elementary school or secondary school."[33] In the understated observation of Kathryn A. McDermott and Laura S. Jensen of the University of Massachusetts, "It is difficult to reconcile these provisions of NCLB with those requiring that curricula and teaching practices be based on scientifically based research." This is an invitation, say the scholars, that "provides an opening for massive federal intervention in state and local decisions about curriculum and teaching."[34]

****

President Bush, echoing the martial language of federal education advocates dating back to the *Sputnik* and NDEA era, said, "We're going to win the war against illiteracy in America."[35] (Physician, heal thyself, one is tempted to respond.) The president made that pledge in a speech in the district of Representative John A. Boehner, future Speaker of the House and a prime sponsor of No Child Left Behind. This was very much a Republican enterprise, no matter that in later years the limited-government wing of the party would distance itself from the act.

In an interview with Patrick J. McGuinn, Republican House Education Committee coordinator Vic Klatt remarked that "NCLB is the precursor of even more federal involvement to come in education."[36] This was, to Bush Republicans, a selling point!

Richard F. Elmore, professor at the Harvard Graduate School of Education, famously called NCLB "the single largest—and the single most damaging—expansion of federal power over the nation's education system in history."[37] Not that Professor Elmore objected to the principle of federal direction of education policy. With Susan Fuhrman, he had called in 1990 for the federal government to "become the leading agent in a broad-scale public discourse about what schools should be doing and how we know whether they are doing it." The feds, he said then, should not limit their input to "jawboning." Rather, Washington, DC should seek "active involvement" and "significant investments" in developing ways of measuring student performance.[38]

NCLB, however, failed Professor Elmore's test. In forcing a "single test-based accountability system for all states," a "single definition of adequate yearly progress," and "a single target date" by which all students in all disaggregated socioeconomic groups must pass the federally mandated tests, NCLB had imposed a test-obsessed pedagogy on every school district in every state in the union.[39]

As a sympathetic scholar, Regina P. Umpstead of Michigan State University, writes in the *Journal of Law & Education*, No Child Left Behind extended "federal authority into areas of education such as teacher qualifications, curriculum selection, and educational assessment that have previously been state or local prerogatives."[40]

Were strings attached? More like ropes and chains. This was conditional spending with a vengeance. It was a top-heavy unfunded federal mandate bearing the imprimatur of that most venerated political entity: bipartisanship. Both parties were eager to force the states to do the bidding of the federal education bureaucracy.

In surveying the prospects of No Child Left Behind, many education policy analysts, as well as those on the ground and close to the action, saw a field of red flags.

Orange County (CA) Department of Education General Counsel Ronald D. Wenkart warned that NCLB could "engulf and overwhelm state and local government."[41] The state of Ohio's education department issued a report pegging the annual cost to the state of compliance with NCLB's mandates at $1.5 billion—a figure far beyond the $44 million that the state would receive from the feds.[42]

Indeed, in NCLB's first year of operation the federal government spiked its Title I spending by $1.5 billion (of a total just shy of $11 billion)—or about how much Ohio expected its annual compliance to cost. Now if they could just find a way to cut the mandate-driven expenditures of the other 49 states to almost zero.

William J. Mathis, superintendent of schools in the Rutland Northeast Supervisory Union of Vermont, calculated that in order to comply with No Child Left Behind, spending would have to be boosted anywhere from 15 to 46 percent in the ten states he studied. Indeed, a serious effort to meet its requirements—which almost every analyst not on the Bush White House payroll conceded was impossible—would have required Title I appropriations of upwards of $80 billion. The states, to put it mildly, were not enthusiastic about forking over that extra $65 billion plus not supplied by Washington. NCLB, it seems, was the unfunded federal mandate to beat all unfunded federal mandates.

For as Mathis writes, the costs of NCLB "reach far beyond the costs of running a testing bureaucracy or buying each teacher a test-prep manual." They also include "the costs of actually teaching children to the new mandated standards."[43] Therein lies a helluva rub.

Even the basic administrative costs outstripped the funds states would receive to implement NCLB. The New Hampshire Association of School Administrators protested that while the state would receive, via the Elementary and Secondary Education Act, $102 more per student under NCLB, the additional cost of implementation was $1,022 per student. Next door in Vermont, administrative costs alone rose 5.3 percent under NCLB. As William J. Mathis writes, "it is a consistent finding that increases in federal appropriations do not cover the increased administrative costs." State after state—Minnesota, Ohio, Hawaii, Indiana, Connecticut—raised the same protest.[44]

The assertion that NLCB was "fully funded," argued Mathis, was absurd. Drawing from seven independent studies at the state level, Mathis estimated state administrative costs due to the law to have risen by between 2–2.5 percent, or by $11.3 billion—rather more than the Bush administration's vaunted Title I boost. State studies also revealed that the total cost of bringing—or attempting to bring—every student in America up to the NCLB-mandated proficiency standards would be $137.8 billion. Add in the administrative burden (minus federal aid) and the cost of fulfilling NCLB comes to $144.5 billion. "[I]t is incontrovertible," concluded Mathis, "that NCLB is not funded adequately" and is, therefore, an unfunded federal mandate of the first order.[45]

Washington was less than impressed by these objections.

Secretary of Education Rod Paige denied that NCLB was an unfunded mandate. He boasted in the *Wall Street Journal* in October 2003 that "President Bush has increased K–12 education spending by 40% since he took office. That's more in two years than it increased during the eight previous years under President Clinton."

It speaks volumes about the Bush administration that its Secretary of Education would take to the pages of the most-read "conservative" editorial page in America to brag about how much more profligate (dollar-wise, that is) the Bush White House was than the Clinton White House. As Paige admitted, the city he was writing from, Washington, DC, was among the largest spenders on public education, per pupil, in the United States, while ranking dead last in math and reading scores on standardized tests. The correlation between spending on education and achievement has never been robust, but somehow the Big

Government Republicans of the second Bush administration were going to defy previous experience. And to those cynics who might doubt the efficacy of No Child Left Behind, Secretary Paige ended his apologia with the most hackneyed yet effective phrase in the modern lexicon of lobbying: he, and the administration, and all those who supported No Child Left Behind, were doing it "for the sake of the children."[46]

The bland reassurances by Bush and Paige that No Child Left Behind was neither unconstitutional nor an unfunded mandate placated Republican members of Congress and some obedient state education officials; others were more skeptical. Including scholars. For instance, L. Darnell Weeden, Associate Dean of Texas Southern University, told a symposium sponsored by the *Thurgood Marshall Law Review* that NCLB was "at best a poorly funded federal mandate and at worst an unfunded federal mandate that probably violates the United States Constitution's federalism principles under the Spending Clause and the Tenth Amendment as well as the specific unfunded mandate provision of the NCLBA."[47]

Although conservative apologists for Republican presidential candidates remind conservative voters every four years that putting the GOP standard-bearer in the White House is essential to the preservation of federalism, it is remarkable how little Republicans cared about NCLB's deviation from the Constitution, from the Tenth Amendment, and the admittedly toothless UMRA that Republicans had overwhelmingly supported, and with such fanfare, during the previous administration of President Bill Clinton. Federalism and the Constitution, it seems, wax and wane depending upon whose party occupies the seats and manipulates the levers of power.

****

The single federal legislator most closely identified with No Child Left Behind was Senator Edward Kennedy (D-MA), whose very name had been a bête noire to Republicans a generation earlier. Many was the direct-mail writer who understood that capitalizing and putting in bold font the name **TED KENNEDY** was the key that opened many a right-wing bank account. Senator Kennedy was a thorough-going centralist whose entire adulthood had been spent in service to the expanding leviathan in Washington, DC. He had precious little concern for preserving the traditional responsibilities of states and localities. And in fact NCLB was "developed with little collaboration with state and local officials," according to Kenneth Wong of Brown University and Gail Sunderman of the Harvard Civil Rights Project.[48]

Even the establishment pundit David Broder of the *Washington Post*, whose columns were always reliable barometers of insider opinion, expressed shock at the eagerness with which George W. Bush was "presiding over the biggest, most expensive federal government in history."[49] Though the GOP still made its ritual obeisances to the ghost of the Ronald Reagan administration, Reagan's (perhaps halfhearted, certainly ineffectual) pledge to abolish the US Department of Education had transmogrified, in the Bush years, to a commitment to enhance, strengthen, and extend the reach of the DoED, and trespass upon state and local education efforts, including state-level reforms that pre–George W. Bush Republicans had heralded as evidence that education policy was best conducted in the fifty state capitals and even at a more local level.

The Bush administration boasted of the bipartisan establishment support for its principal domestic initiative. Secretary of Education Rod Paige, who had been superintendent of schools in Houston, Texas, laid down the preferred narrative of supporters: "Coauthored by prominent political leaders representing multiple ideological positions and both political parties, NCLB represented a new engagement by the federal government in an area previously reserved for the states."[50] There is a certain exaggeration to this, or perhaps it is more accurate to say that Paige was wearing blinders. The "multiple ideological positions" amounted to standard-issue Ted Kennedy liberalism plus the Big Government Conservatism whose fumbling tribune was President George W. Bush. To the left of Kennedy, radical critics of the education establishment condemned No Child Left Behind for its emphasis on standardized testing, and to the right of Bush, libertarian-minded critics attacked NCLB as a profligate and centralizing program that upended the traditional distribution of responsibilities between the national, state, and local governments. The vaunted bipartisanship of the measure meant only that those stuck squarely within the control rooms of the system—the geniuses who also gave us the Iraq War, the Patriot Act, and such "statesmen" as John Edwards and Donald Rumsfeld—approved of No Child Left Behind. It violated none of their deeply held principles because they have no deeply held principles beyond holding onto that power, principles be damned.

In the assessment of Patrick McGuinn of Drew University, NCLB marked a turning point in—or perhaps a last shovelful of dirt piled atop—the federalist principle upon which the US government had been constructed more than two centuries earlier. While federalism once "exerted a powerful restraining influence on the size and character of the federal role in education," wrote McGuinn, "that time appears to have passed." As a result of NLCB, the "U.S. Department of Education now functions as a national schoolmarm, hovering over state school reform efforts and whacking those states that fail to record satisfactory and timely progress toward federal education goals with financial penalties and mandatory corrective actions."[51]

As in previous cases, the acceptance of federal funds—an acceptance to which the states have been conditioned through years of increasing dependence upon such—carries with it the obligation to do the bidding of the federal government. In particular, No Child Left Behind requires those states that accept Title I monies to institute academic standards, subject to approval by the US Department of Education and measurable by annual tests. There is, as its defenders like to assert, a certain flexibility built in: that is, the states design their own tests and standards. Audaciously, the Bush Department of Education claimed that the law actually provided for "increased local control and flexibility, removing federal red tape and bureaucracy and putting decision-making in the hands of those at the local and state levels." The response to this claim ranged from outrage to howls of laughter, for as Kathryn A. McDermott and Laura S. Jensen of the University of Massachusetts noted in the *Peabody Journal of Education*, almost everyone outside the DoED, the Bush administration, and the bipartisan congressional phalanx that passed the law believed that it expanded "federal authority" over K–12 education to an unprecedented and even unseemly degree."[52]

As Secretary of Education Paige explained, No Child Left Behind rested on several premises. First, that the "system"—which he seemed to view as a whole, rather than a medley of 15,000 individual districts within fifty states—must expect of every student a certain level of performance in mathematics and English, and that there must be means of measuring that performance via testing. Second, that those students who do not reach that level of performance need remedial help. Third, that the districts and states composing "the system" must be held accountable to the taxpayers who fund them and the parents who entrust their children to them. Fourth, that such accountability must also apply to those who receive federal education funding.

These are mostly noncontroversial, with the exception of his somewhat unitary view of "the system," which in the past had been relatively decentralized. Paige insisted that NCLB made several concessions to the diversity of the schools and students in this vast country.[53] States, for instance, were permitted to design their own standards for math and English—though these were subject to approval by the feds. States also determine what level of achievement on statewide tests constitutes proficiency. They choose the textbooks and curriculum—well, they do within reason, as the New York City schools would have occasion to learn, as we shall see later in this chapter. In sum, Paige insisted that states enjoyed a degree of flexibility under No Child Left Behind, though whether this was the flexibility of the athlete training under an open sky or the prison inmate exercising in his cell is a matter on which educators and analysts differed.

"I hear the rhetoric about local control and flexibility," said Nebraska education commissioner Doug Christensen in 2003, "but I don't see that. What I see are regimentation and uniformity." Christensen explained to David Broder of the *Washington Post*, "Our classes in [grades three to eight] range from 15 to 18 students. Our teachers know how well every child is doing and every school has its own system for measuring that. We don't want to impose an outside standard that is not necessary. The responsibility for educating our kids is ours, and I am not going to defend some federal requirement unless we think it is good for our kids."[54]

This made Commissioner Christensen an enemy of all that is right and good, according to the Bush education brain trust. The Bush mandarins conceded that forty-eight of the states already had tests and assessments and standards in place by the time of No Child Left Behind, but those tests were administered with much less frequency—only thirteen states mandated annual math and reading exams for all students in grades three through eight, as NCLB did. True, teachers and parents may complain that the consequence of the Bush act was to force teachers to "teach to the test," emphasizing rote learning over other forms of pedagogy, but the feds knew best.

With the wave of its federal wand, Congress and the Bush administration commanded that every student in America be taught by a "highly qualified teacher." The very definition of *highly qualified* had little to do, in truth, with high qualifications. Such teachers had to possess bachelor's degrees and teaching licenses, the latter from their state of employment. This was a guarantee of nothing except that they had jumped through the proper hoops en route to a career in the classroom.

They were also supposed to demonstrate a "mastery" of their subject matter as well as teaching methods.

Many good teachers were insulted by the presumption of the wonks who wrote this legislation. How dare they presume incompetence on the part of veteran teachers? And state education officials, many of whom had already developed methods of grading teachers, wondered where Washington got off in preempting existing measures of teaching ability. They also saw dollar signs—or, rather, seas of red ink, as the wide-scale testing and training necessary for teachers as well as students under NCLB would strain, even overwhelm, state education budgets. The mania for testing was so overwhelming that even the National Education Association—not heretofore known as a bulwark of anti-bureaucratic activism—was moved to song. The NEA's secretary-treasurer Lily Eskelsen penned this ditty in 2004:

> A bureaucrat came to our town.
> At first we thought he jested.
> He said, "When I get through with you folks,
> They'll be no child left untested."[55]

Not exactly "I Dreamed I Saw Joe Hill Last Night" or "We Shall Overcome," but a nice try anyway.

The disconnect between the Beltway-based authors of the act and the teachers, administrators, school boards, and students upon whom the act fell was enormous. The sheer impracticability boggled many outside-the-Beltway minds. The act's sponsors seemed to be unacquainted, for instance, with American geography. Idaho state representative Doug Jones explained, "If a school is deemed in need of improvement and must offer the student an option of attending another school, there simply may not be a place to send the student within 50 miles. Open enrollment may work in Boise, but it certainly doesn't in Fairfield [Idaho: population 417] because there's nowhere else to go."[56]

The rural states protested especially NCLB's mandate that all teachers be "highly qualified" in their subject areas. While such a requirement is easy for outsiders to impose, and difficult to object to—who, after all, wants to defend "moderately qualified" or "poorly qualified" teachers?—when the lofty rhetoric is translated into actual policy affecting real live human beings, it is, quite simply, impossible for many school districts to meet. Washington may have, via No Child Left Behind, demanded that districts force teachers to hold degrees and/or pass tests in the subjects they are teaching, but school districts in sparsely populated areas cannot always comply with that demand.

In October 2003, Democratic governor Bill Richardson of New Mexico and Republican governor Judy Martz of Montana wrote Secretary of Education Paige. (As we are finding, many people wrote Secretary Paige to protest aspects or even the entirety of No Child Left Behind, and they may as well have been writing the Man in the Moon for all the good it did them.) The governors' complaint centered on the "highly qualified" provision of NCLB. They wrote: "The core of the problem is the simple fact that 42 percent of the schools throughout the West are in rural areas. Nearly 33 percent of the students in our nation attend school in towns of fewer than 25,000 people. A rural school with fewer than 100 students lacks similarity to Los Angeles Unified School District. NCLB attempts to treat them the same; they are not. As a result, many rural states and their schools feel as though they have not been considered in NCLB."

A spokesman for Paige responded, via *Education Week*: "We need to give the law a chance to work."[57] In other words, tough luck, though it should be pointed out that Governors Richardson and Martz were not taking direct aim at the very concept of mandates. Their criticism was specifically aimed at the teacher qualification provision; in other parts of the letter to Secretary Paige, they advocated more federal spending on education. This is hardly the formula for a reinvigorated system of local schools.

****

Bryan Shelly of Wake Forest University, writing in *Publius: The Journal of Federalism*, noted that the states, in the main, have been quiescent in recent years on questions of state-federal relations. They have tended to accept whatever prescriptions or proscriptions the feds handed out. Though they may complain about federal overreach, "formal state legislative and legal challenges to federal regulation have been extremely rare."

But the widespread resistance to NCLB "is a notable exception to this pattern."[58] This was one conditional grant and coercive federal mandate that went too far.

There were only scattered murmuring complaints from the provinces as the act sped through legislative channels. The larger establishment bodies registered protests of varying degrees of force. The National Conference of State Legislatures criticized NCLB as a federal encroachment upon the rights of the states. The National Governors Association, after the bill's passage, called it an unfunded federal mandate and demanded not repeal but more funding and a "responsive federal-state partnership"—hardly a call to revolution.[59]

But back in the states and in the school districts, the air was filled with howls of outrage against this unfunded federal mandate and unprecedented power-grab in the field of education.

Five states—Colorado, Illinois, Maine, Utah, and Virginia—passed laws in varying degrees of opposition to No Child Left Behind. Another, Connecticut, sued the US Department of Education over the mandate. In the preponderance of states, legislators debated anti-NCLB bills, thus providing a hearing, if not a sanction, for the resistance movement. In only twelve states did the legislature make not even a peep of protest. These were Alabama, Arkansas, Delaware, Georgia, Massachusetts, Michigan, Mississippi, Missouri, Montana, New York, North Carolina, and Texas.[60]

Evaluating patterns of opposition, Bryan Shelly found that the states with the highest level of resistance to NCLB were those with "relatively large Hispanic populations and low poverty rates." The former, he speculated, is due to the fact that Hispanic children are less likely to speak English as a first language than are white or African American children. Nonnative English speakers, he writes, are "among the most difficult subgroups to bring into compliance" with the AYP, or adequate yearly progress, goals of No Child Left Behind.[61] The requirement that students who have yet to master English must perform at the same level as those who have spoken English since they burbled their first words strikes many as wildly unrealistic, and a matter of wishful thinking trumping realism. It is as if the architects of NCLB thought that the mere utterance of goals made those goals achievable. As years of test results have shown, they do not. (Curiously, Hispanic interest groups have not been outspoken in opposition to NCLB. In fact, La Raza Utah supported the law.)

William Mathis, superintendent of several school districts in Vermont, said that the NCLB mandate requiring schools falling short of adequate yearly progress to pay for their students to employ tutors or transfer to other districts amounted to a "death sentence" for his poorer districts.[62] The costs of such transfers and tutoring would deplete the budgetary resources of these schools.

Recall that the original NCLB legislation mandated that 100 percent of all students in every subgroup—that is, every single child in America—reach proficiency in those academic areas covered by the tests (also mandated by NCLB). No one outside of the most ethereal precincts of la-la land believed that this was possible, but that's what the law required. One suspects that Uncle Sam could appropriate $14.516 *trillion* to the purposes of No Child Left Behind, and it still wouldn't be enough to bring every child in America up to the testing threshold. Different children have different abilities, and no amount of legislating is going to force every child in the country to learn and remember and be able to describe on a test the difference between a cosine and a tangent.

Recall also that a report done for the state of Ohio Department of Education estimated that NCLB would impose an additional cost of $1.5 billion every year, which would rather dwarf the NCLB-targeted annual federal funding of $44 million.

The difference, as Regina R. Umpstead, a supporter of the act, explains, is this: defenders of No Child Left Behind argue that the mandate is funded because federal monies should cover most if not all of the administrative costs associated with the law, among them the costs of testing. Yet critics point out that merely giving and grading tests is in no wise sufficient to meet the NLCB mandate. For there are a raft of costs involved in bringing, or attempting to bring, students throughout a state up to the proficiency levels. Including these costs, as Umpstead concedes, means that "the additional federal funds supplied under NCLB will be vastly insufficient."[63]

As for the relationship of low poverty rates to NCLB resistance, Shelly notes that legal challenges to federal laws are not done on the cheap. The better off a state is, the easier it can afford to mount such a challenge. Moreover, those states whose tribunes spoke openly of noncompliance, or even defiance, were threatened with a reduction of federal funds—a threat that carries extra weight with relatively poor states.

Among those factors that did not influence a state's resistance to No Child Left Behind, according to Shelly, was the relative strength of a state's teacher unions.[64] (Even though the National Education Association was a plaintiff, along with various local school districts, in *School District of Pontiac v. Spellings*, the Michigan NCLB challenge.) Nor did the partisan tincture of a state explain resistance to NCLB. Utah is deeply Republican and Connecticut reliably Democratic; both led the opposition to the Bush education mandate. New York, just as blue, and Alabama, which in modern times is redder than red, complied quiescently.

Like REAL ID and the Motor Voter law, No Child Left Behind permitted the federal government to intrude into matters formerly the realm of the states, and to mandate acts by those states that the feds had no intention of fully funding. How could such aggression by Washington not invite a response, especially from those states that (1) had populations or subpopulations that would have a hard time meeting the act's goals and (2) could afford to mount such a challenge, even at the cost of forsaking some federal aid?

Even so bold an assault on traditional states' rights as No Child Left Behind failed to rouse the fighting spirit in some governors, however. Or it provoked them merely to ask for more money. California governor Gray Davis solicited the signatures of twenty-six Democratic governors in a letter to US Senate leaders complaining that the "states have been shortchanged" in funding of NCLB-mandated programs. Pennsylvania governor Ed Rendell whined, "Don't ask us to test, then leave us without the resources." Michigan governor Jennifer Granholm complained that "The mandates are not funded."[65]

In each case, the gravamen of the complaint is not the mandate itself but rather the fact that the feds are not funding the mandate. The aforementioned trio was all Democrats, it should be pointed out. Few Republicans directly challenged the signature education initiative of a president of their own party, though Nebraska GOP governor Mike Johanns castigated NCLB as "the biggest federal grab in the history of education."[66]

In Wisconsin, which with its La Follette tradition is a state that has combined progressivism, even socialism, with a preference for decentralism, state attorney general Peg Lautenschlager released an opinion in May 2004 that encouraged either the state's Department of Public Instruction or a school district or districts to challenge No Child Left Behind as an unfunded mandate. Attorney General Lautenschlager referenced NCLB's injunction against anything in the act "mandat[ing] a state or any subdivision thereof to spend any funds or incur any costs not paid for under this act."

"The states are entitled to take Congress at its word that it did not intend to require state and local governments to expend their own funds to comply with the detailed and proscriptive federal mandates," wrote the attorney general.[67] Once again, however, state officials and Bush administration officials disagreed on the reach of the mandate.

Should all funds expended within a state to bring its students up to the achievement bar be counted as compliance costs? The states and the feds differed on this question, and always would. Bush spokespeople were quick to boast that as of 2004, Wisconsin was receiving $1.7 billion in federal education monies, or 45 percent more than in Bill Clinton's last year. "Compassionate conservatism"—also known as "Big Government Republicanism"—was in full flower. (Attorney General Lautenschlager eventually filed an amicus brief in the *Pontiac v. Spellings* case.)

Wisconsin's governor at the time, James Doyle, was, by contrast, a profile in cowardice. He was doggedly mute with respect to Attorney General Lautenschlager's anti-NCLB opinion. According to Lance D. Fusarelli, Doyle's timidity was part of a broader range of pusillanimous gubernatorial shrinking from conflict with the feds. A National Governors Association official had remarked that Democratic and Republican governors alike "fear that open, vocal opposition to NCLB will result in retribution from Washington," that retribution being measured in federal funds withheld.[68] This kind of toadying to the powers-that-be is what happens when the feds control the purse strings and the strings attached thereto.

As federalism scholar Christopher J. Deering writes, "many states found NCLB an unfunded mandate at minimum and, for others, a massive encroachment by the federal government into this longstanding preserve of 'states' rights.'"[69] Idaho State senator Gary Schroeder called it "the largest unfunded mandate in the history of the United States."[70] (Power-grabs, it might be pointed out, seem to run in the Bush family. The president's brother, Jeb, then governor of Florida, had pushed for and achieved a state board that had authority "over all [K–12] public education" in the Sunshine State.[71] The members of the board, like the state's education secretary, were all appointed by Governor Bush. In the opinions of the Bush family, it appears, no one is quite so qualified to direct the education of complete strangers as members of the Bush family.)

President Bush seemed almost oblivious to the assault on federalism contained in his prize education law. He consistently framed the debate as between those who favored teaching children the fundamentals (his side) and those who preferred that they grow up wholly ignorant, even unschooled. In his 2004 State of the Union address the president charged, "Some want to undermine the No Child Left Behind Act by weakening standards and accountability. Yet the results we require are really a matter of common sense: We expect third-graders to read and do math at the third-grade level, and that's not asking too much."[72]

This was a deft rephrasing of the argument. If, indeed, the debate was between those who wished to teach math and reading to third graders and those who opposed such pedagogy, then the fix was in. But as hard as Bush and his supporters tried to ignore those fifty entities called the states, those pesky states demanded to be heard.

Bush administration officials boasted—how the Republican Party had changed, at least rhetorically, from the Reagan years!—that federal education spending increased by 35 percent, or about $15 billion, over his first term. But that was far less than the projected cost to the states of the NCLB mandates.

As states of varying hues, from red Utah to blue Vermont, girded up for challenges to the law, its friends in Washington manned the ramparts. Representative John Boehner (R-OH), chairman of the House Committee on Education & the Workforce and the future Speaker of the House, trumpeted a 2004 study by a pro-testing organization called Accountability Works and the self-importantly named Education Leaders Council, which, like Secretary Paige, asserted that "the charge that NCLB is an 'unfunded mandate' is false." Like Paige, the researchers marveled at the increase in federal education funding under President Bush, though its estimates of the amount necessary to meet the mandates and the estimates of the aggrieved states were far apart.

Representative Boehner's press release said that the states were "profiting handsomely from the education spending increases triggered by President Bush's No Child Left Behind education reforms."[73] The implication, therefore, was that the state officials were too dense to understand this, and that all their caterwauling about being unable to meet the federal mandates was at best the result of ignorance and at worst a sly disingenuousness.

They weren't buying Boehner's bland reassurances in Utah, where the superintendent of the Jordan school district, largest in the state, said that NCLB would cost $182 million over the next decade to implement—a rather heftier sum than the annual $2.2 million in Title I funding the district was then receiving.[74]

Legislators in the Beehive State, which gave George W. Bush his largest margin of victory in the 2000 election, 67–26 percent—the sixth time in eight presidential elections in which the state was the most Republican in the Union—threw down the gauntlet to the overreaching feds.[75] In February 2004, state representative Margaret Dayton, an

Orem Republican, saw a Utah House committee unanimously report her bill to opt out of NCLB, thus forfeiting $103 million in federal funds. Eugene W. Hickok, acting deputy secretary of the federal Department of Education, warned Utah state school superintendent Steven Laing that "The rejection of Title I money would result in serious consequences to other programs"—a threat that seemed to constitute a violation of *South Dakota v. Dole*'s coercion-pressure borderline.[76]

If state Republicans were in a rebellious mood, their emissaries to the national government were more conciliatory. Congressman Chris Cannon, a Utah Republican, claimed, somewhat implausibly, that the measure wasn't really a challenge to President Bush but rather to unnamed bureaucrats who "need to figure out Utah does a pretty good job and we want to do it our way."

Representative Dayton's defiant bill did not pass; despite widespread support, when it came time to actually turn down over $100 million too many Utah legislators flinched.

Explaining Bush's trampling over Utah, Kelly Patterson, chair of the political science department at Brigham Young University, said, "Local control. That's the rub. [Bush] had to show national leadership, and that means treading on the states."[77]

Some were easier to tread on than others.

Utah, which the mainstream media often portray harshly as a wilderness of knee-jerk Republican Mormonism, objected to the tread marks. Representative Dayton was back again in 2005 with a slightly less radical bill that would permit the state to ignore No Child Left Behind mandates if they conflicted with state laws or forced the state to spend tax dollars to comply with the demands of the feds. State education administrators were directed to "provide first priority to meeting state goals" if those goals should conflict with those handed down from on high from Washington.[78]

"We can't be expected to fill in the financial blanks, and we shouldn't have to be dealing with federal regulations," explained Dayton. "We have to take our state issues back into our own hands."

The state superintendent of education, Patti Harrington, concurred. "The federal government might not like it, but to wait until a child slips into failure mode is not a wise use of money. We'd rather do it at the front end. NCLB just has it wrong."[79] (Connecticut and Virginia, among others, also insisted that their methods of measuring student proficiency were superior to those dictated by the NCLB mandate.) The Bush administration's coercive federalism had run into a roadblock in the Utah desert—and the only way the coercive federalists knew to react was with supercilious scorn and sputtering threats.

This time the measure passed by wide margins (66–7 in the Utah House and 25–3 in the Utah Senate), and was signed into law by Governor Jon Huntsman. (Huntsman had defeated in the GOP primary the incumbent governor Olene Walker, who had timidly backed off criticism of NCLB, saying, "We cannot afford to lose that amount of money in our public education system."[80]) Utah had defied the Bush administration, which, as the *New York Times* reported, had lobbied against such an act of defiance for fifteen months. The fear was that Utah might be the spark that lit a prairie fire.

Rod Paige's successor as US secretary of education, the abrasive Margaret Spellings, informed veteran US senator Orrin Hatch of Utah that the feds might have to withhold anywhere from $76 to $107 million from Utah's annual federal education appropriation. This was about as subtle as a sledgehammer, and Utah's doughtier solons responded angrily. "I don't like to be threatened," said Salt Lake City representative Steven R. Mascaro. "I wish they'd take the stinking money and go back to Washington."[81]

Even Governor Huntsman, whose feeble 2012 Republican presidential campaign presented him as a moderate, certainly not one of those scary Tea Party types who haunt the dreams of NPR liberals, took aim at Washington. Boasting of Utah's "pioneer ethos," he said that "we are always taken advantage of because we are a consistently and reliably Republican state." But Utah was not going to roll over and take it this time. The state is both fruitful and young; as George Will pointed out, its median age of twenty-eight is eight full years younger than the median age of Americans.[82]

Another state with a disproportionate number of Republicans and conservatives (and, for that matter, Mormons), Arizona, also raised objections to NCLB. Republican state representative Karen Johnson introduced legislation in 2004 that would remove Arizona from under the No Child Left Behind umbrella. "The money that has to be expended is so horrendous that there's no way the state can afford it," she said. She was seconded by House Majority Leader Eddie Farnsworth, also a Republican, who saw the proposal as a potent symbol: "I want to tell the feds they shouldn't be involved in local education."[83]

State education officials, predictably, mouthed the usual platitudes about how local control is preferable to federal control, but then they pointed to the federal aid then flowing to Arizona—$327 million annually—and expressed an even more fervent desire to keep the tap from shutting off. Federalist principles are fine—until they start costing a state's bureaucracy money. Then they are shed like parkas in July. Arizona never did opt out of NCLB.

If in fact federal mandates are that onerous, that budget-draining, that counterproductive, couldn't a state conceivably be better off refusing the king's shilling and doing things its own way?

Lawmakers in Vermont seriously debated following such a course. Then governor Howard Dean "asked school superintendents and local school boards whether Vermont should take" money under NCLB or whether the cost of such nonparticipation would be too great. As the Vermont Society for the Study of Education phrased the question, was NCLB money "worth the disruption to Vermont's high-achieving educational program, the dumbing-down of our standards, excessive testing and federal governmental interference"?[84]

Vermont was already administering its own tests. They were calibrated at a level higher than those generally envisioned by NCLB—that is to say, they actually sought to measure a student's proficiency in the subject at hand rather than merely guarantee that an overwhelming majority of those taking the tests passed the tests. In 2001, noted the Vermont Society for the Study of Education, although Vermont students scored between 22 and 32 percent higher than students in the rest of the country on comparable exams, the higher standards of the Green Mountain State meant that 46.5 percent of its students were adjudged "below standard" on at least one of its tests.[85]

Now, to even the dimmest Statistics 101 student, the fact that 46.5 percent of students scored "below standard" ought to be expected—in fact, that number ought to be slightly higher. After all, half of all students will fall above the median on any given test and half will fall below the median.

But just as all the children are above average in Garrison Keillor's fictional Lake Woebegone, so do some states insist—and in this they are strongly encouraged by No Child Left Behind—that the vast majority of students are above average, and *by 2014 every student in America will be above average*. Vermonters pointed to the states of Texas, whose relatively lax state tests ensured passing rates of up to 90 percent, and Maryland, whose schoolchildren passed its state tests at a rate of just 25 percent. Yet when given identical tests, Maryland's students outperformed those of Texas. Diversity in testing—which includes the right not to administer such tests at all—is consistent with federalism, the original American political arrangement. It is not, however, permissible under NCLB, which mandates the imposition of statewide educational tests and, in setting out a series of punishments for those states with insufficiently high pass/fail rates, offers a powerful, even controlling, incentive to dumb these tests down. Vermont scholars predicted that 80 percent of the state's schools would be judged "failing" under the new federal law—even though Vermont's students regularly outperformed students in most other states on standardized tests.

The Vermont researchers estimated the cost of No Child Left Behind to the state at $158.2 million. (They emphasized that this estimate was conservative.) This sum would cover the costs of testing, remedial instruction, and additional instruction and administration. It represents a 15.5 percent increase in what the state then spent on education. Yet the boost in federal aid to Vermont under NCLB was to be $51.6 million. Thus not only did the NCLB mandate fail to meet Vermont's high educational standards, it was also a drain on the state treasury. The Vermont Society for the Study of Education concluded, "From a fiscal point of view, it is not cost-effective to accept the monies and the obligations that go with them. For a state facing financial problems coupled with deep concerns over the rising costs of education, and with federal financial support in doubt, accepting the federal money is not prudent."[86]

No Child Left Behind was "unworkable and inconsistent with Vermont directions."[87] But under the new federal education dispensation, "Vermont directions" meant nothing. States were not to be trusted to set their own directions in the matter of educating their children. The enlightened federal government had appropriated that responsibility. And Vermont, despite its early resistance to the new law, did not opt out.

In 2004, Virginia, which had instituted a reputedly rigorous Standards of Learning testing regimen in 1998, rebelled against NCLB not only as an unfunded mandate and "the most sweeping intrusion into state and local control of education in the history of the United States," as a House of Delegates resolution (approved by 98–1) asserted, but also as a "ludicrous" preemption of sensible state standards by staggeringly unrealistic federal standards. The Virginia Standards of Learning tested students in third, fifth, eighth, and high school grades in English, history, math, and science. At least 70 percent of a school's test-takers needed to pass for the school to remain fully accredited.

The 70 percent threshold set the No Child Left Behind proponents to baying. NCLB, of course, required that 100 percent of students pass all of its mandated tests. This struck Virginia educators as beyond absurd. As Fairfax County (VA) school superintendent Daniel A. Domenech said, "To expect a youngster newly arrived in this country to take and pass an exam in English, it's ridiculous."

Superintendent Domenech was speaking from experience. But experience means nothing to an ideologue, and the Bush administration was rife with such ideologues.

In response, Acting Deputy Secretary of DoED Eugene W. Hickok told the *Washington Post*, "This law is perhaps a challenge for us to implement, but it is the first comprehensive attempt to make sure that every child everywhere counts. To say no to that is a typical thing for the states to do."[88] One doubts that the contempt federal bureaucrats have for the states has ever been phrased quite so bluntly, but we should thank Mr. Hickok for his candor. In his virtual deification of the federal behemoth—which is working overtime to ensure that "every child everywhere counts," a concept that was apparently brand new to the Bush administration—and his condemnation of the fifty states, whose "typical" attitude toward children is to behave as if they do not count (not, with an eye to the math-challenged, that they *can't* count), Acting Deputy Secretary Hickok provided a succinct and revealing summary of the assumptions behind centralizing legislation. The locals are not only too dense to educate their children, oversee their elections, license their drivers, and monitor those who drink and drive, they are also too morally obtuse even to see the need for any such oversight. Left to their own devices, they would alternately abuse and neglect their subjects—so unlike the benevolent federal government in its treatment of its citizens. Mandates, really, are the only way to see to it that citizens thrive, or even survive.

Hickok's disdain for the states was echoed by Secretary Paige, who in October 2002 issued a diktat that sounded almost totalitarian in its pledge to wipe out resisters. "Those who play semantic games or try to tinker with state numbers to lock out parents and the public," the education secretary warned, "stand in the way of progress and reform. They are the enemies of equal justice and equal opportunity. They are apologists for failure. And they will not succeed."[89]

Close your eyes and listen to these words and they might have come from a Bolshevik commissar. Those who objected to the centralization of education in Washington, to the usurpation of traditional state and local responsibilities by the federal government, to unfunded mandates imposed upon the fifty states of the union, were "enemies" of justice, opportunity, progress, and reform. They were, we may assume, enemies of the people.

Was and is NCLB an unfunded mandate, or was it, as former Secretary of Education Rod Paige said, an entirely proper—indeed, almost kindly and courtly and too mild—use of the federal power?

The evidence from Texas was strongly on the "unfunded federal mandate" side. Writing in the *National Tax Journal*, Jennifer Imazeki of San Diego State University and Andrew Reschovsky of the University of Wisconsin–Madison assessed the "minimum amount of money Texas school districts" would require in order to meet the prescribed goals of No Child Left Behind.[90]

Texas ought to have been the state in which NCLB imposed a lighter burden than on the other forty-nine. It had been a pioneer in statewide standardized testing, and in fact President George W. Bush, who had served as governor of the Lone Star State before moving to the White House, had apparently viewed the Texas educational system as something of a model for his prized No Child Left Behind Act. During the Bush years in Texas, the state's Texas Assessment of Academic Skills tests were given to all students in grades three through eight as well as grade ten. In 2002–2003, the program was retitled the Texas Assessment of Knowledge and Skills and extended to students in grades nine and eleven. Only the seniors, it seems, ducked the testing mania. Such are the rewards of senioritis.

So Professors Imazeki and Reschovsky theorized that if any state could escape the unfunded or underfunded nature of the NCLB mandates, it would be Texas. No such luck. In order to meet the federal goals that would push the Texas standards to the side, the federal appropriation under Title I would have to be "substantially higher" than were the actual appropriations. The Texas example, write the authors, demonstrates that "the federal government is providing only a small portion of the required extra costs" to meet the federal education mandates.[91]

✳✳✳✳✳✳✳✳

The federal share of public spending on education went from 4 percent in 1960 to 10 percent in 1980 and then down to 6 percent in 1990. By 2012, it was back up to 10.8 percent, or approximately $120 billion. (This total includes funding for Head Start and the school lunch program.)[92]

Title I, by far the most lavishly funded No Child Left Behind program, was funded at $10.35 billion in fiscal year 2002. Yet it was authorized in FY 2002 at $27.22 billion. The authorization is the maximum amount that may be spent in a fiscal year upon a program; the appropriation is the amount that is actually spent. The difference between the two is what vexed the educational establishment, which tried to claim that this gap led to the cries that NCLB was not "fully funded." But by that definition, few programs are "fully funded." The authorization almost always exceeds the appropriation. The more relevant question is whether or not the appropriation was sufficient to cover the mandated costs. It was not, by the accounting of the states.

In its first year, NCLB upped Title I spending by 20 percent, which was not even close enough to cover the mandated additional costs to the states. By fiscal year 2005, Title I spending increases were no longer enough to even keep pace with inflation.

By fiscal year 2012, the two largest NCLB grant programs administered by the US Department of Education were Title I Grants to Local Educational Agencies ($14.516 billion), which are targeted to districts with large numbers of disadvantaged students, and Improving Teacher Quality State Grants ($2.467 billion). These sums are nowhere near the amount necessary to meet NCLB goals by the reckoning of any of the states—though the ubiquity of waivers has delayed the crush of these unfunded mandates, at least until the DoED decides to stop granting such waivers. The states cry "unfunded mandate," while NCLB advocates insist that the act is not technically a mandate because states do not have to participate—all they have to do is refuse the federal monies. That this is a practical near-impossibility shows just how deeply entwined state and federal and even local education policy has become.

But perhaps we are letting the states off the hook too easily. Even the most generous estimate of federal spending on education amounts to not much more than 10 percent of total spending on education in the United States. Would a reduction in total education spending in a state of, say, 5 percent really be that disabling? In December 2002, Demeree K. Michelau and David Shreve, writing in *State Legislatures* magazine, remarked, "For its 7 percent contribution to annual K–12 funding, federal law leverages enormous power over state education and fiscal policy."[93] The federal tail was wagging the dog. But the dog, it must be admitted, lets the tail get away with it.

****

The legal challenges to No Child Left Behind fell like pins in a bowling alley.

Connecticut's attorney general Richard Blumenthal filed suit against NCLB, claiming that it was an unfunded mandate, on August 22, 2005. Attorney General Blumenthal asserted that NCLB was saddling his state with $50 million in costs that would not be reimbursed by Washington. While assuring one and all that he agreed with the goals of No Child Left Behind—it would take a brave politician to say we ought to leave some children behind, and Blumenthal has never been accused of bravery—the attorney general threw down the gauntlet. Sort of. "Give up your unfunded mandates or give us the money," he declared, in a very pale echo of Patrick Henry's "give me liberty or give me death" oration.[94]

In *Connecticut v. Spellings*, the Nutmeg State argued that NCLB mandates forced certain costs upon its schools that were not met—were not even close to being met—by the federal appropriations. For instance, the feds sent $5.8 million to the state in FY 2006 to cover the costs of the required assessments—yet Connecticut's assessment-related costs were $14.4 million.[95] As with other states, the cost of collecting and analyzing the data for the mandated NCLB tests was significant. This was an obvious violation of the "unfunded mandate" provision of the act.

Moreover, contended Connecticut's legal spokespersons, the penalties levied against out-of-compliance states were excessively harsh (using the admittedly vague *South Dakota v. Dole* standard). If, as the DoED had threatened Utah, a state that rejected NCLB might lose all its federal Title I funds and not just those specifically targeted for NCLB programs, then Connecticut stood to lose more than half ($175–$184 million) of its total federal education funding ($287–$325 million). "Because states are becoming increasingly dependent upon federal funding for education," notes Regina R. Umpstead, "the U.S. Department's threat to remove most of the federal education funding was coercive," or so claimed Connecticut.[96] The magical line between pressure and compulsion, drawn by the court in *South Dakota v. Dole*, was being breeched.

DoED replied that states did have the right to refuse NCLB funding. And the debate really pointed to an old truth that the states had forgotten in recent decades, with the profusion of federal funding for all manner of activities that had never before seemed within the bounds of constitutional sanction. And that truth is this: he who takes the king's shilling becomes the king's man. Or maybe we should amend that: he who takes the king's shilling performs the king's mandate. If a state becomes dependent upon federal assistance, it places itself in a clearly subordinate position, and should expect to be ordered about as a subordinate.

Connecticut was not exactly an educational slacker. Its students, year in and year out, have scored above the national average on standardized tests. And the state had its own testing system—the Connecticut Mastery Test (CMT)—before No Child Left Behind was ever a vagrant notion in the noggin of George W. Bush. But, you see, the CMT was administered to fourth, sixth, and eighth graders, while NCLB mandated tests for third through eighth graders. And CMT made different provisions for students with disabilities and those for whom English was not a first language.[97] This variety used to be called federalism, but it had no place among the Bush Republicans.

Connecticut v. Spellings ended with a fizzle. The court passed up the chance to consider the constitutionality of the NCLB as unfunded mandate or as excessively coercive under the *South Dakota v. Dole* test because the US Department of Education had not ruled the state out of compliance with the act. Because the DoED was not enforcing sanctions against Connecticut, the district court "lacked subject-matter jurisdiction."[98]

School District of Pontiac v. Spellings, which was the National Education Association's lawsuit against NCLB, challenged the act, claiming that it violated NCLB's own prohibition on unfunded mandates: "Nothing in this chapter shall be construed to authorize an officer or employee of the Federal Government to mandate, direct, or control a State, local educational agency, or school's curriculum, program of instruction, or allocation of State or local resources, or mandate a State or any subdivision thereof to spend any funds or incur any costs not paid for under this chapter." What could be clearer than that? The act itself forbids its interpretation as an unfunded mandate.

To which the veteran observer of government shenanigans can only say, "Heh, heh, heh."

(It gives one a start to see the National Education Association, which has long been a reliable ally of bigger and more intrusive and more centralized government, standing against such centralization in the form of unfunded mandates.)

The costs of administering these tests, compiling and communicating the results, providing for tutors and transfers when schools fall short of making adequate yearly progress, bringing teachers up to the "highly qualified" level, and creating or augmenting programs to ensure (theoretically) that every student is proficient—before and after and summer school programs, more preschool education, and longer days, keeping in mind, of course, that a body of research exists questioning whether *any* of these have lasting results or might even be counterproductive—run, by even the most conservative estimates, well beyond that modest bounty sent stateward by Uncle Sam.

The NEA's suit was filed in Detroit on April 20, 2005, in the US District Court for the Eastern District of Michigan. It was filed on behalf of the school district in Pontiac (a majority of whose 10,858 students were black) as well as the Laredo, Texas, school district (most of whose 23,000 students were Hispanic) and six districts in Vermont (the majority of whose 1,500 students were rural whites). So all the demographic bases were covered.[99] Also tacked on to the suit were the Texas State Teachers Association, the Reading Educational Association, and NEA state branches in Connecticut, Utah, Illinois, Indiana, New Hampshire, Vermont, Michigan, and Ohio.

The plaintiffs asserted that NCLB was an unfunded mandate and thus violated its own anti-mandate proscription. Not that the NEA was turning over some kind of new parsimonious or constitutionalist leaf, mind you. It had no objection to the goals of No Child Left Behind, or to NCLB's extension of the reach of the federal government into state and local educational affairs. Its sole objection to the act was that it was not fully funded. The Pontiac, Laredo, and Vermont school districts, the NEA charged, had been forced to divert funds from other programs to meet the mandates of NCLB. If the US Department of Education would ante up sufficient monies to cover the additional costs, all would be fine.

For its part, the Department of Education denied that NCLB was an unfunded mandate. Rather, claimed department lawyers, the act created a partnership of the federal government and state education departments; it was merely assisting the states and local districts in meeting reasonable goals. The federal government was serving as helpmeet, not dictator. Its guidelines and funding were supplements to the daily educational diet, not the main course. Its aid was meant to ensure that "students make adequate academic progress using educational standards, assessments, and accountability systems developed and implemented by the states."[100] Now, does that sound like a big bad mandate? Heavens no!

On November 23, 2005, Judge Bernard Friedman of the US District Court for the Eastern District of Michigan dismissed the case. Judge Friedman asserted that the act's prohibition upon "an officer or employee of the Federal Government" imposing a mandate upon states or subdivisions thereof did not include Congress, which had a free pass to mandate away. In something of a twist upon the *South Dakota v. Dole* requirement that a condition be clear and unambiguous, Judge Friedman opined that if Congress had intended to pay for costs associated with NCLB, it would have declared its intention to do so in clear and unambiguous language. Connecticut attorney general Blumenthal called Judge Friedman's ruling "virtually incomprehensible."[101]

The plaintiffs appealed to the US Sixth Circuit Court of Appeals in Cincinnati, which, by a 2–1 vote on January 7, 2008, reversed the lower court's decision, remanding the case back to that district court. The Sixth Circuit Court of Appeals found that No Child Left Behind was guilty of "ambiguous" language and thus violated the spending clause of the US Constitution.

The obligations of the states and school districts with respect to academic assessments are spelled out in clear language, but the matter of whether or not the states are responsible for the costs incurred—or if the federal government must meet all such costs—is murky, according to the circuit court.

The Secretary of Education appealed, and in 2009 the judges on the Sixth Circuit Court of Appeals deadlocked, which effectively affirmed the lower court's dismissal of the case.

No Child Left Behind seems to have cleared its hurdles in the courts. Whether it *should* have done so is another question.

Gina Austin noted in the *Thomas Jefferson Law Review* that the US Department of Education is careful to insist that "[t]here are no federal education 'mandates.' Every federal education law is conditioned on a state's decision to accept federal program funds."[102] This, of course, is how the feds typically bend states to the will of mandates: with the lure or the lash of federal monies. *South Dakota v. Dole* is the court's delineation of the boundaries of this federal power. If you recall, the court conceded that "in some circumstances the financial inducement offered by Congress might be so coercive as to pass the point at which pressure turns into compulsion." The court stated that such conditions of aid must be in pursuit of the general welfare, be unambiguous, be related to the federal interest, and not conflict with other constitutional provisions.

Austin asserts that NCLB fails this test almost across the board, though the court would almost certainly find otherwise. Imposing a testing regime on the states may be unwise policy, but improving education would likely fall within the court's definition of the federal interest. Most interesting for our purposes, Austin claims that because NCLB fails to supply the states with the necessary funds to carry out its mandates, the act forces the states to "impose substantial burdens on their own citizenry." And in forcing the states to administer and assess tests and report the results thereof, it intrudes upon the authority of those states in violation of the Tenth Amendment. Moreover, it fails the *coercion* test because, in the case of Utah's threat to opt out, the deputy secretary of education threatened the state with the loss of its $43 million in Title I monies as well as other formula and categorical grants.[103] This would seem to be that mythical point at which coercion passes into compulsion. No state (outside, perhaps, in an Ayn Rand novel) is going to risk losing all Title I funds. This is not to defend the reliance these states have built up on federal aid; in fact, such aid can be weakening and counterproductive. But until that day when education policy is decentralized and returned to the control of local people who best understand local conditions, states simply will not dare cut the cord to Washington. And Washington policymakers know this.[104]

So even if No Child Left Behind passes muster as a legitimate exercise of federal government power under the spending clause, opponents still have recourse to the rather vague "coercion/compulsion" condition established by the Supreme Court in *South Dakota v. Dole*. Denial of significant amounts of federal education funding for noncompliance with NCLB might meet that hazy threshold at which permissible pressure transmogrifies into impermissible compulsion. We know from *Dole* that forfeiting 5 percent of a program's funds does not meet the threshold. Cutting off all Title I education funding, as Connecticut feared, would deprive states of half or more of their federal education funding. On the face of it that might seem rather harsher than the *South Dakota v. Dole* penalties, but the court has in the past given the feds extremely wide latitude in setting conditions upon the receipt of funds.

Moreover, as Regina Umpstead notes, in the case of Connecticut even a complete cutoff of federal education funding would only deprive the state of about 5 percent of its "total educational expenditures." And even in the case of such a cutoff, "Connecticut would retain the real choice and the right to decline federal funding and not participate in the NCLB."[105] Or as a US DoED official told

177

Vermonters in 2004: "You can't call it a mandate. It's a tradeoff if you accept the money."[106]

The obstacles to a successful court case challenging NCLB as an unfunded federal mandate are considerable. As Amanda K. Wingfield writes in the *Loyola Journal of Public Interest Law*, the advocacy groups that have the resources to challenge the law may lack "standing," for the act may not cause them direct injury. States and school districts stand on stronger ground, but the widespread recent granting of waivers from various NCLB provisions may make their cases correspondingly weak: their injuries lies in the future, when the waivers run out.[107]

****

As anyone whose head was not permanently ensconced in the clouds could have predicted, one of the first consequences of No Child Left Behind was a weakening of state-level tests so as to avoid NCLB sanctions. So the mandate was having quite the opposite of its intended effect: it was actually lessening performance-based accountability! Or as researchers McDermott and Jensen said, NCLB had the putatively unintended effect of "defin[ing] proficiency down."[108] For instance, in Texas, which had for years prided itself on its statewide system of testing, the early returns from new tests in spring 2003 were so "grim," according to one member of the Texas State Board of Education, that the board took immediate corrective action. And, no, that corrective action did not translate into more rigorous standards or different methods of teaching. Instead, the board voted to change the minimum "passing" score for third-grade reading from twenty-four out of thirty-six correct answers to twenty out of thirty-six. Otherwise, as Sam Dillon wrote in the *New York Times*, the board feared that "thousands of students would fail the new test and be held back a grade, and . . . hundreds of schools could face penalties" under NCLB.

The Texas two-step—or retreat—was imitated by panicked state boards of education and administrators across the country. In Michigan, which according to Dillon of the *Times* had one of the most stringent sets of academic requirements in the country pre-NCLB, standards dropped like a thermometer in the Arctic once the threat of federal sanctions loomed. When a whopping 1,513 schools failed to record "adequate progress" as per the new NCLB standards, the state jiggered the way such progress was measured. Whereas before Michigan required 75 percent of students to pass the statewide English test before a school was acknowledged to be performing adequately, the threat of NCLB sanctions spurred the state to reduce the threshold to a pathetic 42 percent. Voila! Magically, the number of schools deemed to be not performing adequately dropped from 1,513 to 216. The miracle of No Child Left Behind! Michigan schools are far more adequate than previously reported!

Standards plummeted in other states as well. Colorado was one of them. University of Colorado Professor Robert L. Linn, a former president of the American Educational Research Association, observed, "[S]evere sanctions may hinder educational excellence, because they implicitly encourage states to water down their content and performance standards in order to reduce the risk of sanctions."[109] This was as predictable as the sunrise—yet somehow the savants who conceived No Child Left Behind did not anticipate it.

In New York City, the school system dropped its carefully designed "balanced literacy" reading curriculum in forty-nine low-performing schools because Washington threatened districts that employed such a curriculum with the loss of federal funds unless they forsook the balanced literacy programs for "scientifically proven" curricula approved by the US Department of Education.

At stake was $34 million, which New York City schools chancellor Joel I. Klein called "a significant amount of money for some of our really highest-needs programs."

Other cities, such as Boston and San Diego, refused to bow to the federal dictate. They retained their balanced literacy curriculum. Thomas W. Payzant, superintendent of Boston schools and a former assistant secretary of education under President Bill Clinton, told the *Times*, "The irony is you have got a Republican administration that normally champions local control and opposes any kind of federal involvement in setting prescriptive curriculum for school districts to follow. There ought to be some flexibility in deciding what the best way is to get the results."[110]

So a Clinton education official is condemning the Republican administration that succeeded the Democrat as excessively centralist and hostile to local concerns. It would be ironic, if only it were not so common an occurrence, especially under the second President Bush.

One other legacy of the law is the cheating engaged in by administrators who fear that their districts or schools will fall short of the Washington-mandated mark. In Atlanta, for instance, in the summer of 2011 Governor Nathan Deal released the startling results of an investigation into widespread and systematic cheating on standardized tests within the Atlanta School System. The range and extent of the cheating was astonishing, as was the sudden resignation of Atlanta's previously much-praised superintendent of schools, but the fact that cheating was pervasive should have surprised no one.

The tests were state tests, and those state tests were given, in part, to comply with No Child Left Behind mandates. The cheating had been going on for several years, said investigators, who proclaimed the primary cause to be "pressure to meet targets."[111] Ultimately, those targets can be traced back to NCLB.

When the stakes are so high—potentially, the closing of a school, and the loss of jobs that entails—you can expect cheating as a last-ditch effort to stave off penalties. And even where administrators have the moral fiber to resist dishonesty, the practice of "teaching to the test," which often excludes music, art, and physical education from their rightful place in elementary curricula, has become nigh-universal in American public education.

What has saved school districts from staggering under the NCLB mandate burden has been the increasingly common DoED practice of granting waivers to the states.

From the start, states flooded the US DoED with petitions asking for more time and greater flexibility to meet the (oft unmeetable) goals embodied in the law. To bring *every* student up to a certain level in standardized test taking is, as anyone outside the cloister of a bureaucrat's office knows, simply impossible.

The Bush administration, which gradually came to understand that it had a rebellion on its hands, became more flexible in its imposition of NCLB. Waivers, once as rare as hen's teeth, began to be issued with what might almost be called liberality. Conciliation, not confrontation, became the method of operation. This change was out of necessity, of course, and not any kind of federalist epiphany: when the most loyally Republican state in the union sues the Republican administration in Washington, something is amiss.

After Rod Paige's widely unlamented departure from his post, the Bush DoED cut the states some slack, making it slightly "easier for states to comply with the law's mandates and for more schools to meet annual AYP goals."[112] But there were influential voices that preferred the original Bush act just as it was. For instance, the *New York Times*—whose upper-level staff consists, one can safely say, of extremely few parents of public-school children—lectured editorially that "with No

Child Left Behind, the federal government has set exactly the right goals. It cannot backtrack because the early progress has been rocky. If Washington wavers and begins to cut deals with recalcitrant states like Utah, the effort to remake the country's public schools will fail."[113] How generous of the *Times* to care so much about the children of Utah, a state about which its editorialists are no doubt deeply well-informed.

Motoko Rich of the *New York Times* wondered whether NCLB had "been essentially nullified" by the Obama administration. As Dean Andy Porter of the University of Pennsylvania's Graduate School of Education remarked, "The more waivers there are, the less there really is a law, right?"[114]

As the years passed, and No Child Left Behind became an immovable, seemingly permanent part of the landscape, the early reluctance of the US Department of Education to grant waivers to wavering states became a distant memory. For instance, as of mid-2012, over thirty states had applied for waivers, and these were granted routinely. Indeed, more than half the states in the Union had been granted their requested waivers. The unfunded federal mandate had been delayed—but only delayed.

****

A few Republican members of Congress, catching heavy flak from teachers and parents back home, started to voice tentative criticisms, or reservations, about NCLB late in the Bush administration. In 2007, Representatives Peter Hoekstra (R-MI) and Senator John Cornyn (R-TX) sponsored companion legislation that would permit states to opt out of the mandated testing if either of two conditions was met: (1) approval of such an opting out in a statewide referendum or (2) approval of opting out by two of the following three entities: the governor, the legislature, and the state's highest elected education official. (The Senate bill was considerably weaker and less reliant upon popular opinion.) States choosing to opt out would *not* be opting out of the receipt of federal education funds.

Among the cosponsors of Hoekstra's bill was House Minority Whip Roy Blunt (R-MO), who had supported NCLB and voiced not a qualm when it might have made a difference. A Blunt spokesman said, with a lack of bluntness, that the act was "onerous." Representative Hoekstra, a more forthright foe of NCLB, took on his party's leader more directly. "President Bush and I just see education fundamentally differently," he said. "The president believes in empowering bureaucrats in Washington, and I believe in local and parental control."

The Hoekstra-Cornyn bill to amend NCLB went nowhere. Democrats such as Senator Ted Kennedy remained stalwart champions of No Child Left Behind. Indeed, their only complaint was that it wasn't directing enough federal money to education. For the Republicans, it was simply too late for any effective, or even believable, opposition. A former Bush Department of Education official in the DoED's Gingirchesquely named Office of Innovation and Improvement (which presumably replaced the erstwhile Office of Stagnation and Decline), Michael J. Petrilli, said in 2007, "Republicans voted for No Child Left Behind holding their noses. But now with the president so politically weak, conservatives can vote their conscience."[115] That on-the-mark observation tells you much that you need to know about the strength and integrity of the Republican Party's commitment to federalism.

No Child Left Behind has one indisputable legacy: it furthered the nationalization of American education, the transfer of control over the education of America's children from local school districts and elected school boards, and from state legislatures and governors and (often unelected) state education commissioners, to a federal government that is impossibly remote from individual schools and the problems plaguing them.

Looking back, former Secretary of Education Rod Paige, relieved of the circumspection demanded of a Cabinet officer, was more frank in his assessment of NCLB. He is sick and tired, he says, of state and local education officials whining and moaning about the unfairness of unfunded mandates, the inadequacy of federal aid to meet those mandates, and all the other carps and cavils one hears at a typical conference of educational administrators. Because you know what? Mandates are *good*. Mandates are *necessary*. Without federal mandates, heaven only knows what mischief the local yokels might be pulling. Surely they would fail, for instance, to educate those most in need. "States, districts, schools, or even individual teachers might decide (for any number of reasons) to limit the educational opportunities they provide to special needs students," said ex-secretary Paige in 2006. "The federal mandates . . . are set up in order to provide the assurance that systems, and not just the teachers within them, are meeting the educational needs of students with disabilities."

The situation is no different with the nondisabled. "The same," says Paige, "applies to NCLB. If this federal mandate were stricken, what expectations would our local and state education officials have for student achievement? Would we continue to expect students to read or do math at grade level? Would we keep aspiring to educate all children to high levels?"[116]

Of course not! Teachers, principals, aides, even cafeteria ladies would lie down on the job were it not for the federal whip being applied with due severity. They would expect little of their charges, and in return would receive even less. Why, in the 180 years of the American republic before the Elementary and Secondary Education Act came into being American children seldom attended school, and when they did the boys spent most of their time scaring the girls with frogs and snakes, while the girls spent most of their time in nonsensical prattle. In any case, things were in a very bad state until the ESEA, the Department of Education, *A Nation at Risk*, and No Child Left Behind rode in to save the day.

(The preceding paragraph, while perhaps reflecting the views of the more ardent advocates of federal subsidy of education, is very nearly the reverse of the truth. The decentralized American educational system was the envy of much of the world; to the extent measurable, American students pre-ESEA performed at a much higher level, vis-à-vis students of other nations, than they do today.)

Former Secretary of Education Paige, further demonstrating his boundless faith in the abilities of the national government to achieve great things, also advocated the logical next step: replacing the state-designed tests, which he had instanced as evidence that NCLB was not too centralized, with "national standards and national tests."[117] The Bush administration's trite professions of respect for the rights of states and localities was revealed, as the failure of NCLB became apparent, to be just hot air. Republicans in the Bush era have opted for nationalization over federalism, and for mandates over voluntary choices. The decision was a fateful one for American education.

No one anywhere—except perhaps for George W. Bush—believed that the original deadline of 2014—the date on which every student in every school in America would achieve proficiency in the subjects tested—retained any relevance whatsoever. But through bureaucratic inertia or stubbornness, NCLB was here to stay, at least until at some subsequent reauthorization the education faddists of the day pinned a new name on an old idea: the idea that massive infusions of taxpayers' dollars and the liberal deployment of federal mandates were the cures for what ails American public education.

Notes

1. National Center for Education Statistics, www.nces.ed.gov/fastfacts.
2. Patrick J. McGuinn, *No Child Left Behind and the Transformation of Federal Education Policy, 1965–2005* (Lawrence, KS: University of Kansas Press, 2006), p. 1.
3. H.G. Rickover, "Your Child's Future Depends on Education," *Ladies' Home Journal*, October 1960, p. 100.
4. Max Ascoli, "Our Cut-Rate Education," *The Reporter*, February 20, 1958, pp. 8–9.
5. James R. Killian, *Sputnik, Scientists, and Eisenhower: A Memoir of the First Special Assistant to the President for Science and Technology* (Cambridge, MA: MIT Press, 1977), pp. 73–74, 77.
6. James L. Penick, editor, *The Politics of American Science: 1939 to the Present* (Chicago: Rand McNally, 1965), p. 209.
7. Dwight D. Eisenhower, "Statement by the President upon Signing the National Defense Education Act," September 2, 1958, The American Presidency Project, www.presidency.ucsb.edu/ws.
8. Robert A. Divine, *The Sputnik Challenge* (New York: Oxford University Press, 1993), p. 166.
9. Paul Manna, *School's In: Federalism and the National Education Agenda* (Washington, DC: Georgetown University Press, 2006), p. 9.
10. Ibid., p. 76.
11. McGuinn, *No Child Left Behind and the Transformation of Federal Education Policy, 1965–2005*, p. 33.
12. Ibid., pp. 33, 39.
13. 20 U.S.C. 3403.
14. Manna, *School's In: Federalism and the National Education Agenda*, p. 80.
15. *A Nation at Risk* (Washington, DC: National Commission on Excellence in Education, 1983), p. 5.
16. Manna, *School's In: Federalism and the National Education Agenda*, p. 9.
17. McGuinn, *No Child Left Behind and the Transformation of Federal Education Policy, 1965–2005*, p. 61.
18. Lance D. Fusarelli, "Gubernatorial Reactions to No Child Left Behind: Politics, Pressure, and Education Reform," *Peabody Journal of Education* (Vol. 80, No. 2, 2005): 127.
19. Patrick McGuinn, "The National Schoolmarm: No Child Left Behind and the New Educational Federalism," *Publius* (Winter 2005): 50.
20. Ethan Bronner, "Clinton's School Plan Praised for Goals, if Not Means," *New York Times*, January 19, 1999.
21. McGuinn, "The National Schoolmarm: No Child Left Behind and the New Educational Federalism": 45.
22. McGuinn, *No Child Left Behind and the Transformation of Federal Education Policy, 1965–2005*, p. 101.
23. Elizabeth DeBray, "The Federal Role in School Accountability: Assessing Recent History and the New Law," *Voices in Urban Education* (No. 1, Spring 2003): 58.
24. McGuinn, *No Child Left Behind and the Transformation of Federal Education Policy, 1965–2005*, p. 170.

25. Ibid., p. 179.
26. McGuinn, "The National Schoolmarm: No Child Left Behind and the New Educational Federalism": 57.
27. Elizabeth H. DeBray, Kathryn A. McDermott and Priscilla Wohlstetter, "Introduction to the Special Issue on Federalism Reconsidered: The Case of the No Child Left Behind Act," *Peabody Journal of Education* (Vol. 80, No. 2, 2005): 2.
28. Nicole Liguori, "Leaving No Child Behind (Except in States That Don't Do as We Say)," *Boston College Law Review* (Vol. 46, September 2006): 1033.
29. Fusarelli, "Gubernatorial Reactions to No Child Left Behind: Politics, Pressure, and Education Reform": 121.
30. Title I, "Statement of Purpose," www2.ed.gov/policy/elsec/leg/esea02/pg1.html.
31. 20 U.S.C. 6301.
32. Robert J. Sternberg, "Good Intentions, Bad Results," *Education Week*, October 27, 2004.
33. www2.ed.gov/nclb/landing.jhtml.
34. Kathryn A. McDermott and Laura S. Jensen, "Dubious Sovereignty: Federal Conditions of Aid and the No Child Left Behind Act," *Peabody Journal of Education* (Vol. 80, No. 2, 2005): 46.
35. L. Darnell Weeden, "Does the No Child Left Behind Law (NCLBA) Burden the States as an Unfunded Mandate under Federal Law?" *Thurgood Marshall Law Review* (Vol. 31, 2006): 240.
36. McGuinn, *No Child Left Behind and the Transformation of Federal Education Policy, 1965–2005*, p. 193.
37. Richard F. Elmore, "Unwarranted Intrusion," *Education Next*, Spring 2002, p. 31.
38. Richard F. Elmore and Susan Fuhrman, "The National Interest and the Federal Role in Education," *Publius* (Vol. 20, No. 3, Summer 1990): 161.
39. Elmore, "Unwarranted Intrusion," pp. 31–32.
40. Regina R. Umpstead, "The No Child Left Behind Act: Is It an Unfunded Mandate or a Promotion of Federal Educational Ideals?" *Journal of Law & Education* (Vol. 37, No. 2, April 2008): 200.
41. Weeden, "Does the No Child Left Behind Law (NCLBA) Burden the States as an Unfunded Mandate under Federal Law?": 244.
42. Umpstead, "The No Child Left Behind Act: Is It an Unfunded Mandate or a Promotion of Federal Educational Ideals?": 226.
43. William J. Mathis, "The Cost of Implementing the Federal No Child Left Behind Act: Different Assumptions, Different Answers," *Peabody Journal of Education* (Vol. 80, No. 2, 2005): 93.
44. Ibid.: 101, 103.
45. Ibid.: 113–15.
46. Rod Paige, "It's Not about the Money," *Wall Street Journal*, October 29, 2003.
47. Weeden, "Does the No Child Left Behind Law (NCLBA) Burden the States as an Unfunded Mandate under Federal Law?": 239.
48. Kenneth Wong and Gail Sunderman, "Education Accountability as a Presidential Priority: No Child Left Behind and the Bush Presidency," *Publius* (Vol. 37, No. 3, 2007): 334.

49. David S. Broder, "So, Now Bigger Is Better?" *Washington Post*, January 12, 2003.
50. Rod Paige, "No Child Left Behind: The Ongoing Movement for Public Education Reform," *Harvard Educational Review* (Vol. 76, No. 4, Winter 2006): 461.
51. McGuinn, "The National Schoolmarm: No Child Left Behind and the New Educational Federalism": 67–68.
52. McDermott and Jensen, "Dubious Sovereignty: Federal Conditions of Aid and the No Child Left Behind Act": 40.
53. Paige, "No Child Left Behind: The Ongoing Movement for Public Education Reform": 465–66.
54. Broder, "So, Now Bigger Is Better?"
55. McGuinn, "The National Schoolmarm: No Child Left Behind and the New Educational Federalism": 41.
56. Demaree K. Michelau and David Shreve, "Education Reform from the Top Down," *State Legislatures* (Vol. 28, No. 10, December 2002): 21–25.
57. Alan Richard, "Rural States Concerned about Federal Law," *Education Week* (Vol. 23, No. 8, October 22, 2003): 25.
58. Bryan Shelly, "Rebels and Their Causes: State Resistance to No Child Left Behind," *Publius* (Vol. 38, No. 3, 2008): 444.
59. Wong and Sunderman, "Education Accountability as a Presidential Priority: No Child Left Behind and the Bush Presidency": 343.
60. Shelly, "Rebels and Their Causes: State Resistance to No Child Left Behind": 446.
61. Ibid.: 445, 458.
62. Michael Dobbs, "More States Are Fighting 'No Child Left Behind' Law," *Washington Post*, February 19, 2004.
63. Umpstead, "The No Child Left Behind Act: Is It an Unfunded Mandate or a Promotion of Federal Educational Ideals?": 227.
64. Shelly, "Rebels and Their Causes: State Resistance to No Child Left Behind": 459.
65. Fusarelli, "Gubernatorial Reactions to No Child Left Behind: Politics, Pressure, and Education Reform": 128.
66. Ibid.: 130.
67. Alan J. Borsuk, "No Child Left Behind may not be enforceable, Lautenschlager says," *Milwaukee Journal-Sentinel*, May 13, 2004.
68. Fusarelli, "Gubernatorial Reactions to No Child Left Behind: Politics, Pressure, and Education Reform": 125.
69. Deering, "State Resistance to Federal Mandates: A Cross-Case Analysis," p. 5.
70. Shelly, "Rebels and Their Causes: State Resistance to No Child Left Behind": 444.
71. Fusarelli, "Gubernatorial Reactions to No Child Left Behind: Politics, Pressure, and Education Reform": 123.
72. George W. Bush, "State of the Union Address," January 20, 2004, www.presidency.ucsb.edu/ws/index.php?pid=29646.
73. "New National Cost Analysis Shows States Profiting Financially from No Child Left Behind Act," News from the Committee on Education and the Workforce," February 12, 2004.

74. Michael Dobbs, "More States Are Fighting 'No Child Left Behind' Law."

75. George Will, "In Utah, No Right Left Behind," *Washington Post*, November 11, 2005.

76. Mathis, "The Cost of Implementing the Federal No Child Left Behind Act: Different Assumptions, Different Answers": 114.

77. Ronnie Lynn, "'No Child' rebellion picking up momentum," *Salt Lake Tribune*, February 5, 2004.

78. Sam Dillon, "Utah Vote Rejects Parts of Education Law," *New York Times*, April 20, 2005.

79. Ronnie Lynn, "Bill would buck federal rules on public schools," *Salt Lake Tribune*, February 1, 2005.

80. Fusarelli, "Gubernatorial Reactions to No Child Left Behind: Politics, Pressure, and Education Reform": 130.

81. Dillon, "Utah Vote Rejects Parts of Education Law."

82. Will, "In Utah, No Right Left Behind."

83. "Opt Out of 'No Child Left Behind' plan," Associated Press, February 12, 2004.

84. "The Federal 'No Child Left Behind' Law: Should Vermont Take the Money?" Vermont Society for the Study of Education Policy Discussion Paper, p. 1.

85. Ibid., p. 2.

86. Ibid., pp. 5, 7.

87. Ibid., p. 8.

88. Jo Becker and Rosalind S. Helderman, "Va. Seeks to Leave Bush Law Behind," *Washington Post*, January 24, 2004.

89. Diana Jean Schemo, "States Get Federal Warning on School Standards," *New York Times*, October 24, 2002.

90. Jennifer Imazeki and Andrew Reschovsky, "Is No Child Left Behind an Un (or Under) Funded Federal Mandate? Evidence from Texas," *National Tax Journal* (Vol. 57, No. 3, September 2004): 573.

91. Ibid.: 586.

92. "The Federal Role in Education," US Department of Education, www2.ed.gov/about/overview/fed/role.html.

93. Michelau and Shreve, "Education Reform from the Top Down."

94. "State Sues Federal Government over Illegal Unfunded Mandates under No Child Left Behind Act," Connecticut Attorney General's Office Press Release, August 22, 2005.

95. Umpstead, "The No Child Left Behind Act: Is It an Unfunded Mandate or a Promotion of Federal Educational Ideals?": 210.

96. Ibid.: 221.

97. Liguori, "Leaving No Child Behind (Except in States That Don't Do as We Say)": 1053. For a reconsideration of the wisdom of advancing education for gifted children via federal mandate, see Bruce D. Baker and Reva Friedman-Nimz, "Is a Federal Mandate the Answer? If So, What Was the Question," *Roeper Review*, Vol. 25, No. 1 (Fall 2002): 5–10.

98. Umpstead, "The No Child Left Behind Act: Is It an Unfunded Mandate or a Promotion of Federal Educational Ideals?": 214.

99. Carl Savich, "Unfunded Mandates?: An Analysis of *Pontiac School Board v. Spellings*, the Legal Challenge to the No Child Left Behind Act," June 15, 2008, www.eric.ed.gov/PDFS/ED501713.pdf, p. 3.

100. Umpstead, "The No Child Left Behind Act: Is It an Unfunded Mandate or a Promotion of Federal Educational Ideals?": 209.
101. Michael Janofsky, "Judge Rejects Challenge to Bush Education Law," *New York Times*, November 24, 2005.
102. Gina Austin, "Leaving Federalism Behind: How the No Child Left Behind Act Usurps States' Rights," *Thomas Jefferson Law Review* (Vol. 27, 2005): 352.
103. Ibid.: 353, 364, 366.
104. One dubious assertion upon which defenders of NCLB cannot rest their case is the claim that public education is somehow a fundamental right guaranteed by the US Constitution. The Supreme Court denied that claim in *San Antonio Independent School District v. Rodriguez* (1973). Every state constitution, on the other hand, does guarantee such a right.
105. Umpstead, "The No Child Left Behind Act: Is it an Unfunded Mandate or a Promotion of Federal Educational Ideals?": 223.
106. McDermott and Jensen, "Dubious Sovereignty: Federal Conditions of Aid and the No Child Left Behind Act": 41.
107. Amanda K. Wingfield, "The No Child Left Behind Act: Legal Challenges as an Unfunded Mandate," *Loyola Journal of Public Interest Law* (Vol. 6, No. 2, Spring 2005): 207. One lesser debated provision of the act forced schools receiving NCLB funds to provide the names, addresses, and telephone numbers of students to military recruiters. See Sanja Zgonjanin, "No Child Left (Behind) Unrecruited," *Connecticut Public Interest Law Journal* (Vol. 5, No. 2, 2006). 167–95.
108. McDermott and Jensen, "Dubious Sovereignty: Federal Conditions of Aid and the No Child Left Behind Act": 53.
109. Sam Dillon, "States Are Relaxing Education Standards to Avoid Sanctions from Federal Law," *New York Times*, May 22, 2003.
110. David M. Herszenhorn, "For U.S. Aid, City Switches Reading Plan in 49 Schools," *New York Times*, January 7, 2004.
111. Valerie Strauss, "Shocking details of Atlanta cheating scandal," *Washington Post*, July 7, 2011.
112. McGuinn, "The National Schoolmarm: No Child Left Behind and the New Educational Federalism": 61.
113. Ibid.: 66.
114. Motoko Rich, "'No Child' Law Whittled Down by White House," *New York Times*, July 6, 2012.
115. Jonathan Weisman and Amit R. Paley, "Dozens in GOP Turn against Bush's Prized 'No Child' Act," *Washington Post*, March 15, 2007.
116. Paige, "No Child Left Behind: The Ongoing Movement for Public Education Reform": 466–67.
117. Ibid.: 469.

7

The Help America Vote Act: Good-bye, Lever Machines; Hello, Coercion

The Help America Vote Act is a mandate that can be traced to a single cause; to a single state, in fact; and in the main to a single county: Palm Beach County, Florida, that is, which never before November 7, 2000, and never since has been known as Pat Buchanan territory.

The extraordinary wrangle over the results of the 2000 presidential election had a forensic epicenter in Palm Beach County. If you will recall, the presidential election featuring Republican George W. Bush and Democrat Albert Gore hung on the results in Florida. The television networks jumped the gun, calling the hotly contested state and its crucial twenty-five electoral votes for Vice President Gore before the polls had closed in the western panhandle region of the state, a Republican extremity that lies in the Central Time Zone. Displaying a remarkable fickleness—or irresponsibility—the networks switched their call to Bush after the panhandle voting closed. They eventually removed the state, which had spent the night changing from blue to red, to the undecided column, where it joined New Mexico and Oregon.

Vice President Gore foolishly made a concession call to Bush. He later retracted that concession (which of course had no legal force) when it became apparent that Florida was a virtual deadlock—and that whoever won the Sunshine State would be the forty-third president of the United States.

The next several weeks were a spectacle of bare-knuckled partisan brawling that both parties tried to coat with a democratic varnish. This was politics at its rawest: a battle for power. The constitutionality of the Florida recount became the central legal issue. The struggle, which only ended on December 12, 2000, when the US Supreme Court, in *Bush v. Gore,* ruled that the Gore team's request for a manual recount of certain election precincts would violate the Fourteenth Amendment, did neither side credit. The voters of Florida fared just as poorly in the court (or kangaroo court) of public opinion. They were lampooned as feeble-minded buffoons who couldn't figure out how to punch a hole in a card. Should such cretins really decide so weighty a question as who is to be the next president of the United States? Or so implied a scornful media.

Out of this morass the United States got (1) President George W. Bush and (2) an unfunded federal mandate effectively ordering states and localities to junk some election machinery and use others.

Undeniably, Florida had a voting problem.

The strangest anomaly in the Florida presidential vote of 2000 was found in Palm Beach County. Although the county was not considered fertile ground for the candidacy of writer Pat Buchanan, who was running on the Reform Party ticket, Palm Beach County gave Buchanan 3,407 votes in the initial canvass of Florida. This was, to put it mildly, shocking.

Those 3,407 votes for Buchanan in just this one county represented 19.6 percent of his statewide votes. As Jonathan N. Wand, Kenneth W. Shotts, Jasjeet S. Sekhon, Walter R. Mebane Jr., Michael C. Herron, and Henry E. Brady note in their study "The Butterfly Did It: The Aberrant Vote for Buchanan in Palm Beach County, Florida," in the *American Political Science Review*, Buchanan won just 5.4 percent of his statewide votes in the 1996 Republican primary in Palm Beach County.[1]

As their title puckishly declares, the butterfly did it. The butterfly ballot is the confusing ballot design that Palm Beach County voters struggled with on Election Day 2000. The fact that Palm Beach County did not use a butterfly absentee ballot offers the researchers a "natural experiment." Their finding? "Buchanan's proportion of the [Palm Beach County] vote on election-day ballots is four times larger than his proportion on absentee (non-butterfly) ballots, but Buchanan's proportion does not differ significantly between election-day and absentee ballots in any other Florida county."[2]

What was this elusive and apparently mischievous butterfly ballot? Palm Beach County Supervisor of Elections Theresa LePore designed it, and by November 8, the day after the election, you can bet she wished she hadn't. (For one thing, it earned her the probably unshakeable nickname of "Madame Butterfly.") Supervisor LePore was a registered Democrat, though after the abuse she took for her unwise innovation in balloting she left the party—not that the party wanted her anymore.

She was blamed for Al Gore's loss (as was Ralph Nader and the US Supreme Court—the Democrats were eager to spread blame around to anyone but their own lackluster candidate).

The ballot, which was used only for the presidential choice, resembled a butterfly in that it had a central spine, which contained punch holes for the ten presidential and vice presidential tickets on the Florida ballot, and then it had two "wings," one on each side of the spine (or perhaps we should call it a "thorax" to continue the insect metaphor). These wings featured the names of the candidates, with arrows pointing to the corresponding punch holes. In theory, this was an efficient way to compress a large field of candidates onto a single page. In practice, it was a mess. The first two candidates on the left wing of the butterfly were, respectively, George W. Bush and Al Gore. The top candidate on the right side was Pat Buchanan. But a voter, or at least a somewhat inattentive voter or one with middling eyesight, might easily confuse the punch holes of Buchanan and Gore. That, apparently, is what happened for approximately 2,000 Palm Beach County voters.

With respect to the Buchanan/Reform Party 2000 vote, Palm Beach County, according to Professors Wand et al., was the "largest outlier among all counties in the United States we were able to examine." In other words, the actual Buchanan vote exceeded the expected Buchanan vote by a larger margin—by far—than in any other county in America. Significantly, Palm Beach County was not a Reform Party vote outlier in 1996, the second candidacy of Texas businessman Ross Perot. And Buchanan's campaign manager, his sister Bay Buchanan, scoffed at the Bush camp's suggestion that Palm Beach County was some kind of Buchanan stronghold. The Buchanan campaign "never bought an ad and never paid a visit" to the county.[3]

The researchers noted that if Election Day voters had supported Buchanan at the same rate as absentee voters had, he would have won 854 votes in Palm Beach County among Election Day voters. But he won considerably more than that—3,310 Election Day votes, or 2,456 more than expected.

These extra votes, they further state, came disproportionately from "precincts with high levels of support for Democratic candidates for other offices."

Their conclusion was that the butterfly ballot "caused more than 2,000 Democratic voters [in Palm Beach County] to vote by mistake for Reform candidate Pat Buchanan."[4] These 2,000 votes were considerably higher than the final 537-vote margin of George W. Bush's victory over Albert Gore in Florida. (The initial count had Bush up by 327 votes.) Thus, if Palm Beach County had used a ballot other than the maligned butterfly, Al Gore would have won Florida's electoral votes and the presidency.

Armed with this knowledge, or suspicion, Democrats would push through (with the help of sheepish Republicans) the Help America Vote Act (HAVA). It was overkill and overreaction: a somewhat hysterical response to an admittedly bizarre election dispute.

Before examining the HAVA, we should take a butterfly's tour of vote-counting in America.

****

There was nothing illegal about the butterfly ballot: the Supreme Court of Florida threw out challenges to the ballot during the post-election tug-of-war. But it was wretchedly designed, no doubt about it. Left to their own devices, it's a sure bet no American county or state would ever call upon its lepidopteran pattern again. (Though in this era of "coercive federalism," states and localities are *not* left to their own devices.)

Yet even if one could figure out which candidate corresponded with which punch holes, there was a further practical problem associated with it: "hanging chads," which had the additional burden of a vaguely distasteful name. (Imperfectly punched chads are also called "dimpled" or "pregnant." Ugh.)

Chads are the punched-out part of voting cards. In order for the vote tabulating machines to properly read punch cards, a chad must be fully punched—that is, wholly detached from the card.

Two scholars from the Massachusetts Institute of Technology, Stephen Ansolabehere and Charles Stewart III, confirmed in a 2005 study in the *Journal of Politics* the marked inferiority of punch-card voting. Markedly inferior, that is, if one's goal is to have "every vote count," or come as close as possible to that goal. But their findings also provided a measured vote of confidence for a method of voting that was in the process of being ushered out of existence by the HAVA federal mandate—that is, pulling down mechanical levers in those big, old, solid voting machines in which so many of us cast our first votes.

"Uncounted votes" may sound like a marginal problem limited to the tiny handful of voters who make egregious errors in casting their ballots, but the phenomenon is so well-established that political scientists even have a name for it: "residual votes." These are the "blank, spoiled, or unmarked ballots" that constitute the uncounted votes in any election—the gap, that is, between the total of registered voters who show up and the total votes counted.[5]

Professors Ansolabehere and Stewart, undertaking what they deem "the most expansive analysis that we know of" in regard to the relationship of voting technology to uncounted votes, cast their net across a vast data pool consisting of the available votes for president, governor, and US senator in every US county between 1988 and 2000.[6] They were able to assess the data from about 2,800 of the nation's 3,155 counties. The uncounted votes in these elections were hardly negligible. In presidential elections, the residual vote in the average US county was 2.3 percent; among all voters, the residual vote was 2.2 percent. In gubernatorial and senatorial elections, the residual vote in the average county was 4.2 percent, and the residual vote among all voters was 4.1 percent.

These are not, the authors hasten to point out, the result of widespread intentional abstention. Previous studies have found the intentional abstention rate in presidential elections to be half of one percent; therefore, the residual vote in presidential elections is 2.2 minus 0.5, or 1.7 percent. Given that about 100 million votes have been cast in recent presidential elections, more than a million and a half voters exercise a futile franchise.

The authors examine the most common voting technologies: old-fashioned paper ballots; mechanical lever machines; optically scanned ballots; punch cards; and direct register electronic machines (DREs), which require the voter to "mark choices via a computer interface and the voting machine records them directly to an electronic memory."[7]

Paper ballots, of course, were the original nineteenth-century currency of secret-ballot voting. They are used now only in the most rural and remote corners of the country, though they remain, interestingly, among the most reliable and fraud-proof ways of registering one's vote. (Not that they are infallible. As New York City political chieftain Boss Tweed famously said, "the ballots made no result; the counters made the result.")[8]

The thousand-pound mechanical lever machines on which many Americans came to maturity voting on were first employed in 1892 in Lockport, New York. Called the Myers Automatic Booth, they were soon ubiquitous in cities and were the dominant voting technology for most of the twentieth century. The voter enters the booth, draws the

193

curtain, depresses levers for his chosen candidates, and as he exits the booth he opens the curtain, thereby registering his vote. At the end of the night inspectors record the total vote by examining mechanical counters within the machine.

Lever machines make difficult instruments with which to steal elections. Their interior vote counters are set to zero when the polls open, and this is witnessed by representatives of the parties. Similarly, party representatives are present when the polls close, and the vote count is read aloud. Human oversight makes vote stealing a bad bet with these machines. But, well, they look *old*. Outdated. Tired, even. They just don't fit the computer era.

In the 1960s, the punch card, with its IBM-type bureaucratic feel, was introduced. Its first use was in DeKalb and Fulton Counties, Georgia. The first punch card technology even had the corny futuristic name of Votomatic. Its inventor, Joseph P. Harris, was a political scientist, a product of the University of Chicago who actually got his inspiration from a former student of his at Berkeley who asked if the IBM computer punch card might not make a good ballot. Working with an engineer, Harris created the Votomatic, whose parent company IBM actually purchased in 1965.

Everything about the Votomatic, from its IBM origin to its cheesy handle, bespoke *modern*. Never mind that it was less reliable than those lumbering old lever machines: they were *so* 1930s, while the Votomatic savored of the age of spaceflight, TV dinners, and rock and roll. Robert P. Varni, founder of the company that manufactured Votomatic, claimed that it "has probably had more effect on the country than almost any other product." An exaggeration, to be sure, though in the late fall of 2000, he might have had a case. (As Ken Hazlett, who wrote programs for IBM punch cards, told Ronnie Dugger of *The New Yorker*, "Hanging chad has been with us since the invention of the Votomatic." The art of determining just what a voter meant by the partially punctured card has been called "chadology.")[9]

The dominant force in punch-card and computerized voting, C.E.S., counted a whopping 44.2 percent of the votes in 1984. The potential for genuine mischief was what drove Ronnie Dugger's *New Yorker* investigation, and although he uncovered a handful of cases in which votes had been counted incorrectly by computers—accidentally or otherwise—these were scattered, and involved such relatively benign instances as "soggy, warped, and mangled" cards jamming a computer in Florida, or a county in Illinois in which the votes for state comptroller candidates were transposed. Somehow the prominent role of Illinois in dubious elections failed to take anyone by surprise. For example, in 1982, in certain Chicago precincts "faked punch-card votes were cast in the names of transients, the ill, the incapacitated, and people who had moved away, had died, or had not voted."[10] The first Mayor Richard Daley was dead, but Daleyism lived on.

The 1970s brought the optical scanning of ballots. The ballots were paper and a voter denoted his choice by pencil or marker, but instead of being counted by hand they were scanned by machines. The most recent technological advance—or "advance," as it is distinctly inferior to its predecessors in the critical matter of counting each and every vote—is the direct register electronic (DRE) machine, which requires the voter to either push a button or touch a computer screen bearing the name of his or her preferred candidate. These votes are recorded electronically and then sent to a central vote-counting office.

Professors Ansolabehere and Stewart note that in the disputed 2000 presidential election, the fiasco from which an unprecedented federal voting technologies mandate would emerge, punch cards were the most common method of voting, used by 34.4 percent of American voters. One-quarter of voters cast ballots that were optically scanned, while 17.8 percent used mechanical lever machines. About a tenth of voters used DREs, 8.1 percent resided in counties that used multiple voting methods, and only 1.3 percent exercised the franchise using good old paper ballots. This was a sea change from just twenty years earlier. In 1980, 9.7 percent of voters had cast paper ballots, while mechanical lever machines were used by 43.9 percent of voters.[11] Thus more than half the electorate in 1980 utilized voting technology from the nineteenth century.

Most states featured a mixture of technologies. For instance, in the 2000 election, the breakdown in the bellwether state of Indiana was 36.2 percent punch card, 33.5 percent electronic voting, 23.4 percent lever machine, and 6.9 percent optical scanners. A few states exhibited uniformity: Connecticut's electorate was polled entirely by mechanical lever machines, as was New York's, while Hawaiians, Oklahomans, and Rhode Islanders voted en masse with the aid of optical scanners.[12]

The findings? In presidential elections, "traditional paper ballots produce the lowest rate of uncounted votes (i.e., 'residual votes'), followed by optically scanned ballots, mechanical lever machines, direct register electronic machines (DREs), and punch cards." Matters are not all that different in the case of gubernatorial and senatorial elections.

Again, paper ballots result in the fewest uncounted votes, followed by optically scanned ballots, DREs, mechanical lever machines, and, in their accustomed place at the rear, punch cards.[13]

Voting technologies have "strong and substantial effects on residual votes," declared the scholarly researchers. As noted earlier, "Hand-counted paper does remarkably well." In presidential elections between 1988 and 2000, those voting in counties employing the distinctly old-school paper ballots averaged a residual vote of 1.9 percent, compared to 1.6 percent for voters in counties with optical scanning, 1.8 percent for those with mechanical lever machines, and 2.5 percent each for punch-card and DRE counties. The corresponding rates for gubernatorial and senatorial elections were 2.1 and 3.0 percent for optical scans, 3.2 and 3.8 percent for paper ballots, 3.7 and 5.4 percent for DREs, 3.3 and 4.4 percent for punch cards, and 4.2 and 7.0 percent for mechanical lever machines.[14] (The chasm between the residual vote for president and other offices in the case of the lever machines is explained by the prominent position—upper left corner—of the presidential race on such machines and the more obscure placing of the candidates for other offices.)

The authors write that "paper ballots—the oldest technology—show the best performance."[15] If election commissioners in a county or state are really serious when they mumble the hoary cliché about every vote counting, then they will adopt, or maintain, paper as their voting medium: whether in the form of paper ballots or optically scanned paper. Both technologies are clearly superior to direct register electronic machines. DREs and punch cards produce a considerably higher residual vote. In counting votes, not every method is created equal. (As Ronnie Dugger remarked with amusement, computer-voting advocates call the errors and foul-ups of their machines "glitches," implying that they are minor, even negligible matters.[16])

Election Day fraud is as old as elections themselves. From the 1876 presidential election "victory" by Republican Rutherford B. Hayes over Democrat Samuel Tilden to US Senate candidate Lyndon B. Johnson's theft of the 1948 Texas Senate election (recounted in Robert Caro's *Means of Ascent*), stealing votes is a dishonorable tradition in America, and indeed in any nation with democratic elections. As long as governments wield coercive power over the lives and pocketbooks of their subjects, unscrupulous men and women will pursue that power—often using any means necessary.

Even hand-counted paper ballots offer the opportunity for chicanery. A dishonest election official can discard "inconvenient" ballots or stuff the box with ballots for his preferred candidate. With the maligned punch cards, an iniquitous official might punch out extra chads, invalidating a ballot, or he might take it upon himself to punch out chads in races from which a voter abstained. Yet there are limits to how much damage a single corrupt election official can do. Similarly, the mechanized lever machines have built-in anti-fraud protections: the machine prevents one from "over-voting," or casting more votes than one is permitted in a given race.

Computerized vote counting, however, opens the door to vote stealing on a far more massive scale than does hand counting. Its dangers were first brought to a wide audience by investigative journalist Ronnie Dugger in a much-discussed 1988 article in *The New Yorker*. Dugger warned especially against the DRE technology, which as he noted often makes recounts "impossible, for the program destroys the electronic record of each voter's choices the instant after it counts them."

Dugger's piece seemed alarmist at the time. It echoed the sometimes paranoid political journalism and Allen Drury/Fletcher Knebel novels of the 1960s. He went so far as to ask: "Since, under the state-by-state, winner-take-all rules of the electoral college, a close Presidential election can be decided by relatively few votes in two or three big states, could electronic illusionists steal the Presidency by fixing the vote-counting computers in just four or five major metropolitan areas? Could people breaking into or properly positioned within a computerized-vote counting company . . . steal House or Senate seats, or even the White House itself?" The question sounded a lot less paranoid-conspiratorial after the 2000 election. Most of the experts Dugger spoke to acknowledged that electoral theft was a possibility, if not a probability. Randall H. Erben, assistant secretary of state in Texas, told Dugger, "I have no question that somebody who's smart enough with a computer could probably rig it to mis-tabulate. Whether that has happened yet I don't know. It's going to be virtually undetectable if it's done correctly, and that's what concerns me about it."[17]

After *Bush v. Gore*, folks took another look at Ronnie Dugger.

****

Political scientists have never been terribly interested in matters of voting technology—until the immediate aftermath of the 2000 election, where Florida, and in particular Palm Beach County, served as an object lesson in how *not* to count votes.

Federalism, and the diversity that results therefrom, is a distinguishing characteristic of American governance. It is also one of its strengths. The states serve as "laboratories of democracy," in the conception of Supreme Court Justice Louis Brandeis. The variety of public-policy approaches enable a fruitful experimentation, and permit the states to mold laws and regulations in conformity with local and regional practices. (The Brandeis quote in full, from his dissent in *New State Ice Co. v. Liebmann*: "It is one of the happy incidents of the federal system that a single courageous State may, if its citizens choose, serve as a laboratory; and try novel social and economic experiments without risk to the rest of the country.")[18]

Such diversity bedevils those who prefer a one-size-fits-all approach to public policy. (That one size, of course, just happens to be whatever option such advocates personally prefer.) And so it was post-Florida 2000. "The lack of uniformity of voting technologies was cause for concern among many reformers in the aftermath of the 2000 election," write Ansolabehere and Stewart.[19] The response of these "reformers" was the knee-jerk response of authority-trusting reformers since the Progressive era: bring the weight of the federal government to bear on these individualistic and recalcitrant states and localities. Make them change the way they count votes—*or else.*

To every problem under the sun, it seems, there is a response by the federal government. And this response almost always adds to the powers of that same federal government while reducing those of states, localities, and, as an afterthought, citizens.

Such was the case after the Florida foul-up of 2000.

The Help America Vote Act—and how can one be against a bill with so anodyne a name; *who* is against helping Americans to vote?—was the legislative solution to the problem of Florida. It was a classic top-down mandate: Washington dictates, the states get a few bucks, and local election districts wind up with the headaches of implementing a one-size-fits-all solution to a "problem" that was essentially narrow and localized. The winners were the "policy entrepreneurs" who seized the moment and the well-connected manufacturers of the mandated election equipment. The losers were federalism, the taxpayers, and local election officials.

The Help America Vote Act authorized $3.86 billion to the states to "improve" voting within their jurisdictions. This improvement was focused on trash-canning punch cards and putting the mechanical lever machines out to junkyard pasture. The feds would pick up 95 percent of the cost of new voting equipment, and the states the other 5 percent. It was an offer they couldn't refuse.

HAVA cast its net widely. Given the opportunity to impose voting-technology mandates on the states, there was no way Congress was going to limit its reach to punch cards and butterfly ballots. That's why HAVA addressed everything from voting by the blind to recounts to voter fraud. The result was a bulging grab-bag of top-down election "reforms" that stuck the states and their taxpayers with part of the bill.

The act mandated uniform election technologies and the administration thereof to the fifty states. It sought to ensure, via mandate, that disabled voters could cast their ballots "privately and independently"—that is, in some cases, also expensively. States were ordered to compile computerized voter registration lists. And polling places had to offer provisional ballots to those who showed up to vote but whose names were not on the extant lists.[20]

As with education before No Child Left Behind, the states were already enacting remedial legislation addressing voting technology before the feds blundered into the policy arena with HAVA. According to Sarah F. Liebschutz and Daniel J. Palazzolo, writing in *Publius*, "More than 2,088 election reform bills were introduced in state legislatures, and 321 were passed into law during the 2001 and 2002 state legislative sessions."[21] So quite obviously, the states were responding to perceived inadequacies in vote-counting and election administration.

Florida led the way, in part, as MIT's Charles Stewart III notes, because Governor Jeb Bush, brother of President George W. Bush, wanted to "redeem a reputation that had been besmirched by the controversy."[22] In March 2001, Governor Bush's select Task Force on Election Procedures, Standards, and Technology, created by executive order of the governor on December 14, 2000, the day after Al Gore's final concession, issued a raft of recommendations on voting systems and ballot design, the overall gist of which was to centralize election management in Tallahassee. Most of these were adopted in the Florida Election Reform Act of 2001, which the state legislature passed on May 4, 2001, and Governor Jeb Bush signed into law on May 10. The centerpiece of the reform was the abolition of the much-abused chad, as punch card voting was outlawed. Katherine Harris, who as Florida's secretary of state was at the center of the hurricane in the 2000 dispute, said proudly, "There'll never be a hanging, dangling, or pregnant chad again."[23]

Other elements of the package, which Florida adopted on its own, without the stick of federal mandate, included state aid for voting technology upgrades, reform of absentee and provisional voting rules, the posting of a voter's "bill of rights," and the establishment of voter education and poll worker training programs. The state appropriated $30 million in 2001–2003 for voting technology replacement, voter education, and poll-worker training. The Palm Beach embarrassment had a price tag, and this was only a part of it.

This is not to say that the election reform package was a cure-all. In 2002, the first time the new touch-screen machines were used in Palm Beach County, the undervote in the municipality of Wellington was 3.1 percent, leading county commissioner Tony Masilotti to say, "There seems to be as high a rate of error as there was with the old chad system."[24] Commissioner Masilotti soon had more serious matters to deal with than residual votes, however: in 2007 he went to prison for various illegal land deals.[25] As Susan A. MacManus concluded in her study of "Voter Education: The Key to Election Reform; Success Lessons from Florida," published in the *University of Michigan Journal of Law Reform*, "there is never an error-free election"—no matter how much the government spends on voter education and poll-worker training. Not only do machines malfunction and human beings err, but "switching equipment actually may introduce new opportunities for voter error," as the General Accounting Office noted in a 2001 report.[26]

In addition, Florida's legislature passed and Governor Bush signed the Voter Accessibility Act of 2002, which facilitated voting by the disabled in various ways. For instance, it repealed the state's five-minute limit on voting by any one person, it forced candidates to use closed captions on all television broadcasts, and it mandated the training of poll workers "on issues of etiquette and sensitivity with respect of voters having a disability."[27]

The issue here is not whether these are good ideas or well-meaning but clumsy ideas or examples of political correctness run rampant. They were Florida ideas, crafted and then passed into law by Florida representatives, and funded by Florida taxpayers. Florida was the epicenter of the 2000 election debacle, and Florida took steps to straighten up its own house. *It did not need HAVA.* It did not need a mandate—especially an unfunded, or underfunded, mandate. Florida did not need Washington's stick, or its carrots.

This is a common pattern: the states, which are often affronted and resentful when their turf is invaded by power-grabbing feds, are more than willing to snatch traditionally local responsibilities from towns and cities and counties and make them state concerns. Too often, one's attitude toward decentralizing government depends upon whether one's policy preference is most likely to be enacted at the national, the state, or the local level. Many Americans are situational decentralists, which is a euphemistic way of saying that their principles are flexible in the extreme.

Yet in failing to assert forcefully enough the primacy of state and local over federal reform, the states also opened the way for HAVA. For instance, in February 2001 the National Association of Secretaries of State endorsed a resolution that, while declaring that "the conduct of elections is primarily the responsibility of state and county elections officials," called upon the federal government to come through with funding for election reforms. It asked Congress to

1. Fully fund the continuous update of the Federal Voting Systems Standards developed in consensus with state and local election officials;
2. Fund the development of voluntary management practices standards for each voting system;
3. Promote intergovernmental cooperation and communication among state and local elections officials to facilitate the maintenance of accurate voter registration rolls; and
4. Provide funding to the States to implement the state and local recommendations of this resolution.[28]

It is naïve in the extreme to dun Congress for monies and expect it to merely hand over the funds without taking hold of the leash. Seeing an opening, the nationalizers seized it.

Charles Stewart III observes that "HAVA unfolded after most states had begun, and sometimes finished, their own study commissions." But there was no way the feds were going to leave the issue to the states—federalism, whatever lip service politicos may pay it, is deader than James Madison. And besides, the liberal pressure groups that lobbied for reform at the state level—the League of Women Voters, the NAACP, Common Cause—found HAVA to be a "one-stop-shopping forum to press their cases" for various non-chad-related modifications to election practices.[29] Why lobby the legislatures in Wyoming and Louisiana and Oregon and Vermont when you can, by passing a single bill in Washington, DC, ram your favored policies down the throats of all fifty states?

****

As the 107th Congress convened in January 2001, election-reform bills flooded both chambers. Upwards of 175 separate pieces of legislation were offered to correct perceived shortcomings in voting machines, registration, and election administration.[30] The spectacle of the previous autumn probably made some congressional action inevitable.

The primary Republican vehicle was Senator Mitch McConnell's (KY) Election Reform Act of 2001, which would create a federal commission charged with helping states set and meet "voluntary standards" for elections. The Democrats countered with the Equal Protection and Voting Rights Act of 2001, prime sponsors Senator Christopher Dodd (CT) and Representative John Conyers (MI), a measure that provided funds for and imposed national "uniform and nondiscriminatory requirements for election technology and administration" on the states.[31]

Bipartisanship—which one wag defined as the alliance of Democrats and Republicans against Americans—reigned. The Help America Vote Act, its very title suggesting the federal government as a solicitous Boy Scout helping enfeebled voters across the street and into the polling place, became the compromise engine of election reform. Or, given its dubious premises, maybe that should be "reform."

The House passed its version of the Help America Vote Act on December 12, 2001, by a vote of 362–63. Of the 63 nays, 42 were Democrats, 20 were Republicans, and 1 was an Independent. The Democratic nays generally were drawn from the party's left wing—Dennis Kucinich (OH), Maxine Waters (CA)—while the Republicans were mostly from the party's small-government wing: Ron Paul (TX), Walter Jones (NC), Dana Rohrabacher (CA). The Senate passed its version of HAVA, which went under the how-can-anyone-oppose-this? name of the Martin Luther King Jr. Equal Protection of Voting Rights Act, by unanimous consent on April 11, 2002.

The conference committee that was to iron out differences between the two bills especially wrangled over the Senate's anti-voter fraud provisions, which had been a particular interest of Missouri Republican Christopher Bond, whose state had experienced a bitter and messy US Senate race (not involving Bond) in 2000—one in which charges of voter fraud flew over St. Louis like the swallows at San Juan Capistrano. Senator Bond and his GOP allies insisted that HAVA force the states to require a form of ID—not necessarily photo ID—from those voters who had registered by mail. These ID provisions, which flew in the face of even the most flexible concept of federalism, remained a part of HAVA, and the conference report cleared the House on October 10, 2002, by a vote of 357–48 and the Senate on October 16, 2002, by 92–2: margins not exactly of a Florida-like thinness. (The two Senate no votes came from New York Democrats Clinton and Schumer, who objected to the requirement that those who registered to vote by mail produce ID on their first visit to the polls.) President Bush signed it into law on October 29, 2002.

HAVA was a direct result of the Florida presidential race fiasco. Charles Stewart III notes that "it is clear that without the Florida controversy, a bill like HAVA would not have been seriously considered by Congress, much less passed."[32] Yet as the dissent by the New York senators indicates, "the provisions of HAVA that have ultimately caused the most controversy were prompted by issues that did not arise at all in Florida, and only were introduced in the congressional process through the side door."[33] Those federal mandates causing the controversy were the requirements that (1) first-time voters who registered by mail produce IDs; and (2) that each polling place have the necessary voting equipment to enable handicapped voters to cast their ballots secretly and independently. Curiously, these two "issues" are also subjects on which virtually no hard data exist: we really don't know how widespread voter fraud is, or how formidable a barrier the various methods of voting have been to disabled persons.

The accessibility or inaccessibility of voting places for handicapped persons was a complete non-issue in Florida in 2000. It had approximately zero to do with the outcome or the controversy in the Sunshine State. But it became central to the Help America Vote Act because advocates for the disabled "were immediately drawn to the post-*Bush-Gore* policymaking process as a perfect opportunity to extend their gains." Special provisions for handicapped voters had been enshrined in federal law with the Voting Rights Act of 1965, the Voting Accessibility for the Elderly and Handicapped Act of 1984, and the Americans with Disabilities Act of 1990, but the self-appointed spokesmen for disabled persons staked out a new front in 2001: they insisted upon voting without assistance, which is why every precinct in America is required to purchase a DRE. Now, there is no evidence that these machines have made voting more accessible for the disabled, or that HAVA has increased the voting rate of disabled persons; Charles Stewart III notes that "the disabled are much more likely to cite transportation problems for their non-voting" than they are to blame difficult-to-use voting machines.[34] But as is so often the case with federal mandates, it is the putative good intentions of the law's creators, and not the murkier consequences, that seem to matter most to politicians, and, alas, to voters.

The other major features of the Help America Vote Act were the establishment of grants and payments to the states in order to facilitate the retirement of punch cards and mechanical lever machines; the mandate that polling places provide provisional ballots to voters whose status is uncertain or in question; and the requirement that states maintain computerized lists of registered voters—that is, that every state must create "in a uniform and non-discriminatory manner a single, uniform, official, centralized, interactive computerized statewide voter registration list defined, maintained and administered at the state level." (As Stewart writes, the "centralized voter registry was supposed to improve the quality of the data included in these files— guard against typographical errors, ensure that addresses were valid, etc."—but a 2010 study by Stephen Ansolabehere and Eitan Hersch found these files riddled with errors. Indeed, almost 10 percent of the voter registration records of the fifty states were "invalid"; the figure was 20 percent in Arkansas. Yes, remarkably, clerical bureaucrats make mistakes—even when their acts are mandated by laws with friendly names like the Help America Vote Act!)[35]

Because no new mandate is complete without the creation of an acronym-encrusted bureaucracy to oversee it, the Help America Vote Act gave birth to the Election Assistance Commission, or EAC. (The word *assistance* is kind and gentle, making the EAC sound like a devoted nurse or helpmeet. But just try crossing it.) The EAC replaced the Office of Election Administration (OEA—even the most trivial offices in Washington, DC get their own acronyms), the federal board that previously was responsible for the federal role in administering elections. The new Election Assistance Commission was bipartisan, which is another way of saying it was devoted to the eternal life of the two-party system, those two parties being the Democrats and Republicans. The two-party system is nowhere mentioned or provided for in the US Constitution, but it seems destined to far outlive the rapidly fading Constitution. The EAC is to administer the grants, monitor voting systems, issue guidelines to the states, and otherwise assume responsibilities that constitutionally belong to the states, not the federal government. It lacks the power to enforce HAVA, which is reserved to the US attorney general and, by federal mandate, the states.

HAVA authorized the sum of $3.86 billion, of which $3.032 billion was appropriated in fiscal years 2003 and 2004. These combined

FY '03–'04 appropriations went primarily toward payments to the states to meet HAVA requirements ($2.328 billion) and payments to the states to improve election administration and replace punch cards and mechanical lever machines ($650 million).

Payments for the "improvement" of election administration were made to all fifty states and the territories. Payments for the retirement of punch cards and mechanical lever machines and their replacement by optical scanners or DREs were made to those states that applied for such funds.

Appropriations in FY 2005 and succeeding years were much lower. For instance, in fiscal year 2005 Congress appropriated $14 million for the Election Assistance Commission, $15 million to facilitate access to the polls by the handicapped (administered by the Department of Health and Human Services), and $200,000 apiece for a "student/parent mock election program"—surely a vital function of a constitutional republic: a fake election!—and the Help America Vote College Program. In fiscal year 2006, Congress appropriated $14.2 million for the EAC and $22.1 million for disability access. No money was spent upon fake elections, though a quarter million was available to the Help America Vote College Program. The figures for fiscal year 2007 were $16.24 million for the EAC and $15.72 for disability access; for fiscal year 2008, $16.53 million for the EAC and $17.2 million for disability access—as well as $200,000 for another student and parent mock election. (As if the 2008 Obama-McCain contest wasn't bad enough!) FY 2008 also saw $115 million disbursed to the states in the resumption of payments to meet HAVA requirements. For fiscal year 2009, Congress appropriated $18 million for the EAC and $17.5 million for disability access programs. The mock election monies were boosted to $300,000, and the states received $100 million to meet those still-unmet HAVA requirements. In fiscal year 2010, the HAVA requirements payments fell to $70 million while the mock election funds remained steady at $300,000. The EAC received $16.91 million and the HHS-administered disability programs took in $17.41 million. By FY 2013, the EAC was reduced to $11.5 million and there was "no new money for HAVA grants." The states were now pretty much on their own when it came to maintaining the mandated election machinery.[36]

Under section 101 of HAVA, the states were given block grants to use toward training poll workers; teaching voters how to vote (which had never seemed quite necessary before: either polling procedures have gotten way too complex or voters have gotten way too dumb); and facilitating access to voting sites and machines by the disabled.

Section 102 of HAVA provided for funding to states to replace punch cards and mechanical lever machines—which, as we have seen, have quite different records of success. This was the most controversial, and in the views of many, wholly unnecessary, even counterproductive, mandate.

Section 301 laid down federal standards for voting machines employed in federal elections. As Charles Stewart III of the Massachusetts Institute of Technology notes, "Although Section 301(C) allowed states to retrofit existing equipment to meet the new standards, all states with punch cards and lever machines accepted Section 102 funding."[37] That's called going down without a fight.

As a direct order to the states, HAVA constitutes a federal mandate. Some funding is attached, though whether it is sufficient is an open question, and one on which virtually every state in the union takes the nay side. As such it seems to be an unfunded federal mandate. Now, technically, it only applied to federal elections, but this is a tad disingenuous. The ballot containing candidates for US Senate, House of Representatives, and president is not separate from but blended with the names of candidates for state and local offices. Practically, no state or locality is going to disaggregate these races.

Unlike No Child Left Behind or the national twenty-one-year-old drinking age, under which states maintain, at least in theory, the ability to refuse the federal money and circumvent the mandate, HAVA orders the states to comply with its directives. There is a mechanism by which a state can refuse the funds, but it still must comply with HAVA's requirements. You may have one guess as to how many states have refused the funds. (The answer is zero.)

****

No one really remembers who shot JR or who framed Roger Rabbit, but the doer-in of older voting technologies is clear: HAVA killed the punch card and the mechanical lever machine. It elevated the DRE and the optical scanner to their current place as the dominant methods of voting. In 2000, 11.3 million Americans voted on DREs; in 2008, that number was 39.8 million. In 2000, 41.5 million American exercised the franchise using optical scanners; in 2008, that number was 76.9 million. Over 90 percent of Americans now vote using one of these two technologies.[38] Mechanical lever machines, hand-counted paper, and punch cards are as twentieth century as Hubert Humphrey, VHS tapes, and fax machines.

HAVA doesn't come right out and say, "Use the DRE or the optical scanner." Its mandate is not that crude. But it is just as effective. Any system used in a federal election must "provide for error correction by voters, manual auditing, accessibility, alternative languages, and error-rate standards," as well as "voter privacy and ballot confidentiality."[39] In practice, that rules out mechanical levers and punch cards.

Although HAVA insists that voting systems be auditable, it does not require a paper-ballot trail. This had led to fears echoing those expressed back in 1988 by Ronnie Dugger in *The New Yorker*: namely, that without paper ballots, any recount is liable to manipulation and will inevitably fall under suspicion.

In updating the earlier work he had done on residual votes with Stephen Ansolabehere, Charles Stewart III discovered that HAVA's snuffing of those older systems wasn't exactly an open and shut case of justifiable homicide. Examining data from the 2000, 2004, and 2008 elections, he finds that abandoning punch cards in favor of optical scanning and DREs paid off: "a local jurisdiction switching from punch cards to optical scanning saw its residual vote rate drop by 0.71 percentage points, on average." (The figure for DREs was comparable.)

No real surprise there. We have known for years that punch cards, chads and all, are the least accurate means we have of counting votes. But what of those bulky old mechanical lever machines—the ones that seem as out-of-date as men wearing fedoras or ladies in pillbox hats? Well, HAVA seems to have made a rather serious mistake. For polling places in the 2000, 2004, and 2008 elections, "a shift from a mechanical lever machine to optical scanning is associated with an average *increase* in the residual vote rate of 0.27 percentage points. (emphasis in original)." Teasing out the hard-number implications of this federally mandated shift, Stewart writes, "Roughly, 11.8 million voters in jurisdictions that had used lever machines in 2000 used optical scanners to cast their ballots in 2008. If we apply this 0.27% point residual vote penalty to these jurisdictions, we get almost 32,000 additional residual votes due to the adoption of the newer technologies in those places."[40]

In other words, HAVA's expensive federal mandates didn't even achieve what its advocates assured one and all that they would achieve: they did not reduce uncounted votes, but rather *increased* them. Good riddance to punch cards; but where have you gone, mechanical lever machines? A nation turns its lonely eyes and uncounted votes to you.

So from a Beltway vantage point, the "problem" of dysfunctional voting machines is evidently solved, save for a few million here and there. Having developed a magic bullet in HAVA—and having pointed the gun containing said magic bullet at the states, which had no choice but to comply—the feds have done their duty. But what of the states? How have they complied—and what has it cost them, in dollars and also, less tangibly, in lost or ceded responsibilities? How much have these mandates cost? (Besides the 32,000 extra residual votes due to the abandonment of mechanical lever machines.) The dollars and cents numbers are disputed, of course, with the feds always minimizing the estimated cost and the states coming in with substantially higher estimates.

****

Florida, as we have seen, jumped the gun on election reform. (Though the holders of the gun in Washington did not exempt the Sunshine State from their subsequent coercions.) The state legislature passed a raft of reform measures in early 2001. Among them were requirements that county election supervisors offer voter education programs (to be financed by state taxpayers). HAVA provided further subsidy of such efforts.

New York, in the popular conception, is a state that long ago made peace with big government; the Empire State, in fact, did much to help impose big government on the rest of the United States. Damned Yankees! But just as New York was among the last states to cave in to the Reagan-ordained mandatory twenty-one-year-old drinking age, so was New York one of the holdouts—the last holdout, in truth—against the Help America Vote Act.

The mechanical lever voting machine was invented by a Rochester, New York, tinkerer named Jacob Myers, who received a patent for it in 1889. Voters first used it in the April 12, 1892, election about sixty miles west of Rochester in Lockport, New York. The *New York Times* hailed the machines as palladiums of honest elections:

> The Meyers [*sic*] voting machine had its first test trial in the election here to-day. The Meyers system makes it impossible to buy votes with any certainty that the goods will be delivered. Each voter entered the booth alone, and as he passed in his name was announced and recorded by one of the clerks. One minute was allowed each man for voting, although few required more than from ten to fifteen seconds

to register ballots for between fifteen and twenty candidates. When the voter pressed the knob opposite any candidate's name that knob, with those of candidates for the same office of other parties, was immediately locked, the knob he pressed registering and the others not, thus preventing any fraud on the part of the voter. The saving to the town by using the Meyers machine is very great. By it the number of polling places can be reduced fully half or more, fewer inspectors are required, and the general expenses are materially lessened.

After the closing of the polls the counting compartment at the back of the machine was opened, and inside of ten minutes the clerks had chronicled the entire result of the election that comprehended sixty-four candidates. The process usually occupies about three hours. Inside half an hour returns from national or State elections could be easily ascertained in this State or any other by the use of such a machine.[41]

Lockport, site of the mechanical lever machine's debut, is near Niagara Falls. While the advent of this particular technology was not quite so spectacular as that eighth wonder of the world, the machine did prove as reliable as the nearby cataracts for upwards of a century. New Yorkers saw no reason to change. The state was, as Professor Sarah F. Liebschutz of the State University of New York College at Brockport phrased it in the pages of *Publius*, "[s]eemingly impervious to demands for reform after the presidential election crisis of 2000."[42] Quite true, but then the state and its lawmakers had reason for their imperviousness: the system worked just fine in New York!

New York lawmakers, more so than those of reputedly more conservative states, exhibited an "if it ain't broke, don't fix it" attitude toward election reform. Not much had changed over the previous century of New York elections: the big Lockport-born machines were omnipresent and reliable. They were falling out of favor in other parts of the country—the last phalanx had been manufactured in 1962, and the percentage of Americans who pulled the levers in these machines had fallen to just 13 by 2004—but the two states often parodied as the most prone to fads and innovations, New York and California, were the only ones to still use them statewide.[43]

The machines had their critics, even in New York. They were not infallible. Parts occasionally broke down, and were not always easy to replace. And as one study reported, while being conveyed from warehouse to polling place "bumpy rides take their toll." Don't they, though?

What really did in the mechanical lever machines was their handicap inaccessibility. Or their reputed handicap inaccessibility. As mentioned earlier, the real obstacle to voting by disabled persons is transportation. Making it from home to the polls is the hard part; casting a ballot, even in machines that assume the voter is standing rather than sitting, is much easier to do. But the self-appointed advocates for the disabled castigated these machines as pre-disability-rights throwbacks. In their arguments they tossed out the kind of absurd numbers that sound awfully impressive and that no one ever challenges: for instance, that in 2004 there were "more than 2 million voting-age New Yorkers with disabilities."[44] This is a preposterously high number, unless one is defining "person with disabilities" so broadly as to render the term meaningless. The blind, those in wheelchairs, those lacking arms or legs—their numbers are a small fraction of the "disabled" as estimated by lobbyists for the disabled.

In the wake of the 2000 Florida fiasco, New York governor George Pataki, a Republican, created a Task Force on Election Modernization. New York City mayor Rudolph Giuliani, also a Republican, established a similar task force at the city level. As Professor Liebschutz notes, both recommended the junking of the state's mechanical lever machines on the grounds not that they were unreliable but that they were inaccessible to the handicapped. Yet the New York legislature, after considering the recommendations of the task forces as well as a similar report by Democratic state attorney general (and future governor, then future disgraced governor, and after that future ex-governor) Eliot Spitzer, chose to do nothing. Not because the New York state legislature is resistant to lawmaking, but because, in the words of Professor Liebschutz, "most New Yorkers and elected officials in state and local governments [were] generally satisfied with the voting machines." As Attorney General Spitzer's report observed, New Yorkers "consider the 22,000 old-fashioned lever machines user-friendly and hard to defraud. They do not rely on paper, electricity, or computer programmers, [and] at 950 pounds each, cannot be stolen readily."[45]

In New York, as in Florida, the federal system worked. Floridians had seen just how badly the state, especially Palm Beach County, had bungled the 2000 election, and they responded with legislation. In New York, which may have many problems but electoral screwups are not among them, the legislature considered alternatives to a status quo that was working fairly well and decided to keep on keeping on with the old machines. This, to repeat, is how federalism is supposed to work.

This is how it is *not* supposed to work: federal lawmakers, impatient with leaving important decisions to their "inferiors" in the fifty states, mandated that those states take action—on their own dime, or millions of dimes—to bring their voting systems into compliance with federal diktats.

There was a carrot to go along with the stick: $235.6 million in federal funds for New York to warehouse the old machines, adopt the newer technologies, compile a statewide database of registered voters, and in other ways "educate" voters and inspectors.

The states, as recipients of HAVA funds, were required to draw up and submit to their federal overlords HAVA implementation plans. In New York's case, the plan called for the majority of the federal funds ($140 million) to be applied toward the replacement of the state's 19,843 mechanical lever machines in their 15,571 election districts by voting technologies "which increase . . . the accessibility for persons with disabilities." Access, not accuracy, seemed to be the goal of this "reform" that was forced upon Albany by Washington.

New York planned to use $20 million of the federal pot for the creation of the statewide voter registration database. Another $20 million was to be spent on "voter education," $40 million upon election administration, and lesser amounts on training of inspectors, poll workers, etc.[46] New York is a state with a tradition of home rule—that is, localities, whether at the county, the city, or the township level, are given a say in making the laws under which their citizens live. The HAVA mandate, as Professor Liebschutz points out, undermined this home rule by transferring election powers from the localities to the state government. The state was named certifier of election technology and coordinator of the statewide voter database. It also devised administrative procedures for the fielding of complaints lodged with respect with voting. So HAVA was a force for centralization: not only the centralization of erstwhile state powers by the federal government, but also the transfer of local powers to the state bureaucracy.

In the end, New Yorkers caved. They delayed, but they caved nevertheless. Both the State Assembly and State Senate signed the death warrants for mechanical lever machines by unanimous votes. Jacob Myers, we hardly knew ye. The series of bills, culminating in the Election Reform and Modernization Act, signed into law by Governor Pataki on July 12, 2005, "overturned central features of [New York's] election system in place for more than a century." HAVA had triumphed—despite the "widespread perception that New York's election system was not broken."[47]

The election of 2006 was the first in which substantial numbers of New Yorkers no longer pulled levers behind curtains but rather colored in ballots to be optically scanned or recorded their votes for DREs to tally. The Empire State was the very last to submit to HAVA.

The federal largesse New York received for conforming to the HAVA mandates does not appear close to covering the additional expenses imposed by the act. In "Lever Replacement Costs: New York City Case Study," election analysts Teresa Hommel and Ellen Theisen assessed the cost of machine replacement in New York City alone.

"The costs of replacing lever machines with electronic machines will be enormous," write Hommel and Theisen. "The immediate costs—hardware, software, licenses—will rapidly deplete the City's HAVA funds."

New York City, like the rest of the state, was a mechanical lever town, although people with disabilities voted using "AutoMark" ballots and absentee ballots were counted using optical scanners. Thus the complaint that lever machines discriminate against the disabled, especially those who are unable to stand, was moot. But HAVA, as a federal mandate, was not interested in such fine distinctions. It swept along one and all into a brave new world from which mechanical lever machines had been banished. In the case of New York City, optical scanners were the next stage.

But while HAVA mandated a change—a change that very few of those on the ground thought necessary—it did not provide the funds to fully pay for that change. Analysts Hommel and Theisen noted that $65.42 million in HAVA monies were available to the city as of their writing. (The City had received $85.08 million of the state's $230.51 million HAVA money, or 36.9 percent of the total, and already expended almost $20 million at the time of the study.) The first order of business for Gotham was the purchase of 2,227 scanners and 19,829 booths in which to vote with that modicum of privacy afforded the citizen. (The mechanical lever machines, which are activated when the voter closes a curtain, provide a fuller sense of privacy.)

Surveying a range of estimates of the cost of replacing the lever machines, the authors settled upon a median estimate of $35.45 million—though this number was almost surely low, as it did not include significant costs for which the authors did not have reliable estimates. But the purchase of replacement voting devices is only the beginning. There are annual costs of upkeep and maintenance and training: the median estimate came in at $10.77 million—and again, the authors emphasize that this figure is probably quite low, given the lack of good estimates for other significant associated costs. (These unknown costs are not trivial: they include voter education, storage of equipment and ballots, electricity for charging the machines, and security, training, and transportation of equipment, among others. To take one example, training election workers in New York City is not a matter of merely throwing a photocopied handbook at a few sleepy-eyed poll watchers. Election Day in New York finds from 30,000–36,000 poll workers at their posts. The training costs for poll workers overseeing optical scanners are higher than when the city used mechanical lever machines, and given the turnover in these temporary positions, the training will have to be repeated at every election. HAVA funds will soon be depleted, and yet the training costs will be an annual expense.)[48]

Using these (conservative) estimates, New York City will have drained its HAVA monies by the time this book goes to press. New York is on its own—or sort of on its own. It has had its method of conducting elections dictated by the federal government, but from here on in the city itself must pay for the privilege of such obedience.

In that invaluable journal of federalism, *Publius*, Glen S. Krutz of the University of Oklahoma examined the effect of HAVA on Arizona and Illinois, punch-card-dominated states that, unlike Florida, were slow to join the rush from chads to scanners and DREs.

As Professor Krutz notes, in 2000 a higher percentage of voters cast ballots using punch cards in Illinois than in Florida. In Arizona, meanwhile, the urban counties used optical scanners, but ten of the state's fifteen counties, constituting 20 percent of its population, voted with punch cards.

The factors that influenced whether or not states reformed their own election laws after Florida 2000 but before the Help America Vote Act were, according to the work of political scientist Daniel Palazzolo, eightfold: "(1) the threat of a close election, (2) election law capacity, (3) state political culture, (4) partisan control, (5) the budgetary situation, (6) the influence of interest groups and election officials, (7) recommendations from special commissions, and (8) leadership."[49] States were likelier to enact their own reforms if, following this template, they had close elections, low election law capacity, a moralistic political reform culture, same-party control of the legislative and executive branches, slack budgets, interest groups and officials with reformist agendas, active commissions, and leaders who supported election reform.

213

And what if, as in the cases of Arizona and Illinois, states did not score terribly high on this checklist? Well, that's where the hammer of the federal government came down.

The punch-card counties of Arizona resisted state-level reform. Though outnumbered, they "were intense in their opposition" to a voting-machine switch, which they regarded as expensive and difficult to achieve.[50]

In Illinois, whose political history and climate are more, shall we say, mottled with ethical ambiguities than are those of Arizona, state officials largely denied the existence of any problems with punch cards, even though, as Professor Krutz points out, the state had an "undervote," or "residual vote," of 190,000 in 2000, or a relatively huge 3.9 percent of all votes cast.[51] But the state is closely contested, as Democrats and Republicans each have their strongholds, and to many of the cynical old (and young) hacks in the Land of Lincoln, any talk of "election reform" threatens the status quo, that is, their jobs. So gridlock held, and held fast.

Then along came HAVA.

In Arizona, a state legislature that had hewed to an "if it ain't broke, don't fix it" line on voting technologies changed its tune upon the enactment of the Help America Vote Act. Why? Because, as Krutz writes, "Arizona leaders clearly wanted to take advantage of federal funding ($51.7 million) and were also mindful of the prospective mandates in HAVA."[52] This is a case where both carrot and stick were used by the feds to bend recalcitrant states to their will. Here's the money and here's the whip, said Washington. But as New York found out, the money dries up eventually, leaving the states holding the bag but the feds still holding the whip.

Arizona fell in line. In the summer of 2003 it assented to HAVA. A statewide voter registration database was created, DREs were purchased for disabled voters, and, most importantly and expensively, the punch-card counties switched to optical scanners. (As Krutz remarks, Arizonans distrusted DREs, seeing in them a paper-trail-less nightmare with the potential for fraud and stolen elections.) By the 2004 election all was in place, just as Washington had commanded. The undervote (residual vote) dropped dramatically in the punch-card counties, from 3.8 percent in 2000 to 0.9 percent in the 2004.[53] Optical scanners proved again to be superior to the chad-dappled punch cards—though the underlying philosophical question of Who Decides? remained.

Illinois took more time to fold. It conducted the 2004 election without the oversight of HAVA, as about 7,000 of the state's 12,000 precincts gave voters punch cards on which to commit democratic acts. Still, the undervote (residual vote) dropped from 3.9 percent in 2000 to 1.4 percent in 2004, a decline Kurtz attributes to the state's greater use of optical scanners in the latter year. (He does note that the undervote fell even in the punch-card counties, from 4.3 percent to 3.6 percent, a change he ascribes to voter education measures.)

Illinois caved in, though it held out till 2006. Why the surrender? Kurtz explains that "the lure of $180 million was too great, even for a state with a strong tradition of local control. With mandates coming anyway in terms of election technology, it made little sense to say no to a 95 percent to 5 percent federal-to-state match."[54] This ostensible triumph of "reform," it should be noted, was signed into law by Governor Rod Blagojevich, who was impeached and removed from office by the state legislature in January 2009 for bribery and other acts of corruption. The memorably coiffed "Blago"—who reportedly insisted that an aide carry a hairbrush or comb at all times, in case his pile of hair needed a refresher—was sentenced to fourteen years in federal prison in December 2011. Governor Blago was, perhaps, not exactly the paladin of election reform that HAVA advocates had envisioned, but in politics as in cards, you play the hand you are dealt.

In Illinois, Arizona, and New York, "federal influence and financial incentives" were necessary to achieve the goals—most notably, the junking of mechanical lever machines and punch cards—embodied in the Help America Vote Act.[55]

****

There is a potential (mandated) postscript to the HAVA story. It involves efforts to require that all voting technologies produce a voter-verifiable paper record (VVPR). Many observers were and are troubled that electronic voting machines do not leave a paper record. They fear the possibility of manipulation, mischief, or malfunction. And so, on top of the HAVA mandate, they propose to mandate a verifiable paper trail for these (mandated) technologies.

While this campaign has split the bipartisan coalition that enacted the Help America Vote Act, it nevertheless owes HAVA an enormous debt. For that landmark legislation serves as precedent for those who would have the federal government mandate changes in voting methods at the state and local level. The principle has been established: the feds may use mandates, either gently or with hammer-like force, upon the states. The only question now is who wields the hammer, and for what purpose.

The VVPR push "represents a more coercive brand of federalism," in the judgment of Daniel Palazzolo, Meredith Patrick, and Doug Rubin of the University of Richmond and Vincent G. Moscardelli of the University of Connecticut, writing in *Publius*.[56]

And it may not even be necessary. Just as states such as Florida cleaned up their Election Day acts in the immediate wake of the 2000 spectacle, so have most states sought to guarantee a paper trail for their elections. Between 2003 and 2007, twenty-nine states enshrined VVPR in law. (New Hampshire and South Dakota already had such laws on the books.) At this writing, thirty-one states have adopted their own VVPR laws, without waiting for a dictate from Washington.

These states tend to be Democratic with professional legislatures and "moralistic political cultures," write Palazzolo, Patrick, Rubin, and Moscardelli.[57] Yet while Democrats are often found in the mandated VVPR camp, other elements of the HAVA coalition—disability rights activists, voting machine manufacturers, state and local election officials—stand in opposition. (Some Republicans support VVPR legislation, though they are a minority.)

The primary early VVPR vehicle was a bill introduced by New Jersey Democratic Congressman Rush Holt three months after the passage of the Help America Vote Act. Carrying the benign tag of the Voter Confidence and Increased Accessibility Act, Holt's legislation required that "all voting systems used for electing federal officeholders . . . produce a voter-verified paper record that could be used for a manual audit of votes cast in an election."[58] In other words, electronic voting machines would be required to leave an accompanying paper trail. This would be a mandate on top of another mandate—but for now, it has proved a mandate too far. Holt's bill, reintroduced in subsequent Congresses, attracted a high of 216 cosponsors in 2007–2008, yet it never came before the full House for a vote, nor is it likely to in the near future.

Holt's bill, and related measures, picked up partisan steam in the wake of the 2004 election. Some Democrats charged skullduggery against the Republicans, especially in Ohio. The claim was that DREs had been manipulated to favor the candidacy of George W. Bush against his Democratic opponent, Senator John Kerry. The evidence was not terribly compelling, although in an exceedingly unwise communication,

Walden O'Dell, CEO of the DRE manufacturer Diebold, wrote a letter in which he pledged himself "to helping Ohio deliver its electoral votes to the president."[59] One would think that voting-machine executives might at least pretend to neutrality. The House Judiciary Committee, chaired by Michigan Democrat John Conyers, looked into alleged irregularities in Ohio and elsewhere. Its report, *Preserving Democracy: What Went Wrong in Ohio*, found no irrefutable evidence that the Democrats had lost the election due to Republican voting-machine trickery. (The more plausible explanation was the nomination by the Democrats of a cold, aloof Massachusetts liberal, a kind of Michael Dukakis retread.) But the committee did claim to "have found numerous, serious election irregularities in the Ohio presidential election, which resulted in a significant disenfranchisement of voters."[60] Most of these had to do with provisional and absentee ballots, but there were also reports of electronic machine glitches. Ohio's twenty electoral votes were counted in the Bush column, however, giving the incumbent a 286–251 margin of victory in the Electoral College. Mr. O'Dell was right: Ohio's votes were delivered to his favored candidate.

Fueling the fire was a serious malfunction by DREs in the 2006 election in Florida's Thirteenth Congressional District—the seat occupied previously by former Florida secretary of state Katherine Harris, she of the no-more-pregnant-chads promise. Electronic voting machines failed to register 18,000 votes cast in mostly Democratic precincts in Sarasota County. The county's undervote/residual vote was a whopping 13 percent, or more than six times the undervote in the rest of the district. Something, clearly, was up—or down. The Republican candidate, Vern Buchanan, outpolled by 368 votes Democrat Christine Jennings. Buchanan took the seat. Understandably, Democrats blamed the DREs. Long-time civil rights activist Ralph Neas, president of the liberal interest group People for the American Way, went so far as to say in February 2007 that election reform "has to be the No. 1 domestic priority of the progressive movement."[61] His allies cried, "Remember Sarasota!" Not exactly "Remember the Alamo!" or even "Remember the Maine!" but then the only thing that died at Sarasota was Christine Jennings's political career. (Jennings challenged Vern Buchanan to a rematch in 2008, but won just 37 percent of the vote. The window of opportunity that had opened in the Democratic year of 2006 had closed by 2008.)

The anti-VVPR crowd cast doubts upon the sanity of the DRE skeptics, viewing many of them as "harebrained computer scientists and conspiracy theorists." Until, that is, "empirical studies" by such outfits

217

as the Government Accountability Office, the Brennan Center for Justice, and the National Institute for Standards and Technology (NIST) confirmed the suspicions of the DRE skeptics that the machines are neither failsafe nor entirely secure.[62]

The NIST report, whose draft was made public in November 2006, declared that electronic voting systems "cannot be made secure." The *Washington Post* dubbed this "the most sweeping condemnation of such voting systems by a federal agency," though in best left-hand-not-knowing-what-the-right-hand-is-doing fashion, this apparently leaky system was forced upon many states and localities by the same federal government of which the National Institute for Standards and Technology is a part.

NIST noted that "a single programmer could 'rig' a major election," which is one of those assertions that had theretofore given VVPR supporters a reputation as paranoid conspiracy-mongers. The Institute recommended optical scanners over DREs, but urged that if DREs are used in voting, those systems should provide a "paper summary of each ballot, which voters review and elections officials save for recounts."[63]

VVPR advocates argue that direct register electronic machines, which—along with optical scanners—were forced upon the states and localities when HAVA effectively outlawed punch cards and the much more reliable mechanical lever machines, are an electoral theft just waiting to happen. (Moreover, these machines have been known to freeze or otherwise malfunction.) Without a paper record of each vote cast, they assert, there is simply no way to verify the legitimacy of an election. The only thing keeping political fixers of either major party from stealing a DRE election would be a sense of honor. (You may stop snickering now.) As the quartet of Palazzolo, Patrick, Rubin, and Moscardelli write, "Advocates believe that enabling voters to examine a printed record before exiting the polling place and requiring election officials to use that record to audit a close election are essential safeguards of democracy."[64]

The self-appointed spokespersons for the disabled cried foul. They had succeeded in using HAVA to ensure independent voting by those with disabilities, yet a verified paper trail would require, for instance, that a sighted person assist a blind voter in verifying his or her ballot. "It takes away our right to a secret ballot," an official with the American Association of People With Disabilities told David Broder of the *Washington Post*.[65] Activists for the blind assert that sightless persons can vote most conveniently with DREs.

Mainstream opponents of a VVPR mandate—a mandate, it must be admitted, that is in a way a response to a previous mandate, HAVA—point to what they say are a multitude of problems and complications with the proposed "paper trail." For one thing, if electronic voting screens can freeze, as they sometimes do, so can the printers that produce paper trails.

State and local election officials, in particular, vocalized opposition to a VVPR mandate. Not because they cherish the DREs that, in many cases, the feds had forced upon them, but rather because Representative Holt's mandate was deemed hopelessly unworkable. The flaws in the mandate were manifold. Like all mandates, the VVPR bill emerged from a one-size-fits-all philosophy. South Dakota Secretary of State Chris Nelson criticized the "rigidity of the requirements."[66] Doug Lewis, director of the Election Center in Houston, Texas, told David Broder of the *Washington Post* that "I have no problem with the objective of creating paper receipts. But they have rejected every idea we've offered them to show what might work. I've been at this 40-some years, and I have not seen a piece of legislation worse than this. It is overly prescriptive, overly detailed, a cumbersome monstrosity to deal with."[67]

Sounds tailor-made for the Bush-Obama era!

The absurdity of the debate was captured by Chris Frates, reporting in *Politico*: The Help America Vote Act of 2002 "foisted electronic voting machines on local election officials who didn't want them anyway. When the machines had problems, the officials were forced to defend them. Now . . . they could be required to throw away many of the recently purchased machines and buy new ones."[68]

And then there was the not so small matter of funding. It was, to put it mildly, insufficient. Under the bill, Washington was demanding a paper trail stretching throughout all fifty states, yet it was unwilling to underwrite that paper trail. The center commands; the provinces obey. And pay.

Representative Zoe Lofgren (D-CA), a cosponsor of the legislation, estimated that the total cost of implementation would be somewhere between $300 million and $1 billion. In response to the charge of "unfunded mandate," Lungren and Holt agreed to jack up the federal subsidy to the latter figure. But Doug Lewis of the National Association of Election Officials countered that it would cost at least $3–4 billion, and besides, in the formulation of Palazzolo et al., "the technology required to meet the standards set by Holt's bill had not even been invented."

The battle over a federal VVPR law is a study in how a mandate is defeated. In this case, the states and localities, so often docile and tractable in the face of federal demands, fought back. Mobilized through the National Association of Counties and the National Conference of State Legislatures, they succeeded in keeping a bill with 216 cosponsors—just two congressmen shy of a majority of the US House of Representatives—off the floor. The two abovementioned organizations, along with the National Governors Association; National Association of Secretaries of State; Council of State Governments; National League of Cities; US Conference of Mayors; National Association of Towns and Townships; National Association of Election Officials; National Association of County Recorders, Election Officials, and Clerks; and the International Association of Clerks, Recorders, Election Officials, and Treasurers sent a joint letter to Speaker of the House Nancy Pelosi (D-CA) and House Majority Leader Steny Hoyer (D-MD) protesting that the bill would create "an unfunded mandate of unknown proportions."[69]

They added that even "if the requirements of this legislation were realistic within the specified deadline, state and local governments are understandably skeptical of promises of federal funding for a new, multi-billion-dollar federal mandate for additional election technology and practices."[70]

The mandaters had made a serious mistake in not courting—or even talking to—state election officials. As Kay Stimson, speaking to *Politico* on behalf of the National Association of Secretaries of State, said, "There's a feeling among people who oppose it that they were completely shut out of the process. They weren't consulted when the bill was written; they . . . have the general feeling that they were treated with disdain by Representative Holt and his staff."[71]

The fierce resistance succeeded. Whereas HAVA rolled over its scattered opposition, a mandated VVPR stalled. Federalism prevailed, for once.

Thirty-one states have enacted versions of VVPR, tailored to their own localized circumstances and with the participation of their state and local election officials. Federalism works; the Holt bill was not only unwieldy, in the view of most observers, but it was also unnecessary. Palazzolo et al. note the partisan tinge to the debate, though they remark that "Given the variety of Republican-sponsored election reform bills that did contain federal mandates, it is hard to determine if Republican opposition to the VVPR was motivated more by a principle of institutional federalism or by political convenience."[72]

From Ronald Reagan's imposition of a national twenty-one-year-old drinking age to the Bush administration's hard push for a national REAL ID, taken up in the next chapter, modern Republicans have shown virtually no principled adherence to constitutional federalism. The party in power seeks to centralize power—period. But as VVPR shows, alternative bases of influence, especially at the state and local level, can serve as redoubts from which to assert the rights of states and localities against the federal leviathan.

Notes

1. Jonathan N. Wand, Kenneth W. Shotts, Jasjeet S. Sekhon, Walter R. Mebane Jr., Michael C. Herron, and Henry E. Brady, "The Butterfly Did It: The Aberrant Vote for Buchanan in Palm Beach County, Florida," *American Political Science Review* (Vol. 95, No. 4, December 2001): 794.
2. Ibid.: 799, 793.
3. Ibid.: 803, 793.
4. Ibid.: 795.
5. Stephen Ansolabehere and Charles Stewart III, "Residual Votes Attributable to Technology," *Journal of Politics* (Vol. 67, No. 2, May 2005): 374.
6. Ibid.: 366.
7. Kevin J. Coleman and Eric A. Fischer, "The Help America Vote Act and Elections Reform: Overview and Issues," Congressional Research Service, January 13, 2011, p. 2.
8. Ronnie Dugger, "Annals of Democracy: Counting Votes," *The New Yorker*, November 7, 1988.
9. Ibid.
10. Ibid.
11. Ansolabehere and Stewart, "Residual Votes Attributable to Technology": 373.
12. Ibid.: 372–73.
13. Ibid.: 365.
14. Ibid.: 366, 378.
15. Ibid.: 385.
16. Dugger, "Annals of Democracy: Counting Votes."
17. Ibid.
18. *New State Ice Co. v. Liebmann* 285 U.S. 262 (1932).
19. Ansolabehere and Stewart, "Residual Votes Attributable to Technology": 376.
20. P.L. 107-252. Sarah F. Liebschutz and Daniel J. Palazzolo, "HAVA and the States," *Publius* (Vol. 35, No. 4, 2005): 506.
21. Ibid.: 499.
22. Charles Stewart III, "What Hath HAVA Wrought? Consequences, Intended and Not, of the Post-*Bush v. Gore* Reforms," VTP Working Paper No. 102, April 7, 2011, p. 3.
23. "Another election mess in Florida," *The Economist*, December 7, 2006.
24. Susan A. MacManus, "Goodbye Chads, Butterfly Ballots, Overvotes, & Recount Ruckuses!" May 29, 2003, Electionline.org.

25. "Tony Masilotti Reports to Serve 5-Year Prison Sentence," August 13, 2007, www.wpbf.com.
26. Susan A. MacManus, "Voter Education: The Key to Election Reform; Success Lessons from Florida," *University of Michigan Journal of Law Reform* (Vol. 30, No. 3, Spring 2003): 519–20.
27. Susan A. MacManus, "Implementing HAVA's Voter Education Requirement: A Crisis and a Federal Mandate Improve State-Local Cooperation in Florida," *Publius* (Vol. 35, No. 4, 2005): 541.
28. National Association of Secretaries of State Election Reform Resolution, February 6, 2001, www.nass.org/pubs.
29. Stewart, "What Hath HAVA Wrought? Consequences, Intended and Not, of the Post-*Bush v. Gore* Reforms," p. 4.
30. Ibid., p. 11.
31. Liebschutz and Palazzolo, "HAVA and the States": 501.
32. Stewart, "What Hath HAVA Wrought? Consequences, Intended and Not, of the Post-*Bush v. Gore* Reforms," p. 18.
33. Ibid., p. 16.
34. Ibid., pp. 29, 31.
35. Ibid., p. 24. "Election administration in Wisconsin is handled at the municipal level. Prior to the Help America Vote Act's statewide registration database requirement, municipalities with fewer than 5,000 people did not have to require voter registration." Michael J. Hanmer, *Discount Voting: Voter Registration Reforms and Their Effects* (New York: Cambridge University Press, 2009), p. 63 fn. 11. As with No Child Left Behind, the beleaguered states almost immediately applied for waivers from various HAVA mandates. While the act set a deadline of January 1, 2004, for the building of statewide voter registration databases, a whopping forty states asked for extensions. By 2006, a dozen states still lacked such databases, and by 2008, as Kim Zetter reported in *Wired*, many statewide lists were "plagued by missed deadlines, rushed production schedules, cost overruns, security problems, and design and reliability issues." Kim Zetter, "Voter Database Glitches Could Disenfranchise Thousands," *Wired*, September 17, 2008, www.wired.com.
36. Coleman and Fischer, "The Help America Vote Act and Elections Reform: Overview and Issues," pp. 6–8; Doug Chapin, "Not Dead Yet: President's FY '13 Budget Has (Reduced) Funds for EAC," February 15, 2012, http://blog.lib.umn.edu/cspg/electionacademy/2012/02/not_dead_yet_presidents_fy13_b.php.
37. Stewart, "What Hath HAVA Wrought? Consequences, Intended and Not, of the Post-*Bush v. Gore* Reforms," p. 1.
38. Ibid., pp. 36–37.
39. Coleman and Fischer, "The Help America Vote Act and Elections Reform: Overview and Issues," p. 2.
40. Stewart, "What Hath HAVA Wrought? Consequences, Intended and Not, of the Post-*Bush v. Gore* Reforms," p. 21.
41. "Republicans Carry Lockport," *New York Times*, April 12, 1892.
42. Sarah F. Liebschutz, "The Implementation of HAVA in New York: From Antiques to High Tech," *Publius* (Vol. 35, No. 4, 2005): 597.
43. Ibid.: 599.
44. Ibid.: 600.
45. Ibid.: 605.

46. Ibid.: 607.
47. Ibid.: 611, 614.
48. Teresa Hommel and Ellen Theisen, "Lever Replacement Costs: New York City Case Study," July 20, 2009, www.votersunite.org.
49. Glen S. Krutz, "The Effect of HAVA on Late-to-Innovate States: External Influence on Election Reform in Arizona and Illinois," *Publius* (Vol. 35, No. 4, 2005): 586, 583.
50. Ibid.: 587.
51. Ibid.: 588.
52. Ibid.: 590.
53. Ibid.: 592.
54. Ibid.: 592–93.
55. Ibid.: 594.
56. Daniel Palazzolo, Vincent G. Moscardelli, Meredith Patrick, and Doug Rubin, "Election Reform after HAVA: Voter Verification in Congress and the States," *Publius* (Vol. 38, No. 3, 2008): 515.
57. Ibid.: 516.
58. Ibid.: 517.
59. Ibid.: 519.
60. *Preserving Democracy: What Went Wrong in Ohio*, Report of the House Judiciary Committee Democratic Staff, January 5, 2005, p. 4.
61. Brian Friel, "Remember Sarasota," *National Journal* (Vol. 39, No. 8, February 24, 2007): 44.
62. Palazzolo, Moscardelli, Patrick, and Rubin, "Election Reform after HAVA: Voter Verification in Congress and the States": 520.
63. Cameron W. Barr, "Security of Electronic Voting Is Condemned," *Washington Post*, December 1, 2006.
64. Palazzolo, Moscardelli, Patrick, and Rubin, "Election Reform after HAVA: Voter Verification in Congress and the States": 521.
65. David S. Broder, "A Paper Trail toward Chaos?" *Washington Post*, May 13, 2007.
66. Palazzolo, Moscardelli, Patrick, and Rubin, "Election Reform after HAVA: Voter Verification in Congress and the States": 522.
67. Broder, "A Paper Trail toward Chaos?"
68. Chris Frates, "Local officials take on voting rights groups," *Politico*, May 22, 2007, www.politico.com.
69. Palazzolo, Moscardelli, Patrick, and Rubin, "Election Reform after HAVA: Voter Verification in Congress and the States": 523.
70. Broder, "A Paper Trail toward Chaos?"
71. Frates, "Local officials take on voting rights groups."
72. Palazzolo, Moscardelli, Patrick, and Rubin, "Election Reform after HAVA: Voter Verification in Congress and the States": 531.

8

REAL ID:
The States Fight Back

Throughout the Cold War, Americans, even their politicians, proudly pointed to the lack of a US ID card as a palpable, even poignant difference between the free world and the communist bloc. While they—the morose East Germans, the oppressed Czechs, the grim Russians—had to produce such symbols of subservience anytime a sneering bureaucrat demanded, "Papers, please," we in America were, as a birthright, able to travel, work, even just skylark where we pleased, when we pleased. To borrow from John Huston's film *The Treasure of Sierra Madre*, we didn't need no stinking papers, man.

Indeed, one of the stories Ronald Reagan's champions like to tell is of a Cabinet meeting when the subject of a national ID card was raised by Attorney General William French Smith, who was ostensibly seeking ways to curb the hiring of illegal immigrants. This was, in a way, the perfect end run around civil libertarian concerns about a national ID. Illegal immigrants are, after all, in the country illegally, and discovering that illegality would be considered by most Americans to be a legitimate act of government. But the means of discovering that illegality would have trampled upon the most basic rights of Americans, and introduced an Orwellian instrument that undermined the very liberty the Reagan administration was committed—rhetorically, at least—to protecting.

The tale of the national ID card that wasn't was related most memorably by Martin Anderson, Reagan's domestic policy chief, in his memoir *Revolution: The Reagan Legacy* (1988).

Attorney General William French Smith was the chairman of the administration's Task Force on Immigration and Refugee Policy. The task force presented its recommendations to President Reagan and the Cabinet on July 16, 1981. Among these recommendations was the issuance by the federal government of a national identity card, which, as Anderson writes, was "similar to the internal passports used by the

Soviet Union."[1] This card was to be forced upon every citizen of the United States: it was mandatory. Should it come to be, American citizens, like subjects of the Soviet bloc, would be required to show their ID card whenever government officials demanded, "Papers, please."

In Martin Anderson's telling, Attorney General Smith smoothly and persuasively made the case for a national ID card as a necessary means of controlling illegal immigration in the Southwest. If all US citizens had such a counterfeit-proof card and were required to present it to potential employers, then those in this country illegally would be unemployable.

No Cabinet officers challenged Smith. Anderson, aware that he was breaking the unwritten rule that barred non-Cabinet officials from speaking at these meetings unless spoken to, nevertheless spoke up. "I reasoned that I did not want to be part of an administration that foisted a national identity card on Americans, especially when most of the Cabinet seemed to be quite unaware of what they were doing."[2]

Hey, he figured; what's the worst that could happen? If Anderson were fired for overstepping his bounds, he'd pack up and return to California, which is not exactly Siberia. He raised his hand "directly over the back of the attorney general's head."

Reagan called on him. All eyes—some of them betraying hostility—were focused on him. Anderson began, "Mr. President, one of my concerns about the national identity card is that the Office of Management and Budget has estimated that it could cost several billions of dollars to produce a counterfeit-proof social security card for everyone."

No one so much as blinked an eye at that remark. Several billions of dollars? Heck, the Reagan administration spent that much in its sleep. Mere dollars and cents arguments weren't going to make a whit of difference, especially to an administration that was running up record deficits. But Martin Anderson had an ace up his sleeve.

"I would like to suggest another way that I think is a lot better," he continued. "It's a lot cheaper. It can't be counterfeited. It's very lightweight, and impossible to lose. It's even waterproof. All we have to do is tattoo an identification number on the inside of everyone's arm."

There were gasps and then a long silence, says Anderson. Finally James Watt, the interior secretary, spoke up, "Why, it sounds to me that you are talking about the mark of the Beast. That's terrible." The reference was to the Book of Revelation, specifically 13:16–18:

> And he causeth all, both small and great, rich and poor, free and bond, to receive a mark in their right hand, or in their foreheads: And that no

> man might buy or sell, save that he had the mark, or the name of the beast, or the number of his name. Here is wisdom. Let him that hath understanding count the number of the beast: for it is the number of a man; and his number is Six hundred threescore and six.

Before Attorney General Smith could rebut Anderson and shift the conversation away from end times and the implications of the number 666, President Reagan spoke up, "Maybe we should just brand all the babies."[3]

Laughter filled the room, says Anderson, "and that was the end of the national identification card for 1981." We were saved from "papers, please" by the unlikely combination of a quick-witted libertarian aide and a president who knew his Bible.

The matter of a national ID sunk out of sight for a couple of decades after Reagan's "mark of the beast" put-down. Members of Congress, most notably Representative Bill McCollum (R-FL), occasionally proposed "tamper-proof" Social Security cards, complete with photo, which they obviously envisioned as *de facto* national IDs, but there is perhaps enough historical memory in the Social Security Administration to keep these nine-digit numbers from entirely fulfilling that role.

Social Security numbers were first issued in late November 1936 by local post offices, as there were not yet the Social Security field offices that eventually came to cover the county like zits on a teenager's face. Although the first Social Security record was established for a Westchester County, New York, factory owner's son named John David Sweeney Jr., the lowest number—001-01-0001—was offered, in best New Deal fashion, to a political operative: former New Hampshire governor and then Social Security board chairman John G. Winant. Ex-governor Winant graciously declined the honor—or "honor"—and so the card with the lowest possible combination of numbers was issued instead to Grace D. Owen of Concord, New Hampshire.[4]

Here are two other pioneers for the trivia file: The first American to receive a benefit from Social Security was a man named Ernest Ackerman, who in January 1937 had bestowed upon him a one-time lump sum payment of 17 cents. He likely spent it all in one place. The first American to receive regular benefits was Ida May Fuller of Ludlow, Vermont. To date, over 450 million Social Security numbers have been issued. Approximately five and a half million new numbers are doled out every year, and the Social Security Administration assures us—in case anyone is worried—that no numbers will need to be repeated for several generations.[5] So your number is your own—cold comfort, to be sure, except to eccentric numerologists.

Despite the Social Security number's alleged nonstatus as a national ID, it is used by law enforcement, credit and insurance companies, banks, and state and local as well as federal government agencies as a verifier of identification. It is, seemingly, an inescapable piece of modern American life. But it is not a national ID card, or so the federal government has insisted throughout the years. Which is why politicians who dream of an easier way to track the legal and financial movements of US citizens have sought to come up with a more comprehensive means of keeping tabs on Americans. And that is where REAL ID, which ranks with—maybe even outranks—No Child Left Behind as the most controversial federal mandate of the new millennium, comes in. As Montana American Civil Liberties Union director Scott Crichton says, the Social Security number "was sold as just being used for one purpose, and today it's used for everything. You can't even get some services without divulging it. The REAL ID is that sort of thing, cubed."[6]

REAL ID uses the driver's license, that most common of state-issued documents, as the entering wedge of a national ID. Although driver's licenses are often used to verify a person's identity in manifold ways, their only official use is as proof that an individual is qualified to operate a motor vehicle. The issuance of these licenses has always been wholly and entirely a state matter. Before REAL ID, the feds had occasionally tried to interfere with these licenses, but resistance from the states had proved formidable. For instance, the Illegal Immigration and Immigrant Responsibility Act of 1996 required states to demand of licensees their Social Security number, which the states would then verify and, if they so choose, include on the driver's license. As the Congressional Research Service notes, foes charged that this "could be construed as a step toward a national identification card system."[7] The provision was thereafter repealed.

Like so many surveillance schemes, REAL ID was born, or at least given a serious boost, by the terrible events of September 11, 2001. Eighteen of the nineteen hijackers who seized and crashed the airliners of 9/11 had a form of fake ID, including driver's licenses. Muhammed Atta, for instance, who was one of the murderous hijackers, had obtained a six-year Florida driver's license even though he was in the country on just a six-month visa.

In the frantic and panicked weeks that followed, the homely driver's license was saddled with a new and ominous tag: it was a "breeder document." A piece of paper that, in the wrong hands, could beget all sorts of mischief, up to and including a horrific terrorist attack. The 9/11 Commission, officially known as the National Commission on Terrorist Attacks Upon the United States, released a much-hyped report in July 2004. It included this recommendation:

> Secure identification should begin in the United States. The federal government should set standards for the issuance of birth certificates and sources of identification, such as drivers' licenses. Fraud in identification documents is no longer just a problem of theft. At many entry points to vulnerable facilities, including gates for boarding aircraft, sources of identification are the last opportunity to ensure that people are who they say they are and to check whether they are terrorists.[8]

Congress, in no mood to carp and cavil at recommendations that were said to help prevent terrorist attacks, adopted many of the commission's recommendations as part of the Intelligence Reform and Terrorist Prevention Act (IRTPA) of 2004. (Imagine the courage it would take for a mere member of Congress to vote against a "terrorist prevention" act! The Senate approved it by 96–2; the House by 336–75.)

IRTPA authorized the secretary of transportation to demand of the fifty states that in order for their drivers' licenses to be accepted by a federal agency, they must be tamper-proof (or as tamper-proof as current technology permits) and include name, date of birth, gender, driver's license number, digital photograph, address, and signature. But IRTPA, while encroaching upon this traditional bailiwick of the states, made some allowance for state variations. The feds could not require a uniform design, had to protect the privacy of licensees, and were barred from dictating to a state "the categories of individuals that were eligible to obtain a driver's license or personal identification cards," that is, the states were to determine the eligibility of aliens, legal and otherwise, to obtain licenses.[9]

The federal government was trespassing upon state territory here. But this was not enough—not nearly enough—for the scaremongers of the national security state. The REAL ID Act was to repeal those provisions of IRTPA with which it conflicted. And so we were served REAL ID—as though the hundreds of millions of driver's licenses the states had been issuing since New York pioneered this piece of paperwork in 1910 were fake.

The next step was obvious. As Representative Mary Bono (R-CA), widow of Cher's foil, said, "When we consider ourselves to be at war, people are going to have to recognize that some of their freedoms are going to be gone. Whether we are talking about national ID cards I don't know, or fingerprinting everybody."[10] If Sonny were alive he'd have probably gone straight back to Cher.

The next step, as it turned out, was REAL ID.

****

However noxious, the idea of a national ID card had a powerful champion: Representative James Sensenbrenner, a Wisconsin Republican and chairman of the House Judiciary Committee. Sensenbrenner is famous for being rude, for taking advantage of more privately funded travel than any other member of Congress, and for deriving his fortune from Kimberly-Clark's Kotex feminine hygiene products. (Frank J. Sensenbrenner, great-grandfather of the notoriously thin-skinned Representative Sensenbrenner, began at Kimberly-Clark in 1889 as a bookkeeper and rose to eventually become president and CEO. It was on his watch that Kimberly-Clark began marketing Kotex in 1920. This was a revolutionary product, and one that encountered a good deal of resistance in the marketplace, but Kimberly-Clark's persistence paid off. Like a later Kimberly-Clark product, Kleenex, Kotex became a brand name that doubled as shorthand for an entire market segment.)[11]

Like many heirs to industrial fortunes, the congressman prefers not to think about how he came to be so wealthy. It is said that nothing angers him quite so much as being called "Tex."

With his introduction on January 26, 2005, of H.R. 418, the REAL ID Act of 2005, he also became the most prominent foe of privacy in the US Congress. The provisions of IRTPA, heavy-handed and intrusive as they were, did not satisfy Representative Sensenbrenner. He wanted to take the issue to the next level—that is, to create not just a *de facto* national ID card but a *real national ID card*. Wisconsin has a long tradition of civil liberties–minded Republicans, from the defiers of the Fugitive Slave Act in the 1850s through the La Follette family dynasty of the early twentieth century and up through the limited-government rural Republicans of the modern era. But in pushing REAL ID, Tex Sensenbrenner was standing in a more disreputable Wisconsin Republican tradition: that of Senator Joe McCarthy, "Tailgunner Joe," the hunter of reds under every bed.

(In a bizarre side note, while many sources have chosen an all-caps orthography for REAL ID, its first four letters seem not to stand for anything. Scholars Priscilla M. Regan and Christopher J. Deering write that "no evidence was found to decipher this as an acronym."[12] Apparently its sponsors simply felt that their legislative baby was destined for greatness, for the kind of grandiosity that demands an acronym—like NATO, or TARP, or CETA, or any of the other four-letter un-words that promise national greatness, or at least a great national due bill.)

Sensenbrenner & Co. sought to achieve a national ID by practically nationalizing the state-issued card that almost every American adult has, and that most teenagers even yearn for: a driver's license. In a car-happy culture, this was an ingenious move.

Section 202 of Sensenbrenner's law stated that federal agencies "may not accept, for any official purpose, a driver's license or identification card issued by a State to any person unless the State is meeting the requirements of this section."[13]

This is not a direct order from the federal government, or a direct imposition of federal standards. But it may as well be. "Official purpose" is defined in the statute as including, but not limited to, "accessing Federal facilities, boarding federally regulated commercial aircraft, entering nuclear power plants, and any other purposes the Secretary [of Homeland Security] shall determine."[14]

Except for entering nuclear power plants, these are activities most Americans perform at some time in their lives, and many perform them regularly. And the catch-all at the end of the definition—"any other purposes the Secretary [of Homeland Security] shall determine"—is a virtual carte blanche for the security bureaucracy to further restrict the actions of those who live in recalcitrant states.

According to REAL ID, for the feds to accept a state-issued driver's license, that state must require from the applicant—and verify with the original issuing party—(1) a photo ID (or non-photo ID if it contains the person's legal name and date of birth); (2) a verifiable document with the date of birth; (3) proof of a Social Security number; and (4) a document containing the address of the individual's principal residence. These supersede the prior requirements for such licenses, which varied from state to state. In other words, so long driver's license federalism. Moreover, states must verify an applicant's legal status in the United States, which seems to forbid a state from granting driver's licenses to those who are in this country illegally. (At the time the final—or temporarily final—REAL ID regulations were issued in spring 2008, nine states granted driver's licenses to those who were in the country illegally. As this book goes to press, the number is down to three: New Mexico, Washington, and—in a weakened form—Utah.)

The REAL ID Act also dictates the acceptable forms of technology in the makeup of a driver's license. Each licensee must be photographed, or in the chillingly bureaucratic phrase, be subject to "a mandatory facial image capture."[15] (Ouch! That must hurt! Are Navy Seals involved?) Source documents must be captured in digital images, which must be retained by the states for ten years. Paper documents must be retained for seven years. The Paperwork Reduction Act of so long ago is a distant memory, it seems. States may not issue a license to an individual for a period of longer than eight years.

If a state is so reckless, so lost to outlawry, that it refuses to conform to the REAL ID demands, it must issue its licenses with a "unique color identifier."[16] This is part of the Department of Homeland Security's color-mania. Our country is constantly under some form of color-coded alert, though only a raging paranoid can tell you what the difference is between an orange and a brown alert. (Red alert, we all know, means head between knees and kiss your butt good-bye.)

The states are also required to give access to their ID databases to all their sister states and territories. This effective merging of all data has been roasted as an invitation to identity theft, and the DHS regulatory demand that states submit security plans with respect to their motor vehicle facilities has not allayed such concerns.

Almost as an afterthought, the REAL ID Act authorizes the Homeland Security Secretary to dole out grants to the states to assist them in jumping through this long series of bureaucratic hoops. The grants, it turns out, were meager, not nearly enough to cover the cost of compliance. But when the issue is "security," the mantra is the same as when some piece of legislation is said to be "for the children"—money, especially other people's money, is no object.

Among the staunchest critics of REAL ID was the indefatigable libertarian Republican congressman, Ron Paul of Texas. Representative Paul called the bill a "Trojan horse" that "pretends to offer desperately needed border control in order to con a credulous Congress into sacrificing more of our constitutionally protected liberty." While the measure's sponsors claimed that it would be voluntary, and that states could refuse to conform their driver's licenses to the national standards, "any state that opts out will automatically make non-persons out of its citizens," said Paul. They would be unable to fly, take a train, or enter a federal building. "In essence," said Paul, "in the eyes of the federal government they will cease to exist."

To forbid travel to those lacking the proper national ID, said Representative Paul, is the "hallmark of authoritarian states, not free republics." The whole measure smacks of a "police state," charged Paul, and "should be denounced as authoritarian and anti-American."[17]

It was not, of course. Instead, it passed both houses of Congress easily. It even attracted the support of one of Representative Paul's semi-libertarian Republican brethren: Representative Dana Rohrabacher of California, who in the 1960s was a fire-breathing crusader for liberty. Rohrabacher even refused to consider amendments or the revisiting of the matter. "The bill will not be opened up," he insisted, responding to complaints from state legislators. And disobedience to the federal master will not be tolerated. "Any state that's opting out is opting out in doing their part in solving these national challenges, and I don't have any sympathy for them."[18] Spoken like a true convert to the religion of homeland security.

Passage did require a sly legislative trick. Representative Sensenbrenner's original bill, H.R. 418, passed the House on February 10, 2005, by a vote of 261–161. The yeas and nays split along party lines, with Republicans approving the Judiciary Committee chairman's bill by 219–8 (those eight led by Ron Paul) and the Democrats opposing passage by 152–42. The lone Independent also voted no. But the bill bogged down in the Senate, as even Senator Joe Lieberman (D-CT), the most fervent supporter of anti-terrorism measures—to the point that civil libertarians regarded him as the single most anti-libertarian member of the Senate—criticized the proposal for repealing relevant sections of IRTPA and "impos[ing] on state governments unworkable standards for driver's licenses."[19]

Seeing that REAL ID was mired in legislative quicksand, Sensenbrenner called an audible. Thanks to the Republican leadership in the House, his REAL ID proposal was tacked on to the Emergency Supplemental Appropriations Act for Defense, the Global War on Terror, and Tsunami Relief. The passage of this omnibus bill was a foregone conclusion. Defense bills always pass, as does anything advertised as advancing the "global war on terror." The tsunami relief reference was to the catastrophic Indian Ocean earthquake-spurred tsunami that killed over 200,000 people. As for the Global War on Terror, that referred to the US actions in Iraq and Afghanistan. To vote against this supplemental appropriations bill was to fail to "support the troops," as the cliché had it.

And it was to be insensitive to the suffering of tsunami victims. Who on earth could possibly be in favor of a tsunami? The deck was stacked.

The House approved the emergency supplemental appropriations bill on May 5, 2005, by a vote of 368–58. Those 58 nays were almost all Democratic votes (54), along with 3 Republicans (Paul and Duncan of Tennessee and Coble of North Carolina) and the sole Independent. The Senate then adopted the measure by unanimous vote. REAL ID was set loose upon the land.

Remarkably for such a dramatic step in American privacy policy, Representative Sensenbrenner's REAL ID bill was never the subject of a single congressional hearing, either in the Senate of the House of Representatives. Not one. This makes a mockery of the legislative process, and of the concept of "deliberation." The only deliberate thing about REAL ID was the deliberate contempt Representative Sensenbrenner and his allies showed for traditional American liberties, the rights of the states as protected by the Tenth Amendment, and the Founders' conception of how a bill becomes a law.

The unfunded mandate aspect of REAL ID didn't much concern Tex Sensenbrenner either. Early estimates of the cost of compliance were $100 million—in total, for all fifty states and the District of Columbia combined. As we shall see, this was a ludicrous underestimate. But then when "homeland security" is involved, economic issues fly out the window.

Security is a fig leaf behind which all manner of official mischief can hide. Michael Chertoff, the Secretary of that enormous boondoggle known as the Department of Homeland Security, deftly laid the responsibility for this proposed national ID card not on a power-hungry and aggrandizing federal government but upon Joe and Jane Doe. "The American public's desire for greater identity protection is undeniable," he said, peremptorily. (Who is he to say what opinions are "undeniable"?) REAL ID, argued Chertoff, "will bring some peace of mind to citizens wanting to protect their identity from theft by a criminal or illegal alien."[20] Not to mention—though he almost never failed to mention it—hijackers of the 9/11 variety, who had, he asserted, used 364 aliases and 30 driver's licenses.

The law had "an unmistakable immigration subtext," Shawn Zeller of *Congressional Quarterly* noted at the time of passage.[21] Certainly one of the targets of its authors was illegal immigration. Curbing such had been the ostensible aim of earlier proposals for tamper-proof Social Security cards, too. And interest groups such as the National

Immigration Law Center and the National Council of La Raza opposed REAL ID on the grounds that it was a hardship for immigrants, legal and otherwise.

Yet as Jim Harper of the Cato Institute, author of *Identity Crisis: How Identification is Overused and Misunderstood*, asked, "should law-abiding American citizens really have to carry a national ID to get at illegal immigrants? Just who is the criminal here?"[22] This was the point Ronald Reagan and Martin Anderson were getting at twenty years earlier: Why not just tattoo American citizens? As Harper remarks, enacting REAL ID to catch illegal immigrants and terrorists "would be about as effective . . . as a chainsaw would be at killing flies."[23]

As for the illegals, only the most naïve believer in the omnipotence of the surveillance state would think that they would be unable to use "forgery, fraud, and corruption" to get around the REAL ID obstacle course.[24]

And let's face it. Although the act included other immigration-related provisions (notably changes in asylum and deportation laws and completion of a US-Mexico border fence in San Diego), the heart of REAL ID was the federal mandate regarding state-issued driver's licenses.

The states—or at least some of them—were not fooled. They rose in great roaring opposition to REAL ID as both an unfunded mandate and prelude to a police state. In the Cato Institute's Jim Harper's words, REAL ID was "an unfunded mandate . . . to build a federal surveillance infrastructure."[25] The states were being forced to erect a potentially Orwellian system—and they had to pay for the dubious privilege.

By late 2007, this federal mandate whose cost to the states had been estimated at anywhere from $11 billion to $14.6 billion (and this doesn't begin to cover the cost to American liberties) had been funded by the federal government to the pathetic tune of $38.3 million. In July 2007, an effort in the US Senate to boost by $300 million federal assistance to the states for the purpose of complying with REAL ID failed by a vote of 50–44. The amendment to the Department of Homeland Security appropriations bill was offered by Senator Lamar Alexander (R-TN), something of a REAL ID critic, who nevertheless opined that "insofar as REAL ID goes, we should either fund it or repeal it."[26] Not bad advice. But the Congress, never an institution known for taking good advice, did neither. It would not fund REAL ID, nor would it cease mandating REAL ID. It took the coward's way out—the unfunded mandate. (As a sop, the appropriation to the states to cover REAL ID costs was boosted to a puny $79 million in June 2008.)

The ACLU called the Alexander amendment "sucker money." (The ACLU also called the "unfunded mandate . . . no more than a tax increase in disguise.") The sucker money was just enough to make it seem as if the feds were helping to fund the mandate, yet it was the merest fraction, the tiniest drop in the bucket, of the monies needed to actually implement REAL ID. Speaking with an abundance of hope, perhaps in the wish-is-father-to-the-thought category, ACLU Legislative Counsel Tim Sparapani said, "REAL ID is dead in the water, and it is clear that no amount of money can save it. The only solution to REAL ID is to scrap it and replace it: $300 million does not even come close to covering the costs of the program, and it is not enough to lure Americans to give up their privacy."[27] It would be nice to report that Mr. Sparapani was right on the money, and that REAL ID died a quick death. But the story was not yet over.

****

After 9/11, Larry Ellison, the lightning-rod CEO of Oracle, became the most public nongovernmental advocate of a national ID when he offered—gratis—the federal government the software with which it might compile the database for such an identifier. The American suspicion of government tyranny, he told his employees, had "made it impossible for the government to protect us."[28] "We need a national ID card with our photograph and thumbprint digitized and embedded in the ID card," he declared.[29] Ellison speculated in the pages of the *Wall Street Journal*: "The government could phase in digital ID cards to replace existing Social Security cards and driver's licenses. These new IDs should be based on a uniform standard such as credit card technology, which is harder to counterfeit than existing government IDs."[30]

Ellison was roasted for his suggestion by the dwindling band of privacy and civil liberties defenders—a band that had *really* dwindled in the weeks after 9/11. The Electronic Privacy Information Center (EPIC) printed "Larry Cards," which were handed out to attendees at a privacy conclave. At that EPIC gathering, which was tagged "Security or Surveillance: Technology's Impact After 9/11," Robert Ellis Smith, editor of *Privacy Journal*, warned that even if the progenitors of national ID cards promise that the information they contain will be limited to the bare facts, inevitably their scope will expand. Name, date of birth, address, Social Security number, height, weight, and eye color are only the beginning of the profile.[31] Can anyone seriously believe that if the government has the authority and the power to include biometric data on such licenses—retina scans, hand and fingerprint scans, voice recognition, DNA information, even handwriting and facial recognition—that it will refrain from doing so? The "common machine-readable technology" mandated for these IDs may even include Radio Frequency Identification Chips (RFID), currently used in passports, and which "can be read and tracked from a distance without a subject's knowledge."[32] Your movements, travels, your purchases, your tastes in books and foods and entertainment: hope you don't mind sharing these with Big Brother. The whole shebang promises to be a tyrant's—and a paranoiac's—paradise. Liberty lovers objected, without too much hyperbole, to this "Soviet-style internal passport."[33]

Biometric information has become common as a means of identification within the US military. Businesses, too, have found it to be a sometimes cost-effective method of security, as it permits one to dispense with the expense of security guards. Banks, airlines, credit card companies, and casinos are making use of biometric. Even computers use fingerprint scanners "as a solution for those users who are having a difficult time remembering all of their Internet passwords."[34] Some find the spread of biometric technology in routine business transactions to be portentous and menacing; others welcome it as an efficient means of facilitating exchanges that require a certain degree of security. But when government starts using biometrics, "efficient" takes on a whole new meaning.

Larry Ellison's brazen gambit failed—at first. Even in the midst of the Patriot Act and the Iraq War and the general paranoia about another terrorist attack, few Americans were demanding that they be forced to carry government ID cards. These cards would inevitably become "domestic passports," as Adam D. Thierer argued under the aegis of the libertarian Cato Institute. *Your papers, citizen,* could become a common refrain in everyday life. As Representative Tom Campbell, a California Republican, said, "If you have an ID card, it is solely for the purpose of allowing the government to compel you to produce it. This would essentially give the government the power to demand that we show our papers. It is a very dangerous thing." Thierer concluded, "If federal policymakers begin requiring that all Americans carry a national ID card, it could constitute one of the most significant increases in government power in our nation's history."[35] This is one innovation that runs completely against the grain of the American spirit.

A national ID would be no incremental reform, no footnote in the long volume that is American history. It would be a massive change—a profound shift in the relationship of Americans with their federal government. As identity politics expert Jim Harper explained in testimony to the New Economy and Quality of Life Committee of the Michigan House of Representatives, a national ID card "is not just another in a series of small steps. It would promote tracking and data collection about all citizens."[36] It would be a major landmark in the long road from freedom to something other than freedom: collectivism, paternalism, totalitarianism, or whatever one's ideological predilections lead one to believe.

A certain species of progressive likes to chide the United States for not having adopted dubious reforms that many other nations have saddled their populaces with. National health care; the metric system; conscription—the list usually has a coercive tinge, and gives off the odor of collectivism. A national ID occupies a prominent place on any such census. Most Europeans (Albania, Belgium, Bulgaria, Estonia, France, Germany, Greece, Portugal, Romania, Slovakia, Spain, and others) carry national ID cards, as do the people of Egypt, Gambia, Cyprus, South Africa, Sri Lanka, Bangladesh, Zimbabwe, Indonesia, Hong Kong, Malaysia, Singapore, Israel, India, Thailand, and many more. The list is long and contains countries with varying degrees of freedom. The list has never contained the United States of America, and in fact the Founders of this country would have taken their guns off their mantels had any administration tried to impose a national ID on the men and women of the land of the free and the home of the brave. Traditionally, Americans did not care if every other country in the world forced its subjects to carry proof of identity and produce it every time a police officer or government functionary or civic bully demanded to see it. Such a practice was anathema to Americans—at least until fanatical hijackers crashed three planes into the World Trade Center and the Pentagon, and with that homicidal act seemed to alter, at least among opinion shapers, the very idea of what it meant to be an American.

In the pre-9/11 America, a national ID card was okay for Albanians or Zimbabweans. But Americans? No way!

Not that there were no elite champions of the idea. The *New York Times*, even in the best of times no good friend of personal liberty, editorialized in 2004 that we needed a "serious discussion of how to create a workable national identification system without infringing on the constitutional rights of Americans."[37] That qualification at the end was about as meaningful as saying that one wished to square a circle without depriving it of its qualities as a circle. Sorry, *Times* editorialists, but *it can't be done!* A national ID system is to constitutional rights as an earthquake is to the building that stands upon its epicenter: destruction is the only possible result.

Among the uses to which a REAL ID could be put are the registration and tracking of firearms, employment, movement, the receipt of various government benefits: the list is as endless as the imagination of a bureaucrat. (Well, scratch that. The list is as endless as the ambitions of a power-seeking politico who wishes to change the world.)

And can anyone doubt that forgers and counterfeiters will set their minds to creating fake IDS, whether for traditional reasons—getting underage kids into bars—or more nefarious purposes? As Bruce Schneier, author of *Beyond Fear: Thinking Sensibly about Security in an Uncertain World*, says, "The first problem is the card itself. No matter how unforgeable we make it, it will be forged. We can raise the price of forgery, but we can't make it impossible. REAL IDs will be forged."[38]

"It will not be contained to the purposes for which it was created," adds Robert Smith Ellis.[39] This is a safe bet, and it is why those who cherish traditional American liberties dug in for a long—even epic—fight against the national ID card, which is potentially the most dangerous of federal mandates.

It should be noted that DHS, in its discussion of the federal regulation covering REAL ID, made the cursory declaration that the department "does not intend that REAL ID documents become a *de facto* national ID and does not support the creation of a national ID." It also assures us that the Department of Homeland Security "does not intend to own or operate a database on all driver's license and identification card holders."[40]

Whew. *That's* a relief! Surely we can trust our government to never abuse or misuse the powers it has been granted. Sure, the REAL ID Act in effect creates a nationwide database of all drivers, which is to say virtually all adults. And as sure as the sun rises in the east, there will be weak links in the chain of states in this database. And as sure as it sets in the west, some ostensibly level-headed and practical technocrat will use this weak link to argue that the federal government, which after all has far more experience in security measures than do all the state governments combined, ought to be put in charge of the database, which should be centralized within the Department of Homeland Security. It is hardly paranoia or dark suspicion that leads REAL ID critics to suggest that the card, like the Social Security card before it, will soon be used for an array of purposes, some of which we cannot even begin to guess. Rather, it is history that suggests—that provides overwhelming evidence for—such concerns.

The potential for identity theft and mischief and mayhem on a mass scale are enormous. "[T]he IDs and database will simply create an irresistible target for identity thieves," according to the Electronic Frontier Foundation.[41] The ridiculous conceit that feeding birth certificates and Social Security numbers (which are in the database if not on the ID card) and other documents bearing personal identifying information such as full legal name and permanent address into a nation-spanning database with fifty-plus nodes is somehow going to make us *more* secure boggles the mind. It's an idea that could only be hatched by security theorists who operate at a level of abstraction and detachment from the real world. REAL ID is, in a very real sense, *unreal.*

"The security risks of this database are enormous," says computer-security expert Bruce Schneier. "It would be a kludge of existing databases that are incompatible, full of erroneous data, and unreliable. Computer scientists don't know how to keep a database of this magnitude secure, whether from outside hackers or the thousands of insiders authorized to access it."[42] The mountains of data contained in this haphazard collection would not only be scalable by identity thieves and hackers and crooks of many kidneys, they would be nigh-irresistible. Imagine making the birth certificates of every American citizen available online in a convenient one-stop shop: could there be an easier, more inviting target for the nefarious? As Jim Harper says, "The best data security is not creating large databases of sensitive and valuable information in the first place."[43] The hub that DHS envisions as a central repository of all this personal information would be the Holy Grail of identity thieves; would you really wish to bet the house (literally) that some of them aren't sharper than the employees of the Department of Homeland Security or your local Department of Motor Vehicles?

****

The states were given a Hobson's choice: choose "voluntarily" to submit to REAL ID, to cede traditional state responsibilities to the federal leviathan and, in effect, permit Washington to design your driver's licensing process, in which case the federal government will permit your citizens to board airplanes and enter federal buildings, or hang on to your sovereignty, act as if the Tenth Amendment to the US Constitution were still operative, "choose" not to participate in REAL ID, and sentence your citizens to a kind of third-class status in the United States, as helots who are forbidden (unless they are military personnel) to board airplanes or enter federal buildings. Which is more important to you, the feds seemed to be asking the states: your sovereignty or the liberty of your people? The rights of the states under the Constitution or the right of your citizens to travel freely?

Bureaucratically, REAL ID stumbled out of the gate, though its stumble was largely due to the rebellion brewing in the provinces. The Department of Homeland Security issued draft regulations on REAL ID in March 2007 and its final regulations the following January. The deadline for state compliance was set at May 11, 2008. By that date, DHS threatened, citizens of states that did not issue REAL ID-observant driver's licenses would be barred from flying on planes or entering federal buildings. This deadline was extended to May 2009, then May 2011, then January 2013. The states—those with moxie and true grit anyway—refuse to knuckle under to the mandate, and Congress refuses to repeal it, so it keeps getting extended. But despite howls of outrage from the states, it has not been repealed—yet.

****

REAL ID compelled the states to license drivers using a digital photograph and signature of the license holder and a machine-readable bar code that would contain important information about the bearer. The final regulations issued by the Department of Homeland Security did not mandate the use of biometric technology or radio-frequency identification in the manufacture of REAL ID cards. But this omission, assert critics of the law, does not mean that these features will not be added at some future, perhaps very near future, date. Because "the physical appearance of a driver's license or identification card falls within the purview of the statutory standards," it seems inevitable that technological "advances" will be incorporated into these cards—at the behest of the federal government if the states display any hesitation at all.[44] (Though biometric is not mandated, states are of course free to use this technology on their licenses.)

Moreover, as these machine-readable bar codes would contain the same basic data whether the holder hails from Idaho or New Jersey, the cards would inevitably become *de facto* national IDs. Citizens would be required to produce them for far more than simply boarding planes or entering federal buildings. Being asked to show one's REAL ID would become a common everyday occurrence; at first it would rankle and irritate—even humiliate—many Americans. But people become inured to irritations and humiliations. In time, "card, please," and "yes, sir" would become second nature to Americans—and when that happened, the historical definition of what constitutes an *American* would have changed. And not for the better.

(Because DHS's final regulations did not include encryption of the REAL ID's barcode for reasons of expense—the only time DHS worries about an expense is when it might ensure a modicum of privacy for the average American!—these barcodes would be easily readable by scanners. They will also "generate a trail of where someone has been and at what time," which would seem to be the fulfillment of every dystopian nightmare and fantasy of the last fifty years.[45] To follow a person's path, just follow the swipes of his or her card. The Department of Homeland Security, making nightmares come true since 2002.)

The practical problems posed by a patchwork REAL ID system in which some states comply and some don't could be vexing. What if, asks Todd B. Tatelman of the Congressional Research Service, "an applicant in a compliant state presents a document (i.e., birth certificate or other required paperwork) that requires verification from a non-compliant state"?[46] One assumes that the non-compliant states will not participate in the national database. States may also come into conflict when citizens with (or without) a REAL ID card seek to use it in jurisdictions with different ID standards. Knots and gnarls and convolutions aplenty await—if REAL ID ever stops being deferred and starts getting implemented.

The range of interest groups critical of REAL ID was impressive: Gun Owners of America, the ACLU, the American Conservative Union, Citizens Against Government Waste. The National Coalition Against Domestic Violence opposed it because the requirement that REAL ID contain a subject's permanent address could make it easier for batterers to locate their victims. Even the American Association of Retired Persons (AARP), which has never met a statist measure it didn't embrace, shied away from REAL ID over the very realistic concern that many old-timers (and younger folks, too) would have a difficult time locating their original birth certificates. Were they to be barred from the suddenly not-so-friendly skies?

These groups offered cogent and forceful condemnations of what Barry Steinhardt, director of the ACLU's Technology and Liberty Project, called a "real nightmare" and a "national ID card on steroids."[47] But their collective influence paled before that of organizations by and for political officeholders: the National Conference of State Legislatures, the National Governors Association, the Council of State Governments. The members of these, after all, are working politicos. They are not importunate lobbyists, or ideological crusaders: they are what members of Congress used to be, or may be someday, or can at least conceive themselves as being. They speak the same language, they trade in the same currency. When governors and state legislators lodge serious protests against federal legislations, federal legislators listen.

****

REAL ID would require, in effect, that every holder of a driver's license—new drivers and those who have been on the road for decades, renewing their licenses periodically through the mail—must appear in person at the local Department of Motor Vehicles office. At the time of the bill's passage, about 245 million Americans possessed licenses to drive. The prospect of the vast majority of Americans descending upon the dank gray offices of their local DMV—most of them arriving between the hours of noon and 1 p.m., or lunchtime, the same hours of the day when the harried DMV employees are out to lunch!—boggles the mind. Or at least it boggled the minds of those who might actually have to deal with the consequences. (One suspects that the Sensenbrenners of the world get their licenses via special arrangement.)

This horde of 245 million would flood the DMV offices carrying multiple proofs of their identity. This was the hope, anyway. These proofs would include birth certificates, Social Security cards, photo identifications, and an ID stating the bearer's current address. Now, anyone who has ever dealt with that refractory beast called "the public" knows damned well that not even half of those showing up to renew their licenses would have on them all the requisite paperwork. Some would have a birth certificate but no photo ID. Others would have photocopies of a Social Security card and perhaps a Visa or American Express card. One lady might brandish a twenty-year-old college ID. A man might present his health-insurance card; another man, spelunking through his wallet, might pull out his wedding picture from an old newspaper, or his old prison mug shot. There is no cause to lament this kind of disorganization: it is human nature. It is also, in its way, quintessentially American.

We are a people whose nation was conceived in liberty. We do not respond well to demands for "Papers, please!" We tend, most of us, to the Reagan side of this issue—if not politically, then by instinct. We distrust the motives of those who would make us produce little pieces of laminated paper every time we want to board a plane or a train or a bus or enter a government building. And we are, as a rule, impatient. We do not demand immediate gratification of every need, but we do not always wait patiently—especially if the wait is forced upon us by some external entity, such as a government. Wait in line for the latest Apple computer gadget or tickets to a blockbuster concert or the big game? Maybe. Wait in line to renew in person a driver's license that just the previous year was renewable by mail or online? Fat chance!

Americans used to pity those Russians and Eastern Europeans of the Soviet era, queued up in long snaking lines waiting for a loaf of stale bread or a pint of cheap airplane-fuel-quality vodka. We of the capitalist West would never submit to such indignities! Well, that's what we thought then. Before 9/11 and the "everything has changed" mantra. Before "homeland security" became a phrase associated with the United States of America, not the Union of Soviet Socialist Republics. Topping it all off, REAL ID was going to make Americans pay for the privilege of standing in long government-mandated lines. The federal government, having mandated the program, was not going to pay for the additional personnel and equipment necessary to its implementation. That bill would come due to the taxpayers of the states. And, more directly, to those who were renewing their licenses—which is to say virtually every adult. Higher fees, longer lines, the humiliating experience of having to produce a government-issued card before one could embark on a plane trip or enter a federal building—everything, indeed, had changed.

And those documents were not going to be accepted at face value by the state's DMV workers. Social Security numbers, birth certificates, and the various proofs of one's existence were to be verified with the issuing agency—a requirement that bespoke a seemingly limitless faith in the competence of your typical bureaucracy. And as Patrick R. Thiessen noted in "The REAL ID Act and Biometric Technology: A Nightmare for Citizens and the States That Have to Implement It," a study published in the *Journal of Telecommunications & High Technology Law*, "there is no certainty that a person who is presenting a birth certificate is the person named in the birth certificate, only that the person named in the certificate exists."[48] This rather basic problem might only be solvable by the use of biometric technology, which defenders of privacy regard as an outrageous infringement upon essential American liberties.

Even biometrics are not foolproof. Thiessen details the various problems that have plagued the technology and often rendered it inaccurate. Just as driver's licenses in their current, or old-fashioned, form, could be counterfeited, so is there the potential for impersonation, or in the jargon of biometricians, "spoofing." Spoofers can scan copies of fingerprints or contact lenses to mimic the biometric profile of another person.

And given the vulnerability of the state databases to hackers and thieves, the storage of biometric data is a virtually gold-plated invitation to the dishonest and the greedy. In the assessment of Dave Bixler, informational security officer with Siemens Business Services, "it only takes one leak . . . to irreparably damage privacy—that is one genie that can never be put back in the bottle."[49]

The DMV was charged with keeping paper copies of verifiable documents for seven years and digital images of the same for ten years. All this information was to be fed into a national database that all fifty states and the territories would have access to. The sheer volume of such record-keeping staggers the imagination—and, in the case of those paper documents that must be retained for seven years, it overwhelms storage space, too.

Peter Harkness, columnist for *Congressional Quarterly*, assessed the newly born mandate with gimlet eye. "[T]he new licensing program known as REAL ID clearly will result in . . . national identification cards," he wrote in October 2006. Standardized licenses across all fifty states, identical in many important respects, and all of them fed into a centralized database makes not only for a virtual emporium for identity theft, it also creates what is in effect a national ID card—no matter how loudly its architects protest the term.

"Congress simply unloaded both the political burden and the task of providing them [national ID cards] onto the states, in effect turning state DMV workers into the front-line agents for the Department of Homeland Security," said Harkness.[50] Now, if any government unit has a worse reputation for customer service than the orange-alert everyone-is-a-potential-terrorist Department of Homeland Security, it would be the nation's Departments of Motor Vehicles offices, manned by functionaries who, unfairly or not, serve as comedic shorthand for miserable, unhelpful, overburdened, and unfriendly foot soldiers in the war of bureaucracy on human dignity. But then maybe that's the point.

"The REAL ID Act: National Impact Analysis," a September 2006 report by the National Governors Association (NGA), the National Conference of State Legislatures (NCSL), and the American Association of Motor Vehicle Administrators (AAMVA), estimated that implementation of REAL ID would cost $11 billion over five years, "have a major impact on services to the public and impose unrealistic burdens on states." The authors of the study reached these conclusions after conducting an in-depth survey posing 114 questions to state motor vehicle officials. (Forty-seven of the fifty-one license-issuing jurisdictions responded.) If anything, the "report likely underestimated the full impact of REAL ID," wrote the researchers, for the state officials lacked enough information to reasonably estimate the costs of numerous and necessary actions, among them facility security, transaction costs of federal verification systems, law enforcement training, data privacy protection, customer and public training, and other probable consequences of the new law.[51]

You know you've gone too far in encroaching upon the rights of the states when the American Association of Motor Vehicle Administrators starts sounding radical noises. Well, maybe not quite *radical*, but the AAMVA, which joins highway safety officials and motor vehicle administrators from the fifty states and Canada, is not exactly the ACLU or the Libertarian Party or the Ron Paul for President Committee. But it does jealously guard its turf, and it looked with disfavor upon the attempted conquest of said turf by a ravenous and privacy-trashing REAL ID Act and its bureaucratic booster, the Department of Homeland Security.

Queried by the AAMVA-NCSL-NGA researchers, DMV officials envisioned the re-enrollment of all 245 million driver's license and state ID holders in the fifty states and the District of Columbia to be the single biggest cost—$8.48 billion—of REAL ID. This is not a cost that would have been borne anyway in the absence of the federal law. The state officials reported that, under state laws, only about 13 percent of those who would be applying for licenses in the next five years would have been required to appear in person with the required documentation; the other 87 percent would have been renewals, which usually occur through the mails or over the Internet. Such renewals take only one-fourth the time as do "original issuance transactions."

REAL ID demands that every state require every driver, no matter how long he or she has been on the road, to appear in person at the DMV, brandishing his or her "original" identification documents, primarily birth certificates. Its requirement that all of these licenses must be renewed in person and within five years forces twenty-four of the states to squeeze their lengthier renewal timelines down to five years. As the NGA-NCSL-AAMVA report states, "REAL ID requirements will more than double the workload of state motor vehicle departments . . . by increasing the number of individuals who must appear to renew their licenses and the time it takes to complete each transaction."[52]

The increased workloads due to the REAL ID mandate will force states to hire more employees, increase service hours, expand or create new DMV facilities, purchase more equipment, and institute public education campaigns. Lines at the DMV will grow longer; tempers, which tend to fray in such bureaucratic settings even in the best of times, will grow shorter. As California state senator Don Perata told the San Diego *Union-Tribune*, "Once we start to tell Californians that they have to march to the DMV, show proof of birth and proof of residency, all hell will break loose. No one will look at George Bush to blame. They're going to look at who's doing this—the DMV."[53]

Moreover, the act's foes "argue that DMV agents should not be commandeered to enact the provisions of the REAL ID Act," writes Patrick R. Thiessen, who notes that such commandeering would run afoul of the Supreme Court's ruling in *Printz v. United States* (the Brady Bill case).[54] And, Thiessen points out, the burden on DMV agents is far greater than that imposed on local law enforcement officers under the Brady Bill because the former are entrusted with responsibility for running checks on about 250 million drivers.

The second largest component of the $11 billion bill for the REAL ID mandate is for the new verification procedures, especially the "more than 2.1 million computer programming hours states will need to adapt their systems for new requirements involving eligibility verification, business process re-engineering, photo capture and database design." The NGA-NCSL-AAMVA study pegs this cost at $1.42 billion over five years.[55]

The extensive verification process promises to be a bureaucratic nightmare. As Jim Harper of the Cato Institute says, "the infrastructure for doing this is pretty much imaginary."[56] Applicants—including those who are simply renewing long-held licenses—must produce three identifying documents, which the DMV cannot accept at face value. Rather, the department's employees must confirm the authenticity of each document with the original issuer of that document. This translates to one billion acts of verification over five years. And it's not as if these are all simple computer-to-computer confirmations. Given that there are about 16,000 sources of birth certificates in the United States, by the calculation of the US Secret Service, the comprehensiveness necessary to confirm the authenticity of such documents in every instance is mind-boggling. It cannot be done easily—and short of an unprecedented experiment in the technology of totalitarianism, it probably cannot be done at all.

Verification of eligibility is estimated to cost $408 million over the first five years of REAL ID: of this, operational costs were estimated to eat up $278 million and one-time startup costs the remaining $129 million.[57]

The rest of the costs subsumed under verification of eligibility are

- $48 million for the states to modify or overhaul their record systems— and as the authors of the report note, in the five years previous to REAL ID twenty-one of the states had spent a total of $289 million upgrading their systems—investments that in many cases were nullified by REAL ID.
- $248 million to comply with the mandate that states must begin the process of licensing by capturing a photograph of the applicant (rather than take the inevitably unflattering mug shot after the applicant has qualified for a license, as was the practice in all but seven states). The cost of compliance is understated, explain the authors, since the states will also need to make a "significant investment in facial recognition technology."[58]
- $95 million for system upgrades in order to meet the REAL ID requirement that states verify the "lawful presence" of license applicants; for states that did not previously verify the status of immigrants and those in the country on business or visitors' visas, this requires a substantial investment.
- $242 million to comply with REAL ID's demand that state licenses include a person's "full legal name." This sounds commonsensical, but it would add 1.1 million programming hours to harmonize the multiple variants of many names (Robert, Rob, Bob) into the federally mandated databases which states will maintain.[59]
- $200 million for the states to verify every change of address. Address changes "constitute the largest number of driver record change transactions," said the NGA-NCSL-AAMVA report, and were formerly treated by the states as fairly routine. That is, the changes were fed into the records but the licensee was not required to make a personal

appearance at the DMV, documents in hand, to prove that he or she had moved. Nor were new licenses issued to the person who had relocated. Instead, the change of address was made on the mover's license when he or she renewed. Altering these practices and requiring in-person visits and reissued licenses is a substantial cost, not to mention DMV bottleneck and pain in the licensee's neck.

- $175 million to meet the records retention mandate: that is, states must keep ID documents for at least seven years and images of source documents for at least ten years.[60]

The third largest component of that $11 billion REAL ID mandate is for driver's license and ID design changes. The states would need to spend $1.068 billion conforming to the uniform security configuration dictated by the Department of Homeland Security. And as the NGA-NCSL-AAMVA report notes, "If all DL/ID cards have the same basic configuration, counterfeiters will only need to overcome one configuration to be able to counterfeit any jurisdiction's card."[61] As is so often the case, decentralizing decision making and permitting a diversity of approaches to a problem is the best guarantor against a large-scale fiasco. One of the many flaws in the one-size-fits-all model is that if it is hacked or hijacked, all those who have been broken to the unisize bit have to pay the price.

The fourth and smallest component of the $11 billion mandate is support costs, which include training for workers in the detection of fraudulent IDs, employee background checks, and certification of the states by DHS every three years.

The National Governors Association, the National Conference of State Legislatures, and the American Association of Motor Vehicle Administrators are not exactly known as the three horsemen of the revolution. Indeed, in the aggregate they are about as threatening to the status quo as a jelly doughnut. So while their analysis suggested that REAL ID was a burdensome and misguided and unfunded federal mandate, they offered "workable alternatives" and assured their federal overlords that "It is our intention to work towards implementation of the act in a cost-effective and reasonable manner." They asked for an easing of certain requirements and the amending of the more draconian regulations. This the Department of Homeland Security was willing to do—to a point. A very sharp point. One gets the sense, from the text of this report, that a primary grievance was money: that is, it was the "unfunded" part of "unfunded mandate" that was the most bothersome. "We also urge Congress to appropriate sufficient funds to allow states to implement the act," concluded the NGA-NCSL-AAMVA report.[62] This does not give off the whiff of gunpowder and rebellion. That came from other sources.

****

Despite some second thoughts from Congress, where bills to repeal or modify REAL ID were subsequently introduced by Senators Daniel Akaka (D-HI) and John Sununu (R-NH) and Representative Tom Allen (D-ME) but not passed, the real action was beyond the Beltway.

No sooner was REAL ID enacted into law by a compliant, mostly unquestioning Congress than the states—or at least those states with enough gumption to assert their rights—rose in protest. For REAL ID was an underfunded federal mandate that usurped a traditional activity of the states and threatened the people of resisting states with, to paraphrase Ron Paul, federal nonpersonhood.

Sponsors made the absurd claim that these standards were somehow voluntary, but as the Congressional Research Service admitted in its April 2008 report "The REAL ID Act of 2005: Legal, Regulatory, and Implementation Issues," "while REAL ID does not directly impose federal standards with respect to states' issuance of drivers' licenses and personal identification cards, states nevertheless appear compelled to adopt such standards and modify any conflicting laws or regulations to continue to have such documents recognized by federal agencies for official purposes."[63] These were about as voluntary as paying one's income tax is voluntary.

The response from the states was immediate and vigorous. In August 2006, the National Conference of State Legislatures resolved at its annual meeting that REAL ID, as an unfunded mandate, should either be fully funded or repealed. (A conservative subset of state legislators, the American Legislative Exchange Council, or ALEC, had a Homeland Security Task Force which opposed REAL ID and shared a model anti–REAL ID resolution with its members.)

Not that every governor or state legislator sounded like Tom Paine. The then chairman of the National Governors Association, Arkansas Republican Mike Huckabee, who was to become a national figure two years later when he ran for the GOP presidential nomination, hedged his criticisms of REAL ID in a way that separated him from the more vocal opponents.

"It's absolutely absurd," Huckabee told the *New York Times*. But his boldness immediately weakened. "The time frame is unrealistic; the lack of funding is inexcusable." So a little more time and money would fix everything? Well, maybe not *everything*. We had to ask ourselves, continued Huckabee, "whether this is a role that you really want to turn over to an entry-level, front-line, desk person at the DMV." Governor Huckabee then gave up the game: "If we're at a point where we need a national ID card, then let's do that," he said. "But let's not act like we're addressing this at a federal level and then blame the states if they mess up. There's not a governor in America that wants that responsibility."[64]

It would be hard to find a weaker-kneed critique of REAL ID than that given by Huckabee.

But Governor Huckabee and the moderate, even milquetoast national organizations of state officials did not speak for all governors, all state legislators, or even all motor vehicle administrators. Consider, for instance, South Carolina governor Mark Sanford, a Republican who had gained political fame when as a member of the Contract of America House of Representatives Class of 1994 he actually acted upon the principles he had campaigned on. (Imagine that!)

Sanford, as a member of Congress, earned notice as that rare representative who walks it as he talks it. He ran as a fiscally conservative proponent of term limits, and he voted against most spending bills. He voluntarily left the House after three terms. He term-limited himself: imagine that.

Returning to South Carolina, Sanford won election as governor on a platform of cutting the abundant pork in that state's budget. He served two terms in that office but his second term was clouded by an embarrassing scandal in which he was revealed to have used state travel funds to dally with his mistress in Argentina. (He had told his staff that he was "hiking the Appalachian Trail," which became the hot euphemism of 2009.)[65]

But his disgrace and downfall cannot blot out Governor Sanford's energetic and eloquent leadership of the anti–REAL ID movement.

On March 31, 2008, Governor Sanford sent a five-page letter to Homeland Security Secretary Michael Chertoff. It became one of the canonical texts of the anti-national ID card, pro-privacy movement. It is thus worth excerpting at some length. Governor Sanford began by informing Secretary Chertoff that South Carolina, working by its own lights, had largely met the requirements of the REAL ID statute without any poking or prodding from the feds:

South Carolina has proactively taken steps, without prompting from the federal government, to establish one of the most secure driver's licenses in the country. South Carolina is already in compliance with nearly all of the REAL ID requirements. In fact, the Department of Homeland Security (DHS) has recognized that South Carolina has coincidentally met more than 90 percent of REAL ID's requirements—well ahead of the projected implementation deadlines and far in advance of many other states. As a result of this work, we now electronically verify social security numbers of license applicants with the Social Security Administration; we require applicants to provide documents to verify citizenship or show authorized presence in this country; we tie the validity of licenses to the length of authorized stay in the U.S.; we provide our employees with AAMVA-approved fraudulent document training; we have a documented exceptions process; and we have now enhanced the physical security of our field offices. As you know, we require a criminal background check for every employee at our Department of Motor Vehicles (DMV) that includes screening through state and federal law enforcement agencies. We also have an internal affairs operation that guards against and monitors potentially fraudulent documents issued by our employees. We also recently established a consumer hotline to provide fraud reporting 24 hours a day, seven days a week. In addition, we have a written security plan that has established defined benchmarks in moving our state towards more secure operations in the issuance of driver's licenses.

Also, as a result of a major systems upgrade in 2002, our DMV now uses a state of the art computer system that employs a "one customer, one record" relational database. Data security is achieved through various levels of network, application, and database security features, and it contains controls to easily provide and monitor access of authorized users. Given that security is constantly evolving, the new system allows our DMV to continue to enhance the security of our license processes as new threats arise.[66]

In other words, South Carolina was making secure its driver licensing practices just fine without any help from Secretary Chertoff. And because the state legislature had passed, and the governor had signed, a law forbidding the state from implementing REAL ID, South Carolina had no intention of begging the approval of DHS. Governor Sanford went on to elucidate his personal reservations about REAL ID. First, he noted, REAL ID was passed without any real debate in Congress. "Does it make any sense," asked Governor Sanford, "to begin a *de facto* national ID system without debate? As a practical matter, this sensitive subject received far less debate than steroid use in baseball." But then members of Congress could grandstand on the subject of bulked-up sluggers hitting home runs; forcing every American to carry a national ID card is considerably less sexy a topic.

"Second," wrote the governor, "at some point someone has got to draw a line in the sand with regard to unfunded federal mandates. Based on the broad array of groups from across the political spectrum that oppose REAL ID, if there was ever a federal mandate on which to draw that line in the sand, this seems to be it. In fact, the bipartisan National Conference of State Legislatures classified REAL ID as 'the most egregious example' of unfunded federal mandates."

Noting his own eye-opening experience in Congress, Governor Sanford ventured to predict that the DHS's modest estimates of the cost of REAL ID—it pegged it at $9.9 billion as of March 2008—would miss their mark by some distance, but even if that estimate were accurate, the federal financial contribution to this mandate was a pittance. "It seems to me," wrote the governor, that "there is something wrong when the federal government imposes the burdens of creating a national ID system on the states—but only pays for two percent of the cost." This is standard operating procedure for the feds, but it has to stop, said Governor Sanford. We are drowning in red ink, yet the mandates keep on coming. "[I]f the federal government thinks a national ID card is necessary, then, after debating its merits, they should pay for it—after determining they *can* pay for it."[67]

The language of fiscal responsibility fell on deaf ears. The Department of Homeland Security, which already had achieved infamy as the biggest dispenser of pork in the federal government, was not particularly sensitive to concerns about either federalism or spending. As for the $116 million bill Sanford asserted the feds were sticking South Carolina with—well, that is the price of security, Secretary Chertoff would say. So is the enormous increase in DMV wait times that would result. Governor Sanford claimed that the average wait in a South Carolina DMV office was fifteen minutes. That would lengthen to between one and two hours were the state to bow down to REAL ID, he averred.

But the governor was not finished. The price of REAL ID exceeded tax increases and eroded federalism and prolonged waiting times. It also struck at a core American value. Wrote Governor Sanford,

> REAL ID represents another step against a limited federal government. Our greatest homeland security is liberty and, yet, based on the history of civilizations, its biggest threat is found in a central

government that is too powerful. Our founding fathers were explicit in reserving first to individuals, then to states, all powers that were not expressly delegated to the federal government. As mentioned, they did this because they considered the biggest threat to liberty a large federal government and, as a consequence, they put in place checks on its prerogative—one of the greatest of which is the power of individual states. REAL ID upsets the balance of power between the federal government and the states by coercing the states into creating a national ID system for federal purposes. Given its requirement to board a plane or enter a federal building, it would also change the balance of power in something as seemingly insignificant as a visit to a member of Congress. As a former member of the U.S. Congress, I had countless meetings with constituents whose personal details I knew nothing about—and this was a good thing. Their background was not the issue, my stand on a given matter was. The First Amendment guarantees Americans the right to assemble and petition their government, and in it there has never been a qualification that said, "Only if you have a REAL ID card." On this, I think it would be best to let the Founding Fathers original work stand.[68]

Let the Founding Fathers' original work stand. Now there's a radical idea for you. But then if we had let their original work stand, "unfunded federal mandates" would be as alien an oxymoron as "camera-shy celebrity" or "reality TV intellectual."

Governor Sanford also objected to the REAL ID–mandated national computer network through which the states and Washington, DC, could share information on licensees. Mistakes, the governor said, happen. So do thefts. So "does it really make sense to put all this information into a central database rather than have this information housed independently across fifty states? I find it difficult to believe that our privacy will be *more* protected by housing the fifty states' licensing information in Washington."

Sanford ended this extraordinary letter—extraordinary in its detail, in its thoroughness, and in its overwhelming rejection of a federal law ostensibly protecting "national security," a phrase that usually induces would-be objectors to shut up—with a caution against the "grave consequences to the taxpayer, privacy interests, and civil liberties in our country if we continue with Real ID in its present form." After all, he concluded, "America's greatest homeland security rests in liberty."[69]

The South Carolinians had hoped to "rattle the cage" of those birds in Washington, said state senator Larry Martin, but Chertoff and company were insulated against any such rattling. Governor Sanford had raised privacy concerns about the REAL ID, but legislators seemed more upset about DMV waits. As Senator Martin predicted, "There won't be a parking lot at a DMV in South Carolina that can hold the customers waiting in line simply to get a driver's license renewed."[70]

Twenty-one states passed anti–REAL ID legislation in various forms; in eleven others anti–REAL ID bills passed one chamber of the state legislature but not the other. So loud was that roar of objection from the states that for a time, it actually froze the homeland security state—but only for a time. Assistant Secretary of Homeland Security Richard Barth conceded in 2007 that "No, we are not going to be blocking the citizens of noncompliant states from doing things like flying." The Assistant Secretary spoke too soon. Or too honestly. DHS spokespersons denied that Barth's admission was department policy. He had gone too far—he had seemed to say that the threat underlying the entire REAL ID program was, at its heart, hollow. "The bottom line is that we have not backed off anything," explained DHS flack Laura Keehner. "We will enforce REAL ID."[71]

Perhaps. But you will notice that the people of all fifty states are still flying on planes, six years after Ms. Keehner's threat. The mandate is stalled, though not because the Department of Homeland Security has suddenly wakened to the importance of liberty.

Missouri state senator Jim Guest, sponsor of Missouri's noncompliance with REAL ID law and a leader of the national group Legislators Against REAL ID, called the plan "a direct frontal assault on the freedom of citizens." Nor did he trust the secrecy-obsessed bureaucratic behemoth in whose clumsy paws REAL ID reposes: "Homeland Security has total control," said Senator Guest; "there is no judicial or legislative control over this."[72] Like the most fervent and passionate foes of REAL ID, he concentrated on its potential as a tool of tyranny. "I love my freedom," said Senator Guest. "I love my country, and we're heading down a road here that would take away many of the things we take for granted. If we had to start carrying a card around—if we lost our freedom not to—I don't think we could ever get that back."[73]

The fear that Americans were losing a fundamental freedom, and that we were entering a Dark Age of obedience to an out-of-control surveillance state, motivated much of the opposition within the states to REAL ID. Yes, the unfunded nature of the mandate nettled, and seemed to be the linchpin of the issue for many on the administrative side, but the real heat came from liberty-lovers.

Maine was the first state out of the gate. In January 2007, legislators in the Pine Tree State passed by overwhelming numbers (137–4 in the

House and unanimously in the Senate) a resolution refusing compliance with and demanding the repeal of REAL ID, which they asserted would cost the state $185 million in what amounts to a "massive unfunded federal mandate," in the words of Hannah Pingree, Democratic House majority leader.[74] The Senate Democratic majority leader, Elizabeth H. Mitchell, spoke in the classic diction of federalism: "The federal government," she charged, "may be willing to burden us with the high costs of a program that will do nothing to make us safer, but it is our job as state legislators to protect the people of Maine from just this sort of dangerous federal mandate."[75]

The coercive federalism of the Bush administration had renewed in Democrats an appreciation for states' rights. In this sense, and perhaps this sense alone, George W. Bush really was a "uniter." Paul Posner called REAL ID "coercive and centralizing federalism," and if anything is going to rouse the states from compliant stupor, it is coercive centralism.[76] At least that is the case if the concept of federalism has any relevance left in it.

Alaska state senator Bill Wielechowski, who sponsored the law forbidding his state from spending any money on REAL ID compliance, said, "From an Alaskan perspective, we don't like big government—the federal government, in particular—telling us what to do here. We felt that if enough states stood up very strongly to the federal government, it would be extremely difficult for it to impose this kind of mandate on air travel."[77]

Senator Wielechowski voiced the libertarian concern about the malignant potential of REAL ID. "It is the beginning of a surveillance society," he said. "It's very easy to see where this goes." Where it goes, he speculated, was toward DNA and retinal scan databases and national gun registries. All sorts of personal behaviors could be tracked with such cards, including the smoking, drinking, and fat consumption habits of the holder. While defenders of REAL ID will say that such fears are groundless, can anyone honestly look at the ever-more intrusive nanny-state lobbies and say that these groups would *not* seek to collect information on such habits—*for our own good*, of course.

To make matters worse, the feds were sticking the states with the bill. "If the federal government . . . wishes to create a society that really is big brother, we don't want to pay for it," Senator Wielechowski said.[78] The ban on air travel for those who failed to get their REAL ID would hit Alaska especially hard, said the senator. "This is a state sovereignty issue," Wielechowski said, and in the Last Frontier, it transcended petty partisan differences. As the *Juneau Empire* pointed out, opposition to REAL ID consisted of "an unusually united front" of "left and right," with House Democratic Leader Beth Kerttula calling the mandate "very frightening" and "another way for the government to intrude in people's lives" and Republican governor Sarah Palin concurring with Kerttula and signing the bill into law just months before she became a national figure.[79] (Palin would join the GOP national ticket led by Senator John McCain, who never met a "war on terror" restriction of liberty he didn't like. The Alaskan legislature, one suspects, Senator McCain would have regarded as lily-livered appeasers of Islamic terrorism.)

Down the Pacific Coast, the state of Washington barred implementation of REAL ID unless and until (1) it was fully funded by the feds (the state estimated a $50 million annual cost for the first five years) and (2) privacy protections were embedded in the program. As Washington state senator Mary Haugen said, "This is a huge mandate on us with big costs and significant privacy concerns. . . . It's totally unrealistic."[80]

The legislation passed by a 95–2 margin in the Washington House, drawing support from the fiscally conscious and those dedicated to civil liberties. The American Civil Liberties Union of Washington was a supporter; its legislative director, Jennifer Shaw, called REAL ID a threat to "personal privacy" and a "bureaucratic nightmare."[81] You have to say this on behalf of REAL ID: it had the rare talent of bringing left and right together, as legislators of all stamps and factions stood up for the personal liberty and state sovereignty that the plan menaced.

Washington state representative Toby Nixon, a Republican, warned of a "national citizenship database," and added, tongue perhaps not entirely in cheek, "I can just hear the black helicopters arriving now." At the opposite end of the spectrum—or just across the way, if in fact the spectrum is closer to a circle—was liberal state representative Kathy W. Stein, a Kentucky Democrat, who said, "New Hampshire—is their state slogan 'Live Free or Die'? We're more of a guns, God, gays, and gynecology state. But this is one of those issues where the extreme left, which I'm always characterized as, and the extreme right meet." Representative Stein was jesting to make a point, but we have come to a pretty pass when objecting to a national ID card is taken as evidence of extremism. Politicians like state representatives Stein and Nixon are much more traditionally American than are the timid, go-along-to-get-along types who muffle their objections to legislation of the REAL ID ilk because they don't want to raise hackles or jeopardize funding.

For instance, despite Representative Stein's nod to the Granite State, New Hampshire's Senate president at the time, Republican Theodore L. Gatsas, supported REAL ID, offering by way of explanation, "I'd hate to see the people from New Hampshire heading to Florida in the week of vacation and not be able to get on the plane."

That's the spirit, Senator Gatsas! Knuckle under to the most improbable threat! Don't stick up for your state when the convenience of snowbird vacationers is involved!

Senator Gatsas should not be taken as typical of his state. Representative Neal M. Kurk, like Gatsas a Republican, charged, "If you say you can't board a plane without a REAL ID driver's license, it's not that far of a stretch to say you can't do other things unless you have this type of identification. It reminds us all of *1984* and more importantly, 'Papers, please,' in the Nazi era." (According to the *New York Times*, REAL ID foes in New Hampshire "staged a rally with Nazi regalia and fake checkpoints."[82] A bit of an overstatement? Sure. But then as Barry Goldwater remarked in 1964, extremism in the defense of liberty is no vice, and moderation in the pursuit of justice is no virtue.)

Representative Kurk spoke for New Hampshire state pride, as well, a vanishing commodity in this age of centralized power. Upholding the license-plate ethos of the Live Free or Die state, he declared: "This small state cannot be coerced or bribed into abandoning the principles embodied in its state motto."[83]

The Arkansas legislature charged that REAL ID "wrongly coerces states into doing the federal government's bidding by threatening to refuse to the citizens of noncomplying states the privileges and immunities enjoyed by the citizens of other states."[84] It also noted that REAL ID technology could "convert state-issued driver's licenses into tracking devices"—a truth whose *1984*-ish flavor sounds less far-fetched with each passing year.[85]

Even harsh critics of illegal immigration weren't buying REAL ID as a panacea. Georgia state representative Mitch Seabaugh, one such critic, nevertheless called REAL ID "a slap in the face of the states." What especially galled him was the way that the feds were not only sticking the states with the bill for this mandate, but they were also going to create logjams in department of motor vehicle offices across the country. And it wasn't James Sensenbrenner who would be dealing with irate customers! As Representative Seabaugh said, "Individuals are going to stand in line for hours, realize they don't have the right documents, and it's going to be us that has to deal with that."[86]

Priscilla M. Regan of George Mason University and Christopher J. Deering of George Washington University, writing in *Publius*, found that the states most likely to pass resolutions objecting to REAL ID were "the relatively less populous and less wealthy states," which would be especially hard hit by unfunded mandates; the "more conservative states," whose political traditions upheld the rights of states vis-à-vis the national government; and those states with "stronger privacy orientations."[87]

Thus Florida and California failed to pass anti–REAL ID laws or even give the matter serious consideration. Big wealthy states, it appears, aren't too much troubled by the prospect of Big Brotherism. And New York State obediently bowed to the federal dictate, never bothering to seriously debate REAL ID. Governor Elliot Spitzer sure didn't use a REAL ID card when patronizing high-priced prostitutes, the revelation of which led to his resignation from office. Yet the New York City Council approved an anti–REAL ID resolution.

But objections to REAL ID sometimes broke through the complacent hum even in those rich and populous states with a culture of paternalistic liberalism. Massachusetts attorney general Martha Coakley, who later was to lose to Republican Scott Brown in a shocking upset in the race to succeed the late Senator Ted Kennedy (D-MA), testified before the Joint Committee on Veterans and Federal Affairs that the verification and database design provisions of REAL ID would force the states to pay for 21 million additional personnel hours of computer programming. Even in Massachusetts, that seems like a lot of extra government spending.[88]

The absence of funding for the mandate extends beyond DMV offices, beyond state record-keeping bureaus, beyond the complications of verification, beyond federal intrusion into a realm traditionally left to the states. Officials in states that had permitted illegal immigrants to gain licenses complained that these persons were not going to forego driving just because they lacked a piece of paper; instead, they would drive illegally, without licenses, and as outliers on the road would cause increased safety hazards.

In the years since the early outrage, some states have made peace with this federal usurpation; servility, if it is practiced enough, becomes a habit. But fifteen states have laws on the books that prohibit compliance with REAL ID: Alaska, Arizona, Georgia, Idaho, Louisiana, Maine, Minnesota, Missouri, Montana, New Hampshire (the Live Free or Die state was among the first to sound the alarm over what many of its denizens considered a police state measure), Oklahoma, Oregon, South Carolina, Virginia, and Washington. The Arizona law, strangely enough, was signed by then governor Janet Napolitano, who morphed into "Big Sis," the ominous Secretary of Homeland Security in the Obama administration.

Not that Big Sis had much choice. Governor Napolitano had tried to cut a deal with Homeland Security Secretary Michael Chertoff that would permit Arizona to issue enhanced-security driver's licenses—a move that Arizona privacy advocates saw as stealth compliance with REAL ID. (Enhanced licenses, which some proposed as a milder version of REAL ID, use radio frequency identification technology.) But when in spring 2008 the Arizona House passed a noncompliance bill by 51–1 and the Senate approved it 21–7, the governor did not exactly have the constituency for a veto. (The excuse of the single House member who voted against the rejection was particularly pathetic: "We have to be able to board airplanes," he whined. But he was no match for the enthusiastic sponsor of the bill, Republican representative Judy Burgess of the piquantly named Skull Valley, Arizona, who called for "a REAL ID tea party at the statehouse.")[89]

The rejections were bipartisan. Montana governor Brian Schweitzer, a Democrat, signed into law a bill directing "the Montana Department of Justice not to implement" REAL ID and "thereby protest the treatment by Congress and the President of the states as agents of the federal government and, by that protest, lead other state legislatures and Governors to reject" REAL ID. The Big Sky State was hoping to start a prairie brushfire. As Governor Schweitzer said, "The best way for Montana to deal with the federal government on this issue and many others is to say, 'No. Nope. No way and hell no.'"[90]

The Montana law of April 2007 was the strongest rejection yet of REAL ID. Passed unanimously by both houses of the Montana legislature, the noncompliance law was an act of defiance by a state with a frontier ethos and deep suspicion of Washington's motives. The projected cost ($11 million to start) and the absence of funding for the mandate were secondary concerns; foremost was REAL ID's assault on personal liberty. "Our right to be left alone is being chipped away and we've drawn the line here in Montana," said Representative Brady Wiseman of Bozeman, sponsor of the House bill.[91]

The right to be left alone: this is a diminishing right in an America of surveillance cameras and healthcare mandates. But the Montana State Constitution, in Article II, Section 10, states that the "right of individual privacy is essential to the well-being of a free society." People who value their privacy will be reluctant to share personal, financial, even biometric data with a state government that is linked to a nationwide database. Retinal scans, to put it mildly, cramp Montanans' style. (Before we praise the Montanans too lavishly, depicting them as a peaceful army of latter-day Samuel Adamses, it should be noted that Wiseman's bill was enacted instead of a more radical measure—a bill nullifying REAL ID that had been introduced by Representative Diane Rice. Nullification, the act of a state declaring a federal law null and void because unconstitutional, was proposed by Thomas Jefferson as a response to the Alien and Sedition Acts of the John Adams administration. It was later championed by South Carolina senator John C. Calhoun with regard to high federal tariffs and by abolitionists throughout the North as a way of invalidating the Fugitive Slave Act of 1850.)

Governor Schweitzer was not in a mood to accommodate the feds. He said that Montanans "don't think that bureaucrats in Washington, DC ought to tell us that if we're going to get on a plane we have to carry their card, so when it's scanned through they know where you went, when you got there and when you came home. This is still a free country and there are no freer people than the people that we have in Montana."[92]

This is a language of the old liberty-minded America, a language that must have sounded as foreign as a Swahili hymn to Homeland Security Secretary Chertoff and Vice President Cheney.

In a letter to Colorado governor Bill Ritter, Governor Schweitzer said that Montana's action "[s]ent a strong message to Washington that this unfunded mandate needed to be repealed." He called for solidarity among the states: "If we stand together, either DHS will blink or Congress will have to act to avoid havoc at our nation's airports and federal courthouses."[93]

Illinois, which had lagged in compliance with the Help America Vote Act for different reasons, objected, in a not terribly forceful way, to the REAL ID mandate. Its House and Senate passed nonbinding resolutions in mid-2007 rejecting the mandate, which Illinois secretary of state Jesse White estimated would cost the state $150 million over its first five years. Secretary White was dismayed by the state legislature's action, or the threatened action, or the phantom action, though one wonders why. For what good is a nonbinding resolution, which is itself a declaration of powerlessness, of lack of seriousness? White's office, which oversees motor vehicle branch offices in Illinois, had been under fire for the glacial pace at which its employees worked. His spokesman predicted that the adoption of REAL ID without federal funding would lead to even greater chaos in DMV offices, as the number of Illinoisans who would be showing up to obtain or renew licenses over the next five years would jump from 8.5 million to 12.5 million or more. The state would need to hire at least 300–400 new workers to make REAL ID real in the Land of Lincoln.[94] And given that this is Illinois, by common acclamation the most politically corrupt state in the union, there might be just a *wee* bit of padding thrown in for good measure.

One did hear broader objections to REAL ID in Illinois, though, at least from the civil liberties community. ACLU of Illinois communications director Edwin C. Yohnka warned readers of the *Chicago Sun-Times* that not only would the Orwellian scheme prolong the wait at the DMV, it would also be a gift to identity thieves. He referenced Secretary of State White's testimony before the state House Appropriations Committee that in one month alone, there were "58,300 unauthorized attempts to access the self-contained Illinois driver information database."

Illinois used stronger privacy and encryption protections than were required by REAL ID. So what would happen, asked Yohnka, when the state's driver information database was shared with those of other states—and not only other good red-blooded American states, as he pointed out, but dubious states and faraway territories such as "Alaska or Guam"?[95]

It would be open season on Illinois drivers! Guamese identity thieves would break into the territory's driver database and presumably run up Congress-sized credit card bills. Alaskan computer hackers would steal the vital information from virtuous Chicagoans and stick them with the bill for feasts of salmon and seal meat and—why not?—Baked Alaska. You get the picture.

Yet Mr. Yohnka's concerns were legitimate. The shared database would be only as strong as its weakest link. And while the DHS denies that the database is national because the states have some flexibility in designing the way information is exchanged, the fact that such exchange is compulsory—state privacy laws be damned—gives this assertion the lie.

In addition to the aforementioned states with REAL ID noncompliance laws on the books, ten others have passed resolutions denouncing REAL ID: North Dakota, South Dakota, Nebraska, Illinois, Tennessee, Arkansas, Colorado, Utah, Hawaii, and Nevada.[96]

Passage of this legislation tended to happen in clusters: the strongest wave came after the Department of Homeland Security's March 2007 proposed rules for implementation. After a nine-month gestation period, the rules became "final" in January 2008, and a new wave of rejections washed over REAL ID.

Six states—Arkansas, Washington, Hawaii, Nevada, South Carolina, and Tennessee—included in their rejection or objections to REAL ID a demand that the program, if implemented, be fully funded by the federal government. And fifteen of the states—Maine, Idaho, Montana, North Dakota, Georgia, Illinois, Missouri, Colorado, Nebraska, Arkansas, Hawaii, Nevada, South Carolina, Tennessee, and Louisiana—finger the unfunded mandate as a specific concern about the law.

As Professors Regan and Deering note, the stated reasons for rejecting REAL ID were plentiful. In addition to its status as an unfunded mandate, REAL ID was also tagged as being a violation of the Tenth Amendment (Arkansas, Georgia, Missouri, Oklahoma, Nebraska, Tennessee), a Brady Bill–like "commandeering" of the states by the feds (Montana, Missouri, Tennessee, Louisiana), the product of insufficient deliberation by Congress (Idaho, Arkansas, Hawaii, Georgia, Illinois, Colorado, Nebraska), an invitation to identity theft (Maine, Idaho, North Dakota, Hawaii, Illinois), a way to make state DMV officials responsible for enforcing federal immigration laws (Idaho, Arkansas, Hawaii, Illinois, Nebraska, South Carolina), and, most commonly, an expensive proposition (Maine, Idaho, Arkansas, Montana, Washington, North Dakota, Hawaii, Georgia, Illinois, Missouri, Nevada, Colorado, Oklahoma, Nebraska, South Carolina, Tennessee, Louisiana). Other concerns itemized in the various state resolutions included REAL ID as an invasion of privacy, a national ID, an ineffective way of preventing terrorism, an unwise exposure of state databases and creation of a massive national database, a trampling on the Bill of Rights, and a violation of the liberties of religious persons who object to being photographed. (These include the Amish, Old Order Mennonites, and some Muslims and adherents of Native American religions.) Those who oppose REAL ID are clearly not grasping at straws—they are, instead, overwhelmed by good reasons for their objections. The challenge is whittling these down into manageable form.[97]

In their monograph in *Publius*, Professors Regan and Deering suggest that the fact that REAL ID is an unfunded federal mandate was not, by itself, enough to goad the states into such a broad popular front of opposition. Nor was the violation of privacy represented by this radical advance in the surveillance state enough to have sparked such widespread resistance. But together—and with the added fillip of state legislators feeling put upon and disregarded by the federal leviathan—the combination was potent enough to create a broad alliance that transcended conventional political arrangements and pointed to a new, perhaps more sensible political grid, in which "conservatives" who cared about federalism and frugality joined with liberals who cared about privacy—and in this junction they found kindred spirits: liberals who were just as dedicated to upholding the rights of states in our federal system, and conservatives who worried about the encroachments of the national security state upon the privacy of the individual. Such an alliance seems powerful enough to have delayed, if not entirely derailed, the advent of a national ID card in America. One wonders what else this alliance might be capable of. (Significantly, such an alliance of left and right, of economic conservatives and personal-liberties liberals, never really coalesced around opposition to the mandatory twenty-one-year-old drinking age, or the Help America Vote Act, or No Child Left Behind, though there were stirrings in the late-blooming resistance to NCLB). Thus REAL ID stands as the primary instance of the states blocking an unfunded federal mandate—in this case, one that had the entire federal government, from the security complex to an almost unanimous bipartisan Congress, behind it. The possibilities boggle the mind—and would no doubt worry the nationalizers and centralizers of both parties and, indeed, the Washington, DC establishment. The battle against REAL ID just may show federalists and independent liberals the way to defeat the ravenous, power-hungry, mandating federal government.

****

REAL ID was born, as Shawn Zeller of *Congressional Quarterly* wrote, in a union of Bush administration national-security officials and those in Congress and without who favored a crackdown on illegal immigration. But eventually others were attracted to it, particularly, in Zoeller's pungent phrase, "advocacy groups with a pronounced stake in a centralized federal identification regime," especially "anti-drug activists and homeless groups." If this sounds like a match made in civil liberties hell, it was. Liberty, to these groups, was at best a nuisance, at worst an evil to be extirpated by a powerful bureaucratic state.

Calvina Fay, Executive Director of the Drug Free America Foundation, gushed that "the link between fraudulently obtained ID cards used by drug dealers and the proliferation of methamphetamine production makes a compelling additional argument" for a national ID. National IDs will be no more counterfeit-proof than state IDs were, but it is true that a totalitarian system can keep closer watch on citizens—the law-abiding as well as the scofflaw—than can a government based in liberty and the consent of the governed. As for those self-appointed advocates for the homeless, they got with the program in the professed belief that it would somehow shield the homeless from identity theft. Henry Buhl, who founded something called the Association of Community Employment Programs for the Homeless, told Zeller that criminals "fraudulently obtain driver's licenses using the names and Social Security numbers of the homeless, who are often unaware their identities have been stolen."[98] Just how common such practice is we are left to guess, but one suspects it is the sort of "crisis" that might make a decent 90-second story on a local news channel. Is it really so great a problem as to necessitate the adoption of a national ID card, which runs contrary to the basic philosophy undergirding the Constitution of the United States?

Just five days after the Department of Homeland Security promulgated its January 2008 final rules for the implementation of REAL ID, a DHS mandarin gave us, perhaps unintentionally, a glimpse into the totalitarian potential of this national ID card. Stewart Baker, DHS Assistant Secretary for Policy, told an audience at the Heritage Foundation, an establishment conservative think tank in Washington, DC, that among the many and varied and magically manifold uses to which REAL ID could be put would be as a requisite ID for any American wishing to buy over-the-counter cold medicine such as Sudafed. Yes, that's right, Sudafed. In the world of Mr. Baker and the DHS, you, as an ordinary American citizen, would have to produce a national ID card when you bought something over the counter at your local drugstore.

The War on Drugs supplied Assistant Secretary Baker his rationale. "If you have a good ID . . . you make it much harder for the meth labs to function in this country," he told the Heritage audience.[99] Sudadfed, you see, can be used to concoct homemade methamphetamine. And so one war (that on Terror) feeds another war (that on Drugs), and the victim is the liberties of the American citizen. And we skid further down the slippery slope.

Perhaps the real lobbying push behind REAL ID came from technology firms that stood to profit from the government contracts to be let.

When federal grants are to be had, the potential grantees will form a potent force in favor of the expenditure. And in this case, they had a ready-made noble purpose to stand behind: national security. Keeping us safe. Safe from terrorists, from identity thieves, from illegal aliens. Dwight Eisenhower once said that if Americans crave security above all else, they should just check into a prison cell, but Eisenhower lived in a different time. (A time when threats such as the Soviet Union and Nazi Germany were rather more potent, it would seem, than the threats posed by Sudafed and ragtag bands of fanatical Muslim terrorists.)

The military industrial complex against which President Eisenhower warned in his famous farewell address has expanded apace since Ike left the White House in 1961. And it has added a third leg—a technology complex whose executives and lobbyists tend to be former military officers who "retire" around the Beltway, where they take up residence as suppers at the public trough.

Those who would profit from REAL ID are determined to not let a few whining libertarians spoil their big paydays. The contractors who see gold where others see chains have put on conferences and meetings of the minds where panels of bureaucrats and lobbyists discuss how best to overcome public resistance to REAL ID. Jim Harper noted a September 2007 conference at the Renaissance Hotel in Washington, DC, where REAL ID promoters met to consider such subjects as "Bringing Your Public Onboard."[100] (That was directed at DMV officials.) This conference, which bore the menacing name of Government ID Technology Summit 2, brought together bureaucrats from the US Department of Homeland Security, various state departments of motor vehicles, and executives with sundry technology firms that would perform the lucrative task of making REAL ID real. The conference was sponsored by such vendors.

For instance, the lead sponsor was Digimarc, which describes itself as

> the leading provider of driver license issuance solution [sic] and your safe passage to REAL ID compliance. Digimarc's comprehensive secure ID solutions protect citizen identities, secure commercial transactions, entrance ([sic!] Surely they mean "enhance"?) homeland security and personal safety. Currently, Digimarc systems produce more than 60 million personal identification documents annually. Including two-thirds of U.S. driver licenses and secure ID's for more than 25 countries. The company has guided its customers through every major transition in driver license history, including digital IDs, and digital watermarking as a covert, machine-readable security feature.

Gee, might Digimarc have a stake in the outcome of the REAL ID struggle? How public-spirited of them to sponsor a conference featuring twenty speakers whose titles include registrar of motor vehicles for the Commonwealth of Massachusetts, systems administrator and project coordinator for the Colorado Department of Revenue, director of revenue for Missouri, deputy director of the California Department of Motor Vehicles, commissioner of the Georgia Department of Driver Services, and the list goes on, up to and including the director of REAL ID for the US Department of Homeland Security. These are the people Digimarc will sell to if the proponents of REAL ID can overcome public hostility and suspicion. No wonder they want to bring the public onboard!

The cosponsors of Government ID Technology Summit 2 included Visage, which boasts that it

> offers a comprehensive set of products and solutions for protecting and securing personal identities and assets. Leveraging the industry's most advanced multi-modal biometric platform for finger, face and iris recognition, our solutions provide a circle of trust around all aspects of an identity and the credentials assigned to it—including proofing, enrollment, issuance and usage. With the trust and confidence in individual identities provided by our solutions, government entities, law enforcement and border management agencies, and commercial enterprises can better guard the public against global terrorism, crime and identity theft fostered by fraudulent identity.

Now, what was that assurance that REAL ID did not mandate biometrics, so therefore they would not be used? Someone had better tell Visage before the company wastes any more money on sponsoring REAL ID conferences!

Another cosponsor of Government ID Technology Summit 2 was NXP, which confessed to being

> an independent semiconductor company with a fifty-year history of providing engineers and designers with semiconductors and software that deliver better sensory experiences for mobile communications, consumer electronics, security applications, contactless payment and connectivity, and in-car entertainment and networking. NXP's identification technologies are designed to track inventory, improve logistics and protect people's information-driven lives. Our technologies can be found in everything from Radio Frequency Identification (RFID) tags that authenticate medicines, to e-ticketing systems that cut commute times and e-passports that fight identity theft and increase border security.

Once again, someone had better tell NXP that those who are charged with selling REAL ID to a wary public and skeptical states have assured us that Radio Frequency Identification is not essential to REAL ID, and that we are foolish worrywarts if we think RFID is coming to our driver's licenses. Hmm, doesn't it seem as though these big technology companies waste a lot of money promoting REAL ID when the technologies they sell won't even be part of the new identification system? They should pay more attention to Department of Homeland Security press releases!

Finally, the sponsor of the speakers' panels was the rather more well-known JPMorgan Chase, which advertised itself to participants as a company that

> provides treasury solutions to over 3,000 state governments and municipalities, helping them with purchase, travel, fleet and integrated cards, tax processing, enterprise content management, electronic benefits transfer (such as food stamp and WIC payments), disaster preparedness, child support payments, unemployment insurance, and license, fee and violations processing. JPMorgan Chase is also listed on multiple GSA Schedules, including: GSA Schedule 520 - Financial and Business Solutions (FABS), GSA Schedule 36 - Office Imaging and Document Solutions and GSA Schedule 874 - Mission Oriented Business Integrated Services (MOBIS), which allow federal agencies to contract directly with JPMorgan Chase.[101]

One wonders what the original J.P. Morgan would think of his namesake company battening on food stamp and WIC transfers, child support payments, and the fees for federally mandated driver's licenses that function as national ID cards. John Pierpont Morgan was no saint, but U.S. Steel, the *New York Times*, General Electric, and the various other firms he helped to finance and organize were rather more impressive than the red-tape winders and subsidy beggars that assembled to plan their assault on the Homeland Security budget under the guise of "making us secure" by forcing every American to carry a national ID card.

****

The constitutional objections to REAL ID are fourfold: (1) that it violates the Tenth Amendment, which reserves to the states or the people all "powers not delegated to the United States by the Constitution"; (2) that it infringes on a citizen's right to travel by denying the traveler the right to board a plane without a REAL ID card; (3) that by requiring a digital photograph it violates the First Amendment rights of certain religious persons (Amish, Muslim women) whose faiths forbid such photographs; and (4) as Governor Sanford explained, that by restricting access to federal buildings by those without a REAL ID it violates a citizen's First Amendment right "peaceably to assemble, and to petition the government for a redress of grievances."

We have, in chapter 2, rehearsed the Tenth Amendment arguments respecting unfunded federal mandates. In *New York v. United States*, the low-level radioactive waste case, the US Supreme Court declared that "States are not mere political subdivisions of the United States." The federal government cannot conscript state governments to act as its agents.

The later "Brady Bill" case of *Printz v. United States*, which built upon *New York v. United States*, found unconstitutional the provisions of the Brady Handgun Violence Act that forced state and local officials to perform federal background checks on those who wished to purchase handguns. It "is an essential attribute of the States' retained sovereignty," said the Court, "that they remain independent and autonomous within their proper sphere of authority."[102] The feds cannot force state officials to enforce and administer federal laws. Given that the issuance of driver's licenses has always been regarded as within the "proper sphere of authority" of the states, a Tenth Amendment challenge to REAL ID would seem to hold promise. Just as county sheriffs and state police officers could not be forced, under the Brady Act, to conduct background checks for the feds, nor can employees of county clerks or state departments of motor vehicles be forced to act as agents of the federal government in enforcing REAL ID. (The burden on these state and local employees, who must process driver's licenses for close to 250 million people, is far greater than what would have fallen upon the police officers who were to have conducted background checks on handgun buyers under the Brady Act.)

As Legislative Attorney Todd B. Tatelman of the American Law Division of the Congressional Research Service wrote in the CRS report on REAL ID in April 2008, one can make a plausible constitutional case that "because the issuance of drivers' licenses remains a function of state law, the minimum issuance and verification requirements established by the act, even if limited to federal agency acceptance, constitute an effective commandeering by Congress of the state process, or a conscription of the state and local officials who issue the licenses."[103]

Michael J. Allen, in the *Seattle University Law Review*, argues that "Although the federal government claims that the Act regulates the federal government, the practical effect of the statute is upon the apparatus of state governmental power. State legislatures will need to enact laws to implement the standards established by REAL ID; state executive agencies will need to conform their administrative policies and practices to the strictures of the statute. If the Act effectively compels state governments, then it coerces states in violation of the Constitution."[104]

In other words, REAL ID is vulnerable on Tenth Amendment grounds, just as the Brady Bill's gun-control background check was. In striking down REAL ID on such grounds, the court would collaterally defend the less well-defined right to travel. And it would define a line beyond which permissible federal guidance crosses into unconstitutional mandate making—funded or not.

(Amusingly—if one has a macabre sense of humor—the DHS, in its January 2008 rules regarding the implementation of REAL ID, somewhat implausibly claimed to have listened to the concerns of the states, respected the Tenth Amendment, and drafted these rules "in the spirit of federalism" and in an attempt to "balance state prerogatives with the national interests at stake."[105] It says something, one supposes, about the continued relevance, at least in the American imagination, of federalism and the Constitution, that even the most flagrant violations thereof are camouflaged as if they have passed the kosher test and been found consistent with our nation's founding principles.)

Tatelman, for one, sees any challenges to REAL ID resting on one's "right to travel" as more problematic.[106] Such a right is nowhere enshrined in the Constitution, but neither is the right to breathe, and that is (mostly, or so far, anyway) uncontested.

Michael J. Allen points out that the Articles of Confederation, the first blueprint of national governance and the predecessor to the Constitution, guaranteed that the people of every state "have free ingress and regress to and from any other State."[107] Although this language did not make the transition to the Constitution when it was written in Philadelphia in the late spring and summer of 1787, the US Supreme Court, not to mention two hundred and twenty-five years of the republic, has found a tripartite "right to travel." First, a citizen has a right to travel freely between states. Nebraska cannot refuse to admit you just because you hail from Wisconsin. Second, a citizen of one state who is visiting another state enjoys all the "privileges and immunities" enjoyed by citizens of the state he is visiting. He can't be treated as a second-class citizen. And third—and occasionally controversially—a new citizen of a state cannot be treated differently than those who have lived in the state longer.[108] (This doctrine is the basis for striking down, for example, Alaska's former practice of awarding long-term residents larger shares of its Permanent Fund, or oil pipeline money.)

The right to travel would seem to be a clear and unhampered right of all Americans, regardless of whether their states of residence comply with federal mandates in the devising of driver's licenses, but there is a catch: the government's argument that such restrictions are justifiable in light of safety and security considerations would likely meet with the court's approval—just as, for instance, highway tolls have been upheld. Moreover, because a REAL ID–less passenger would have an alternative—a passport or military ID—that would permit him to board a plane, CRS attorney Tatelman speculates that the court would find the requirements of REAL ID within the bounds of constitutional permissibility.

Citing passports as the REAL ID alternative raises a new set of objections. According to the US Department of State, about 110 million Americans have valid passports.[109] This is well under half the population—in fact, at 37 percent it is not much more than one-third of Americans. The reasons for this seemingly low number vary, but two stand out. First, many Americans have no desire to travel to a foreign country, so they do not need a passport. Second, they can be expensive. At present the Department of State charges $110 for a passport, and there are additional local costs depending upon the photograph one wishes to use. The applicant will usually end up spending in the neighborhood of $150 for a US passport. This may not seem like a lot of money to the cosmopolitan travelers inside the Beltway, but to ordinary Americans $150 is real money. Should the expenditure of such a sum be necessary to the REAL ID–less American citizen who wishes to board a flight to visit Aunt Sissy, or who must enter a federal building for a legal matter? Passports also routinely take weeks, even months, to be issued. What does the passport-less citizen do when he has to quickly book a flight to travel to a loved one's funeral? In addition, under REAL ID, the cost of a driver's license might eventually rival that of a passport. Citizens for Government Waste estimated that the fee for a license could zoom from the then typical—though by now low—$10–$25 up to $90, which would pinch the pocketbooks of lower-income and senior citizens.[110]

The third constitutional objection to REAL ID—that the mandatory image capture violates the First Amendment rights of certain religious groups—strikes at only one piece of the REAL ID puzzle. The court has given mixed signals on this issue. Quite possibly these religious groups deserve accommodation, but "[g]iven REAL ID's strong basis as both an anti-terrorism and fraud prevention statute," writes Tatelman, "it appears that the government would have a strong argument that a compelling interest does exist for not granting any exceptions to the act's requirements."

Finally, there is the case that REAL ID violates the right of the people peaceably to assemble, and to petition the government for a redress of grievances, as provided for in the First Amendment. Specifically, it prevents those who wish to do so *anonymously*. Must one provide government-issued identification in order to, say, travel to a demonstration? Tatelman, for one, thinks that the indirectness of such a violation would be an insufficient hook on which to hang a legal challenge to REAL ID.[111]

(The commerce clause might offer constitutional justification for REAL ID because licensed drivers motor from state to state. As telecommunications law specialist Patrick R. Thiessen notes, the Supreme Court tea leaves are of varying hues. While the court, in *United States v. Lopez* (1995), found interstate commerce an insufficient peg on which to hang the Gun Free School Zones Act, it upheld, in *Gonzalez v. Raich* (2005), the seizure of a paltry six marijuana plants from a Californian's home because the home growing and consumption of marijuana "had a substantial effect on the supply and demand of the national market."[112] Interestingly, the plaintiff was supported not only by the usual libertarian and anti-drug law outfits, but also by the attorneys general of Alabama, Louisiana, and Mississippi.)

So the Tenth Amendment is probably the strongest constitutional grounds upon which to oppose REAL ID. Michael Allen sees the Tenth Amendment as the basis of any successful constitutional challenge to REAL ID. It would "preserve state sovereignty against federal coercion while also protecting the liberty of the People against encroachment upon their right to travel and to access the federal court system." In defending the rights guaranteed the states, the Tenth Amendment also provides protection for those individual rights (to travel, to assemble) that REAL ID tramples. This strategy would "assert federalism as a principled and effective bulwark against invasions of citizen liberty by the federal government where existing individual rights jurisprudence, rooted in substantive due process and equal protection, may prove an inadequate defense."[113]

Patrick R. Thiessen, too, encourages a legal challenge to REAL ID based on the Tenth Amendment and using *Printz* and *New York* as the bulwarks: the former, because state DMV workers cannot be conscripted as agents of the federal government, and the latter because "Congress overstepped its powers by not providing adequate funding for the Act's provisions and then imposing a punishment on that state's citizens."[114]

Embedded within a Tenth Amendment challenge is the unfunded federal mandate quality of the act. As the Electronic Frontier Foundation, a nonprofit that defends free speech and privacy in the digital world, declares, "REAL ID won't just cost you your privacy. The federal government didn't give the states funds to implement the law and overcome its many administrative burdens so the billions of dollars in costs will be passed down to you in the form of increased DMV fees or taxes."[115]

But the unfunded federal mandate that is REAL ID is protected by that alleged mandate reform that is in bald fact an enabler of mandates: the Unfunded Mandates Reform Act of 1995.

Is REAL ID an unfunded federal mandate? Undoubtedly it is. It dictates a course of action to the states in an area that has traditionally been a purely state realm. And while it is careful to leave a fig leaf of "choice" in the matter, in practice, the consequences are so far-reaching—forbidding air travel by citizens of noncompliant states—that its mandate is essentially iron-clad. And as for the funding part, not even the most oleaginous Homeland Security flack dares suggest that the meager federal appropriations cover anywhere near the cost to the states of the act. The states, we are left to understand, should be grateful to the feds for this supreme instance of coercive federalism. So grateful that they should be happy to pay for the privilege of standardizing their driver's licenses.

The toothless Unfunded Mandates Reform Act of 1995 almost surely exempts REAL ID from its mild strictures. While the costs it imposes easily exceed the UMRA threshold, Section 4 of UMRA exempts regulations that are "necessary for the national security." While such critics as Ron Paul and the ACLU deny that federal dictation of driver's license standards is "necessary for national security," the Department of Homeland Security begs to differ. Whether or not REAL ID in fact bolsters or weakens the national security is an open question, but the intent, clearly, is of national-security origins. Then again, a sophistic government mouthpiece can argue that almost anything the federal government does is related to, or an outgrowth of, that protean phrase "national security." For the record, DHS did, in its final rule, claim that it had "analyzed the cost to the states, considered alternatives, and solicited input from state and local governments."[116] The state and local governments would deny this, and the "cost to the states" was underestimated exponentially, but then the Department of Homeland Security is not exactly a stickler for the letter of the law.

Even if one could put aside the many potent objections to REAL ID as an unfunded mandate, a trespass upon the Tenth Amendment, a wholesale violation of privacy, and an unworkable bureaucratic mess— even if, that is, one cared not a whit or a fig for the Constitution or personal liberties—REAL ID is still a bad bargain. The aforementioned Jim Harper, testifying before the Senate Committee on Homeland Security and Governmental Affairs and the Senate Judiciary Committee, used the DHS's own numbers to project that the "value" of REAL ID in delaying or deterring a future 9/11 type attack would be between $2.24 and $13.1 billion—numbers that range from far shy to significantly shy of the Department's own 2007 claim that implementing REAL ID would cost $17 billion.[117] (And this last number is a serious underestimate according to the NGA/NCSL/AAMVA survey.)

Of this $17 billion, the lion's share ($11 billion) would be the responsibility of the states, while the other $6 billion would be paid for by the—no, not the federal government that handed down the mandate—but the *citizens* of the states in their dealings with the expanding bureaucracy necessary to the program's implementation. (DHS later revised its estimates downward. Its final regulations pegged the cost of implementation at $9.9 billion—a pretty fantasy that fit in nicely with the department's practice of keeping its distance from what one Bush administration official called "the reality-based community.")

****

The Department of Homeland Security's final regulations of January 29, 2008, totaled 280 pages and made note of more than 21,000 comments. The deadline for compliance was set at May 2008, or less than four months later. It slackened regulations just a bit—some drivers wouldn't have to show up at the DMV to get their new licenses till 2017—but for the most part, the most dedicated protectors of the rights and responsibilities of the states still viewed REAL ID as impossibly onerous and malignant to boot.

Resistance from the states to this unfunded mandate—which REAL ID is, no matter what the pettifoggers of the UMRA choose to call it—set the Department of Homeland Security on its heels. Delay followed delay. The first deadline for compliance, May 11, 2008, came and went, and the people of South Carolina and Idaho and Maine and other refractory states still boarded airplanes by showing their state-issued IDs. This despite considerable huffing and puffing by the bombastic DHS Secretary Chertoff, who said at a March 6, 2008, press briefing, "I'm not bluffing about May 11 . . . the law makes it clear . . . if you don't get a waiver then you're going to have—a driver's license will not be acceptable for federal purposes as an ID."[118]

Notice the out Secretary Chertoff provided himself: a waiver. The REAL ID Act authorized the granting of extensions to those states requesting such. Every state did, and so the deadline was pushed back to December 31, 2009, and again, and again. The letters from the states requesting extensions were not necessarily of a subordinate, beseeching character. Indeed, several states "made clear in their letters . . . that either due to existing state law, or other concerns regarding REAL ID in general, that their request for an extension is not to be viewed as an indication that they intend to fully implement the requirements of REAL ID." For instance, New Hampshire's request of March 26, 2008, flatly stated that "New Hampshire is . . . currently prohibited by law from implementing the REAL ID Act." DHS Assistant Secretary Stewart A. Baker, pretending not to have read the very plain words of the New Hampshire letter, replied that "[u]nder the statute, the Department can only grant an extension of the compliance deadline. Therefore, I can only provide the relief you are seeking by treating your letter as a request for an extension."[119] In other words, I'll pretend that you didn't just tell the Department of Homeland Secretary to take a flying leap at a rolling donut and we'll grant you the extension that you did not request. Sometimes willful ignorance is the better part of bureaucratic valor.

A second extension was also built into the rules. If by October 11, 2009, a state was in an undefined "material compliance" with the law, an extension could be granted till the new deadline of May 10, 2011. That was later pushed back to January 15, 2013, and as this book goes to press it has been extended *at least* another six months. Yet as the deadlines came and went, just a single state—Florida, not exactly known as the model of administrative competence—was in complete compliance with REAL ID.

Further delays and waivers and modifications of REAL ID are missing the point, says Bruce Schneier, who recommends instead "the simple change that would do the most good: scrap the REAL ID program altogether."[120] It is costly, an unfunded and possibly unconstitutional mandate, and it won't work to boot. It's a program that only a Constitution-deaf technocrat could love.

Notes

1. Martin Anderson, *Revolution: The Reagan Legacy* (San Diego: Harcourt Brace Jovanovich, 1988), p. 273.
2. Ibid., p. 275.
3. Ibid., pp. 276–77.
4. "Social Security Numbers: The First SSN and the Lowest Number," www.ssa.gov/history.
5. www.ssa.gov/history/hfaq.html.
6. "Montana is Trying to Fight Off the National ID Card," *Montana Lawyer* (Vol. 32, No. 6, February 2007): 6.
7. Todd B. Tatelman, "The REAL ID Act of 2005: Legal, Regulatory, and Implementation Issues," Congressional Research Service, April 1, 2008, p. 1.
8. National Commission on Terrorist Attacks upon the United States, July 22, 2004, p. 390.
9. Todd B. Tatelman, "The REAL ID Act of 2005: Legal, Regulatory, and Implementation Issues," p. 2.
10. Adam D. Thierer, "National ID Cards: New Technologies, Same Bad Idea," Cato Institute *TechKnowledge*, September 21, 2001, www.cato.org/publications/techknowledge/national-id-cards-new-technologies-same-bad-idea.
11. "Frank J. Sensenbrenner," Paper Industry Hall of Fame, www.paperhall.org.
12. Regan and Deering, "State Opposition to REAL ID": 500.
13. P.L. 109-13, Section 202.
14. P.L. 109-13, Section 201.
15. P.L. 109-13, Section 202.
16. Tatelman, "The REAL ID Act of 2005: Legal, Regulatory, and Implementation Issues," p. 5.
17. Ron Paul, "The National ID Trojan Horse," February 15, 2005, www.lewrockwell.com.
18. Pam Belluck, "Mandate for ID Meets Resistance from States," *New York Times*, May 6, 2006.
19. Michael J. Allen, "A Choice That Leaves No Choice: Unconstitutional Coercion under REAL ID," *Seattle University Law Review* (Vol. 32, 2008): 236.
20. "DHS Releases REAL ID Regulation," Department of Homeland Security Press Release, January 13, 2008.
21. Shawn Zeller, "REAL ID Act Makes State Officials Really Angry," *CQ Weekly*, September 11, 2006.
22. Jim Harper, "Rejecting National ID," *American Spectator*, February 7, 2008, www.cato.org.
23. Jim Harper, Testimony before the New Economy and Quality of Life Committee of the Michigan House of Representatives on the Federal REAL ID Act of 2005, October 25, 2007.

24. Jim Harper, "Rejecting National ID."
25. Jim Harper, "The REAL ID Act: An Update," Cato Institute *TechKnowledge*, October 8, 2007.
26. Anne Broache, "Senate Rejects Extra $300 Million for REAL ID," July 27, 2007, http://news.cnet.com/Senate-rejects-extra-300-million-for-Real-ID/2100-7348_3-6199220.html.
27. "ACLU Cheers Failure of REAL ID Sucker Money Proposal," press release, July 26, 2007, www.aclu.org/national-security/aclu-cheers-failure-real-id-sucker-money-proposal.
28. Declan McCullagh, "The Oracle of National ID Cards," October 27, 2001, www.wired.com.
29. Thierer, "National ID Cards: New Technologies, Same Bad Idea."
30. Declan McCullagh, "Closer to a national ID plan?" February 17, 2003, http://news.cnet.com/2010-1071-984792.html.
31. McCullagh, "The Oracle of National ID Cards."
32. "Montana Is Trying to Fight Off the National ID Card."
33. Karl Beisel, "New Hampshire can stop the coming federal police state," Manchester (NH) *Union-Leader*, April 25, 2006.
34. Patrick R. Thiessen, "The REAL ID Act and Biometric Technology: A Nightmare for Citizens and the States That Have to Implement It," *Journal on Telecommunications and High Technology Law* (Vol. 6, 2008): 494.
35. Thierer, "National ID Cards: New Technologies, Same Bad Idea."
36. Harper, testimony before the New Economy and Quality of Life Committee of the Michigan House of Representatives on the Federal REAL ID Act of 2005.
37. "A National ID," *New York Times*, May 31, 2004.
38. Bruce Schneier, "REAL-ID: Costs and Benefits," *Bulletin of Atomic Scientists*, March–April 2007, www.schneieir.com.
39. McCullagh, "The Oracle of National ID Cards."
40. Tatelman, "The REAL ID Act of 2005: Legal, Regulatory, and Implementation Issues," pp. 28–29.
41. "REAL ID," Electronic Frontier Foundation, www.eff.org/issues/real-id.
42. Bruce Schneier, "REAL-ID: Costs and Benefits."
43. Harper, testimony before the New Economy and Quality of Life Committee of the Michigan House of Representatives on the Federal REAL ID Act of 2005.
44. Allen, "A Choice That Leaves No Choice: Unconstitutional Coercion under REAL ID": 238.
45. Regan and Deering, "State Opposition to REAL ID": 490.
46. Tatelman, "The REAL ID Act of 2005: Legal, Regulatory, and Implementation Issues," p. 20.
47. "Maine Calls for Repeal of National-ID Act," Reuters, *Washington Post*, January 26, 2007.
48. Thiessen, "The REAL ID Act and Biometric Technology: A Nightmare for Citizens and the States That Have to Implement It": 488.
49. Ibid.: 497.
50. Peter Harkness, "REAL ID: Reality Check," *CQ Weekly*, October 2, 2006.
51. "The REAL ID Act: National Impact Analysis," National Governors Association, National Conference of State Legislatures, and the American Association of Motor Vehicle Administrators, September 2006, p. 2.

52. Ibid., pp. 6–7.
53. Harkness, "REAL ID: Reality Check."
54. Thiessen, "The REAL ID Act and Biometric Technology: A Nightmare for Citizens and the States That Have to Implement It": 502.
55. "The REAL ID Act: National Impact Analysis," p. 9.
56. Harper, "The REAL ID Act: An Update."
57. "The REAL ID Act: National Impact Analysis," p. 9.
58. Ibid., p. 11.
59. Ibid., pp. 12–13.
60. Ibid., p. 14.
61. Ibid., p. 16.
62. Ibid., p. 20.
63. Tatelman, "The REAL ID Act of 2005: Legal, Regulatory, and Implementation Issues," Summary.
64. Belluck, "Mandate for ID Meets Resistance from States."
65. "Hiking the Appalachian Trail," www.urbandictionary.com.
66. Governor Mark Sanford to Secretary Michael Chertoff, March 31, 2008, http://epic.org/privacy/id_cards/sc_dhs_033108.pdf. In *Condon v. Reno*, the Supreme Court upheld the Driver's Privacy Protection Act of 1994, which barred state DMVs from sharing certain information obtained from applicants for driver's licenses. (Some states had made it a practice to sell the names, addresses, phone numbers, and automobile-related information to insurance companies and direct marketers.) The DPPA restricted such actions by the states. South Carolina filed suit on Tenth Amendment grounds; the Supreme Court unanimously upheld the Driver's Privacy Protection Act of 1994 as a legitimate exercise of the commerce clause. See the testimony of Roger D. Cross on behalf of the American Association of Motor Vehicle Administrators before the Senate Appropriations Committee Subcommittee on Transportation, April 4, 2000, for a treatment of *Condon v. Reno*–related privacy issues.
67. Ibid.
68. Ibid.
69. Ibid.
70. Seanna Adcox, "'REAL ID' could hit roadblock," *Spartanburg Herald-Journal*, March 8, 2007.
71. Alexandra Marks, "Why states are resisting on plan for REAL ID," *Christian Science Monitor*, November 5, 2007.
72. Dennis Behreandt, "Pushing National IDs," *The New American*, July 9, 2007, p. 16.
73. Marks, "Why states are resisting on plan for REAL ID."
74. "Maine Calls for Repeal of National-ID Act."
75. Stacy A. Anderson, "Maine lawmakers reject national ID," *Los Angeles Times*, January 26, 2007.
76. Regan and Deering, "State Opposition to REAL ID": 486.
77. Alan Greenblatt, "Get Real," *State Legislatures*, September 2010, p. 25.
78. Alan Suderman, "Lawmakers oppose national ID by opposing funds for it," *Juneau Empire*, February 15, 2008.
79. Pat Forgey, "Lawmakers spur REAL ID opposition," *Juneau Empire*, March 25, 2008.

80. Matt Sundeen, "The REAL ID Rebellion," *State Legislatures* (Vol. 34, No. 3, March 2008).

81. "Washington Governor Signs Bill Rejecting REAL ID," press release, American Civil Liberties Union, April 18, 2007.

82. Belluck, "Mandate for ID Meets Resistance from States."

83. Regan and Deering, "State Opposition to REAL ID": 487.

84. Behreandt, "Pushing National IDs," p. 16.

85. Allen, "A Choice That Leaves No Choice: Unconstitutional Coercion under REAL ID": 242.

86. Zeller, "REAL ID Act Makes State Officials Really Angry."

87. Regan and Deering, "State Opposition to REAL ID": 498.

88. Testimony of Attorney General Martha Coakley before the Joint Committee on Veterans and Federal Affairs, June 14, 2007, www.realnightmare.org/images/File/Testimony%20of%20Attorney%20General%20Coakley%20on%20Real%20ID%20Act.pdf.

89. "Legislature votes to opt Arizona out of REAL ID program," Associated Press, *Tucson Citizen*, June 12, 2008.

90. Behreandt, "Pushing National IDs," p. 16.

91. "Montana Is Trying to Fight Off the National ID Card."

92. "Governor signs bill defying U.S. ID law," *Billings Gazette*, April 18, 2007.

93. Governor Brian Schweitzer to Governor Bill Ritter, January 18, 2008, http://governor.mt.gov/brian/RealID_080118.pdf.

94. David Mendell, "State backs U.S. ID foes," *Chicago Tribune*, June 7, 2007.

95. Edwin C. Yohnka, "REAL ID Act could be real nightmare for privacy," *Chicago Sun Times*, May 19, 2007.

96. www.realnightmare.org.

97. Regan and Deering, "State Opposition to REAL ID": 483, 485.

98. Shawn Zeller, "An Uphill Battle against REAL ID Rules," *CQ Weekly*, January 21 2008.

99. www.theregister.co.uk/2008/02/05/real_id_for_cold_ medicine.

100. Harper, "The REAL ID Act: An Update."

101. All conference descriptions from www.government-id-summit.com/Sponsors.asp. As an aside, let's hope that Digimar is much better at issuing secure licenses than it is at writing promotional material.

102. *Printz v. United States.*

103. Tatelman, "The REAL ID Act of 2005: Legal, Regulatory, and Implementation Issues," p. 8.

104. Allen, "A Choice That Leaves No Choice: Unconstitutional Coercion under REAL ID": 252.

105. Ibid.: 255.

106. Tatelman, "The REAL ID Act of 2005: Legal, Regulatory, and Implementation Issues," p. 10.

107. Allen, "A Choice That Leaves No Choice: Unconstitutional Coercion under REAL ID": 258.

108. Tatelman, "The REAL ID Act of 2005: Legal, Regulatory, and Implementation Issues," p. 9.

109. http://travel.state.gov/passport/ppi/stats/stats_890.html.

110. "REAL ID: Big Brother Could Cost Money," Citizens Against Government Waste, January 24, 2007, www.rinf.com/news/oct05/realid.html.

111. Tatelman, "The REAL ID Act of 2005: Legal, Regulatory, and Implementation Issues," pp. 13–14.
112. Thiessen, "The REAL ID Act and Biometric Technology: A Nightmare for Citizens and the States That Have to Implement It": 503.
113. Allen, "A Choice That Leaves No Choice: Unconstitutional Coercion under REAL ID": 264, 266.
114. Thiessen, "The REAL ID Act and Biometric Technology: A Nightmare for Citizens and the States that have to Implement It": 507.
115. "REAL ID," Electronic Frontier Foundation, www.eff.org/issues/real-id.
116. Tatelman, "The REAL ID Act of 2005: Legal, Regulatory, and Implementation Issues," p. 16.
117. Harper, testimony before the New Economy and Quality of Life Committee of the Michigan House of Representatives on the Federal REAL ID Act of 2005.
118. Tatelman, "The REAL ID Act of 2005: Legal, Regulatory, and Implementation Issues," p. 16.
119. Ibid., pp. 16–17.
120. Bruce Schneier, "REAL-ID: Costs and Benefits."

9

Will Mandates Never Cease?

Paul Posner, author of the first scholarly volume on unfunded mandates, concludes that "federalism is largely a secondary value, overshadowed and often overwhelmed by other, more primary goals."[1] What was once the linchpin, the essential element, of the American system is now barely an afterthought.

Efforts to rein in or repeal mandates have largely faltered. As early as 1984, the Advisory Commission on Intergovernmental Relations recommended the repeal of crossover sanctions, among them the 55 mile per hour speed limit mandate and the highway beautification act penalties, on the grounds that such provisions are "excessively coercive and confrontational in character."[2]

No one listened to ACIR. The mandate way is just too tempting.

There is a bold and forthright and airtight way to slay the dragon of the unfunded federal mandate: a constitutional amendment. In the early 1990s, when the issue achieved its high-water mark of prominence, Representative Paul Gillmor (R-OH) proposed in the *Harvard Journal of Legislation* an amendment to the Constitution that would read,

> Section 1. The Congress shall not enact any provision of law that has the effect of requiring any State or local government to expend non-Federal funds to comply with any Federal law unless the Congress reimburses the State or local government for the non-Federal funds expended to comply with the Federal law.
>
> Section 2. Section 1 shall not prohibit the Congress from enacting a provision of law that permits a State or local government to choose to expend non-Federal funds in order to receive Federal funds.[3]

Representative Gillmor's was a spirited effort to remove the mandate millstone from 'round the necks of wearied state and local government officials. He concluded, "Unfunded federal mandates are repugnant to our constitutional scheme, for they force state and local governments to be subservient to the federal government. These mandates' boundless power to usurp state and local authority runs afoul of our notion of federalism, and their significant effects on state budgets and decision making power can prove disastrous."[4]

Stirring rhetoric, for a politician, but Representative Gillmor's amendment went nowhere. In states from Texas to Washington, proposed constitutional amendments banning states from imposing unfunded mandates on counties, cities, and towns are live issues, but in our nation's capital, the amendment route—that is, the most comprehensive and effective route—is closed to traffic. For now.

Benjamin J. Cardozo School of Law at Yeshiva University professor Edward A. Zelinsky is a leading scholar of unfunded mandates who argues that they are a result of structural deficiencies and thus must be addressed not by weak palliatives but by a constitutional amendment. Transparency and providing legislators with greater knowledge of the cost, even existence, of mandates will do little, says Zelinsky, for "The problem is not that mandate-imposing legislators are poorly informed but that they are poorly monitored."[5] Zelinsky proposes a bracing tonic: nullification. That is, legislators at lower levels of government would be empowered to refuse compliance with mandates imposed by higher levels of government if they are not "fully compensated" by that higher level. "[O]nly conferring upon lower tiers of government the constitutional power of prospective nullification" of unfunded mandates, Zelinsky concludes, "can decisively deter such unfunded mandates."[6]

Granting states and localities such powers of self-defense would be, in our nationalizing era, a radical move, but it is in keeping with a Jeffersonian interpretation of the American polity, under which the strength of the country resides in its small self-governing constituent parts rather than in an all-powerful central state.

The damage done to federalism by the rush of unfunded federal mandates of the George W. Bush years is, if not incalculable, considerable. Bush's centralizing policies "mark a major turning point toward a more insistent, demanding federal role," wrote Posner.[7] The presidency of Barack Obama, who is no one's idea of a federalist, has neither advanced nor impeded the march of mandates. (Though the Obama Department of Education has been more liberal in granting waivers from the absurd dictates of No Child Left Behind.)

Over thirty years ago, Mayor Ed Koch of New York City issued an alarm about the way that mandates were undermining basic American values: "Throughout its history, this nation has encouraged local independence and diversity. We cannot allow the powerful diversity of spirit that is a basic characteristic of our federal system to be crushed under the grim conformity that will be the most enduring legacy of the mandate millstone."[8]

Despite UMRA, despite greater awareness of the cost, in dollars and in constitutional soundness, of unfunded federal mandates, they show no real sign of abating. Or to use Koch's metaphor, the millstone grows no lighter.

Advocates of federalism occasionally see signs of hope in these nationalizing times. Back in 1990, as the coercive federalism of the Reagan administration had disabused thoughtful conservatives of the illusion that electing Republicans would decentralize governmental affairs, ACIR executive director John Kincaid expressed hope that the pendulum might shift, and that just as the "evils of centralization" in the Soviet Union had led many progressives to see the virtues of decentralization abroad, so might they open their eyes to analogous problems at home.[9] That did not happen. Progressives and conservatives went merrily along, mandating through Democratic as well as Republican administrations.

Yet the intermittent opposition to the most intrusive and expensive mandates, such as REAL ID and No Child Left Behind, suggest that there exists a constituency for federalism. We shall soon see if a new generation of federalists can mount an effective counterattack on the mandate mandarins.

Notes

1. Posner, *The Politics of Unfunded Mandates*, p. 54.
2. *Regulatory Federalism: Policy, Process, Impact and Reform*, p. 278.
3. Paul Gillmor and Fred Eames, "Reconstruction of Federalism: A Constitutional Amendment to Prohibit Unfunded Mandates," *Harvard Journal on Legislation* (Vol. 31, 1994): 410.
4. Ibid.: 413.
5. Edward A. Zelinsky, "Unfunded Mandates, Hidden Taxation, and the Tenth Amendment: On Public Choice, Public Interest, and Public Services," *Vanderbilt Law Review* (Vol. 46, No. 6, November 1993): 1358.
6. Ibid.: 1396.
7. Posner, "The Politics of Coercive Federalism in the Bush Era": 408.
8. Koch, "The Mandate Millstone": 57.
9. Kincaid, "From Cooperative to Coercive Federalism": 152.

Index